CRUEL AUTEUR

AFFECTIVE DIGITAL MEDIATIONS
TOWARD FILM-COMPOSITION

#WRITING

Series Editor: Cheryl E. Ball

The #writing series publishes open-access digital and low-cost print editions of monographs that address issues in digital rhetoric, new media studies, digital humanities, techno-pedagogy, and similar areas of interest.

The WAC Clearinghouse, Colorado State University Open Press, and the University Press of Colorado are collaborating so that books in this series are widely available through free digital distribution and in a low-cost print edition. The publishers and the series editor are committed to the principle that knowledge should freely circulate. We see the opportunities that new technologies have for further democratizing knowledge. And we see that to share the power of writing is to share the means for all to articulate their needs, interest, and learning into the great experiment of literacy.

OTHER BOOKS IN THE SERIES

Derrick N. Mueller, *Network Sense: Methods for Visualizing a Discipline* (2017)

CRUEL AUTEURISM

AFFECTIVE DIGITAL MEDIATIONS TOWARD FILM-COMPOSITION

By bonnie lenore kyburz

The WAC Clearinghouse
wac.colostate.edu
Fort Collins, Colorado

University Press of Colorado
upcolorado.com
Louisville, Colorado

The WAC Clearinghouse, Fort Collins, Colorado 80523

University Press of Colorado, Louisville, Colorado 80027

ISBN 978-1-64215-002-5 (PDF) | 978-1-64215-018-6 (ePub) | 978-1-60732-918-3 (pbk.)

Printed in the United States of America

Library of Congress Cataloging-in-Publication Data

Names: Kyburz, Bonnie Lenore, author.
Title: Cruel auteurism : affective digital mediations toward film-composition
 / by Bonnie Lenore Kyburz.
Description: Fort Collins, Colorado : WAC Clearinghouse, [2019]
 | Series: #writing | Includes bibliographical references and index.
 | Identifiers: LCCN 2018047485 (print) | LCCN 2018059947 (ebook)
 | ISBN 9781642150025 (pdf) | ISBN 9781642150186 (ePub)
 | ISBN 9781607329183 (pbk : alk. paper)
Subjects: LCSH: Motion pictures in education. | Motion picture authorship.
 | English language—Composition and exercises—Study and teaching.
Classification: LCC LB1044 (ebook) | LCC LB1044 .K93 2019 (print)
 | DDC 371.33/523—dc23
LC record available at https://lccn.loc.gov/2018047485

Copyeditors: Don Donahue
Designer: Mike Palmquist
Cover by Than Saffel
Series Editor: Cheryl E. Ball

This book is printed on acid-free paper.

The WAC Clearinghouse supports teachers of writing across the disciplines. Hosted by Colorado State University, and supported by the Colorado State University Open Press, it brings together scholarly journals and book series as well as resources for teachers who use writing in their courses. This book is available in digital formats for free download at wac.colostate.edu.

Founded in 1965, the University Press of Colorado is a nonprofit cooperative publishing enterprise supported, in part, by Adams State University, Colorado State University, Fort Lewis College, Metropolitan State University of Denver, Regis University, University of Colorado, University of Northern Colorado, Utah State University, and Western State Colorado University. For more information, visit upcolorado.com. The Press partners with the Clearinghouse to make its books available in print.

Contents

Acknowledgments vii

Introduction 3

Chapter 1: Hope 23

Chapter 2: Fear 49

Chapter 3: Desire (I). 73

Chapter 4: Desire (II). 91

Chapter 5: Pleasure. 121

References 145

Index 157

Acknowledgments

I thought I'd write a book some day, but I had no idea it would be this book. Like many creative projects, this one flickered ambiently in my path for some time, just shimmering with promise but elusively withholding . . . until it was right in front of me, illuminated and waiting on me to answer the call. I know. But so, though I labored to write it, it seems to have sort of happened. In the midst of some of the worst years of my life, my love for the creative, critical, and pedagogical film work I'd been doing was honored and valued by my dear friend, colleague, and editor, Cheryl E. Ball. She is a miracle, and I will be forever grateful for her faith in me. Similarly, magically, Mike Palmquist signed on, sharing Cheryl's faith and creating a path. Never once doubting any of it was my most beloved, the best person I know and my own dear husband, Mike Kyburz. How many silly edits did he watch and applaud? How many conference presentation prep cycles did he endure? Impossible to say. He is my spiritual and creative partner, and I will never be able to express how lucky I am that we found each other. He was there with me when I started my Teaching Assistant's gig at the University of South Florida. I was writing about chaos theory while my secret desire to work with film in my writing classes began to grow in the light of the knowledge that Bob Haas (another TA) mostly showed films in his classes. WHAT?! Mike was there when I defended that chaotic dissertation, and my kind and generous committee (Joe Moxley, Phil Sipiora, Silvio Gaggi & Betsy Hirsch) bestowed my PhD upon me as my father, Gerald Clifton Surfus, sat weeping, prideful and red-faced, barely able to contain himself in the corner of the room. He didn't. Contain himself. He collected himself, requested that the committee stay for a bit longer, and delivered the story of my purple hair and my expulsion from another university, several years in my past. He'd earned that story because of his profoundly loving and deeply forgiving move to send me back to college for another try, and I will never ever be able to say or do enough to warrant his good deed, but this book is nice, and he would hate it because he hates my writing, but so. Mike was there for that. He was there for the afterparty, patiently locking (rolling?) eyes and eating pizza with my mom, Mary Adeline Surfus, while Dad regaled us all with the story we'd just lived in that conference room, "Remember when they asked you this . . . and you answered that?!!" Mike was there when I shot scenes, when I screened my short films at MLA, CCCC, NCTE, WSRLC, and other conferences. We texted back and forth as I heard eloquent colleagues articulating ideas that seemed to suggest that what I was doing wasn't simply nuts. Doug Hesse, and Kathleen Blake Yancey, both in their CCCC's Chair positions, delivered talks on literacy shifts that emboldened me. Both Doug and Kathy also encouraged me individually. They are champs. Mike and I dined out with Trish Roberts Miller, who was an early figure in my short film status update, and has been indefatigable in her support of my work. Others featured in that film also shared meals with us; Ron Brooks in Las Vegas ("who ARE these rich, beautiful people?!"), Cynthia Haynes and Jan Rune Holmevik in North Carolina, Victor Vitanza, in LA, Chicago, Memphis, and more. Even earlier, my USF crew gave their support. Todd Taylor once helped me rig sound for a giant ballroom in New York for a CCCC presentation I had the honor of sharing with the brilliantly sublime Geoffrey Sirc, and Anne Frances Wysocki, our very own design goddess who didn't even blink when I accidentally knocked an entire pitcher of ice water over and onto her new MacBook Pro (!) but swiped left on the mess and urged me to proceed. Other USF support evolved in the form of a lovely friendship with a woman who helped me through the loss of my father and some pretty furious compositional activity; Julie Drew is the best magic girl listening and empathizing friend a girl could want. I love you, Julie, and I could not have said "good-bye" to Dad and survived without you. Sid Dobrin, Andrea Greenbaum, Joe Hardin, Raúl Sánchez, . . . what to say. I love you idyots!! My new colleagues at Northern Illinois University—especially the brilliant mentor-friend, Michael Day—thank you! The support from my talented, loving, humane, and indulgent friends and colleagues has been everything, and while I would love to here unspool the longest list with all the stories, I've got to wrap this thing. Unspeakably generous, brilliant, creative, and fabulous film-compositionists and others supporting the kinds of work that manifested this book, I invite you to read their stories in these pages. If you don't see your name here, please know that I didn't want to Hilary Swank you, but I do thank you (unbearable attempt at humor). Mike won't need to read this book (though all are welcome!) because he's lived it with me, as we've shared the work and the play with our willing collaborators and ALL THE REASONS, Aoife Bell Frances Coakley, Matilda Mae Coakley, Fiona Rose Coakley, Emily S. Coakley, and Joe Coakley. We came to be with you and you gave us everything that matters. We'll never have enough ways to thank yo and express all that you mean to us. In many ways, you've provided one of the most vital "zones of optimism" (thank you, Lauren Berlant!) within which we've been able to compose ourselves, and I, this book. Thank you. Thank you all.

CRUEL AUTEURISM

AFFECTIVE DIGITAL MEDIATIONS TOWARD FILM-COMPOSITION

Introduction

Cruel Auteurism sounds like a thing you'd want to avoid. I hope instead that you come to see it as an illustrative characterization of our investments in digital filmmaking as engaging rhetorical practice. Toward this end, this book highlights both problems and promises associated with a pedagogical and scholarly area of rhetorical activity I've been calling "film-composition." Using affect theorist Lauren Berlant's (2011) concept of "cruel optimism" to articulate the findings of my archival, analytical, and experiential methods, *Cruel Auteurism* describes a cultural shift within the discipline, from the primacy of print-based arguments, through an evolving desire to generate cinematic rhetorics, toward increasingly visible forms of textual practice currently shaping composition classrooms, rhetorical pedagogy, and digital scholarship.

This book has emerged from my experience as a rhetorician, compositionist, and DIY ("do it yourself") digital filmmaker. I've been tempted to claim that my methodology is ethnographic, and I may refer you to ethnography's capacious and ambiguously available qualities where I feel I'm veering toward the overly personal perspective. For the most part, I have been powerfully lit by Berlant's (2011) concepts, and I rely on her affective lens as an appropriate guide. *Cruel Auteurism* is not strictly an ethnographic report, though some qualitative characteristics of ethnography shape my appreciation for the affects that animate the timeline onto which I am mapping my arguments via Berlant's concept of "cruel optimism," a phrase she coined to articulate a kind of damaging desire that generates a troubling yet potentially hopeful state of affairs. Articulating the more hopeful end of the spectrum is Berlant's more promising "zones of optimism," (2011, p. 48) spaces within which relations of cruel optimism are bearable due to the pleasures of certain affective flows and occasional material byproducts. The timeline I generate moves dynamically across the spectrums of "cruelty" and "optimism."

Beginning with hope, and moving through fear, desire, more desire, and pleasure, the book articulates the history and emergence of film-composition. Not merely an object for analytical study, film-composition creates new scenes within which to practice our rhetorical craft, scenes that may feature revisions of our lives, possibly even to discover new "mode[s] of enfleshment," (Berlant, 2011, p. 128),[1] so profound are the affective intensities asso-

---

1   Here, I intend a subtle reference to David Cronenberg's (1983) *Videodrome*. More directly, my access to this term is via Berlant's Chapter 4, "Two Girls, Fat and Thin," from *Cruel Optimism*, where Berlant (2011) discusses strategic, post-traumatic choices regarding corporeal being (pp. 121–159).

ciated with the work (cue new materialisms). Digital filmmaking provides obvious, visible reflective spaces and tangible frames for sensing and theorizing our affective attachments en route to the production of filmic arguments. Throughout these processes, the sensorium delights at the thrillingly expansive range of modal options for enacting our hopes, worrying our fears, pursuing our desires, and reanimating longstanding pleasures. Berlant's (2011) turn to film in her own work helps explicate this potential. In her discussion of Luc and Jean-Pierre Dardennes' (1999) film, *Rosetta*, she recasts a critical view of citizenship so that it is not so neatly defined as "an amalgam of the legal and commercial activity of states and business and individual acts of participation and consumption" but, more generously, hopefully, as "an affective state where attachments that matter take shape" (2011, p. 163). Tracing a line of flight from within an overdetermined notion of citizenship in capitalist culture, Berlant highlights the chaotic experiences of everyday life, intimating that our attachments may render promisingly and potentially via critical, even unwitting intervention because "the affects of belonging are all tied up with what happens at the point of production" (2011, p. 163). Exactly. And while Berlant is analyzing a fictional cinematic narrative, she is clear to enumerate the potential for works of this kind to render meaning for our experiences of everyday living (as we produce, resist, remix, revise, and otherwise generate selves, communities, cultures).

Of course, we need not turn to affect theory to see that cultural texts matter. However, studying the formation, intensity, and duration of the affective attachments of participating within culture via certain cultural texts suggests that we should. Obviously, the project of Cultural Studies has made its lasting mark in Composition,[2] so the need to examine the fact that fictional narratives reflect, produce, and reproduce culture is unnecessary. Nonetheless, toward populating this timeline, it's interesting to note that many historical backchannels in Composition worked toward similar effect. A 1973 *NCTE/CCC Workshop Report*, under the heading, "The Popular Arts and Introductory Courses in English" features Gary Harmon, Irving Deer, and Harriet Deer proclaiming that "[t]he popular arts are important in themselves" because they "usually focus upon the crises of our times and thus reveal the nature of our society" (pp. 311–312). The workshop concluded:

> *Resolved*: Because the Popular Arts form our dominant culture and clearly reveal its values, the CCCC should give more attention to evaluating them in a rigorous and disciplined

---

2   See Julie Drew's (1999) careful review of the many voices—*i.e.*, James Berlin, Diana George, John Trimbur— articulating this convergence, in "(Teaching) Composition: Composition, Cultural Studies, Production." *JAC, 19*(3), 411–429.

way, and should encourage integration into curricula now dominated by the Fine Arts. (Harmon, Deer, I. & Deer, H., 1973, p. 312)

This historical, backchannel detour wants to remind us. Berlant's (2011) more contemporary reading on attachments as evolving through in-process experience hints at an ongoing form of critical making to which we in Composition are increasingly committed. I enthusiastically trace these sorts of claims— on the value of digital filmmaking as production of self (re)orientation, community attachment, and cultural disposition—throughout *Cruel Auteurism*. Affect theory helps me in retracing my experiences as a digital filmmaker even as I work to lay out an emergent history of film-composition.

Mine is a material hope, affectively experienced. My project is about doing, making, and sensing. I have made films driven by a desire to illuminate rhetorical phenomenon for all the players involved in my cinematic projects (participants, subjects, performers, students, audiences, myself, and other scholars). I have sought to highlight things that we, in the field, are doing, and what some are possibly missing or for some reason(s) evading or otherwise not doing ("Video?! Anyone can make a video!"). In hindsight, I see that as I have been making films and writing and publishing about the work, I have been operating within a network of similarly oriented filmmaking peers, within an immersive, mulitmodally-oriented rhetoricity.[3] And yet, "auteurism." The scholar who produces films as digital scholarship has often been of necessity a kind of auteur, singularly isolated and seemingly non communal, yet aiming for rhetorically and culturally moving texts that matter to ourselves and to our field. The latter part of this equation upholds the more critically valuable aspects of auteurism that early auteur/auteurist theorist Francois Truffaut hoped to articulate, though many still see the term as pejoratively tied to a retrogressive isolationist, that sad sack, that left-in-the-dusts of recedingly blown modernist winds, the tired old individual composer. I use the term "auteur" for how it articulates my own experience of development, which involved pursuing my desire through internal grants, personal funding, and weekend workloads that overtook any semblance of "free time" one associates with weekends "off." I use the term because when I started making films as digital scholarship and toward pedagogy, I did so on a crew of one. A strictly focused, at times lonely DIY quality has informed my experience of film work in Composition. This is perhaps because film production remains as yet a small niche, not widely funded in ways that allow for extensive support (i.e., crews, studios). Thus, cruel, limited by a missing sense of

---

3   Briefly, "rhetoricity" is a "web of relations" that enables rhetorical action. See Detweiler (2014). "What Isn't Rhetoricity?" *Rhetoricity* (Podcast).

community and collaborative peers, isolated within new scenes of compositional activity and the comforting familiarity of discursive conventions, and challenged by working somewhat beyond disciplinary identification, genre conventions, and the comforts of peer response that validates. *Cruel Auteurism* wants to help provide a sense of community for existing and would-be film-compositionists, affording them a sense that this (digital filmmaking as rhetorical scholarship and pedagogy) is a thing.

"Auteur," though?

True, the directorial metaphor of "auteur" might seem to suggest radical constraints due to an outdated notion of a singular composer with precious individual vision, a notion complexified by our contemporary sense of composers as constellations within larger, concatenous universes of discourse, responsive to rhetoricity's persistent call. But the term "auteur" has always been far more complex than its variously reductive readings might suggest. Introducing the comprehensive, *Auteur Theory/Auteurs* collection for the British Film Institute (BFI), David Sharp (2002) contextualizes the auteur, explaining,

> a considerable European tradition that says that film-makers develop recognisable styles, unfettered by a studio system (even if they work within one) and the finished film expresses their own philosophy of life, thoughts, politics and worldview distilled into their own creative output. This has quite a lot to do with the creation of works of art (films), and film being seen in the light of this tradition. (p. 1)

Does the "auteur" of digital filmmaking, digital pedagogy, and digital scholarship work with, through, or toward a particular style? Often, yes. Does she work somewhat beyond institutional constraints and through immersive ecologies? Frequently, yes. Does his work articulate through a particular ideological lens? Undeniably so (and, in fact, the work of many film-compositionists is to render explicit their politics, toward their rhetorical aim). In many ways, the birth of the term "auteur" seems to me a recognition of film's rhetoricity, the notion of a director working forcefully toward particular rhetorical goal (shot-by-shot, scene-by-scene, set design object-by set design object) rather than "merely" his or her quirky stylistic tendencies (though they are obviously interrelated). In fact, the BFI collection hints that auteurs are more like *focused rhetors rather than isolationistic divas* through its aggregation of books, articles, and case studies. Brief bios of famous auteurist directors expose a variety of distinct rhetorical perspectives. Summarizing the "auteur" conflict, and toward a definition for this work, an "auteur" is considered a director whose personal vision is so powerful that it becomes a kind of critical signature identified with the "author" of the work—notice the concepts of identification and style, here. The term and its conceptual uptake are associated with the emergence of the French New Wave, the writings of film critic and theorist André Bazin, and an influential 1954 essay by director Francis Truffaut, entitled "A Certain Tendency of French Cinema" in which Truffaut discusses directorial *creative vision* as a trait associated with powerful filmmaking. In doing so, Truffaut sought to disrupt the notion of a precious unique diva and instead to point to *signature filmmaking for its cultural and politically relevant nature.* Rather than merely to single out a group of precious darlings for special merit (though he did do just that), Truffaut attempted to infuse the French New Wave with a sense of the seriousness of style and vision (delivery and rhetorical purpose). Truffaut insisted upon the critical importance of film as public rhetoric. Sound familiar? Composition, particularly through an infusion of Cultural Studies, has similarly asserted the cultural value of many of its mattering works.

In many ways, questioning the notion of "personal" vision is rendered somewhat less urgent by theories on selfhood associated with the postmodern turn, theories that are by now well established in Composition scholarship (Brodkey, 1994; Dobrin, 2011; Hardin, 2001; Kent, 1999; Miller, 1991). Additionally, studies in collaborative composing suggest that the mythically "solitary writer" is particularly undone as we contemplate filmmaking practices. In a study that "answers the research call to explore filmmaking as an exemplar for collaborative creativity," Robert M. Gonzaléz (2008) explained that communication is demonstrably essential to collaborative creativity, that against traditionally narrow views of compositional activity, "creativity is storied" through processes that are dynamic, situated, and social: "Creativity is shared, not possessed; collaborative creativity emerges within human drama; and collaborative creativity lives and finds its meaning in performance" (p. v). Gonzaléz studied "making-of-documentaries" (MODs) in order to replay the communications that revealed collaborative creativity's sociality. Here, we see how film affords us insight into the rhetorical nature of film's compositional backstory. Gonzaléz explains

> First, there is an undeniable intimacy of tone in these interviews, inviting me to lean in to listen more closely. Second, most MODs are enhanced with cinema verité-style video footage that wanders through sound stages, foreign shooting locations, and pre-production design facilities, inviting me to wander along, too. Third, the professional film artists who speak on MODs—directors, designers, composers, crew members, and actors—share technical details of how specific

scenes were designed, filmed, edited and scored, inviting me
to be a part of the inside story. (2008, p. 2)

It seems to me that the ability to watch (for scholarship) and screen (for pedagogical purposes) MODs provides a kind of ethnographic insight into how
films are made to radiate their rhetorical purposes. We get a sense of a vibe that
goes beyond a singular vision, though we may also discern auteurist flourishes
through certain repeating signatures (the color palettes of Wes Anderson films
have, for example, generated a variety of infographics and humorous memes
even as they accurately review Anderson's idiosyncratic choices[4]). Gonzaléz
elaborates the value of MODs to further reveal process-oriented communications, illuminating them as

> richly valuable resources for studying, analyzing, and argu-
> ing the importance of communication in collaborative cre-
> ativity. As resources for studying communication, they are
> stories of events told from multiple points of view; they draw
> connections across individuals, communities, and history;
> they portray human interactivity as dramatic and engaging;
> they are stories shaped rhetorically by both tellers and docu-
> mentarians. (2008, pp. 2–3)

In other words, MODs enable us to see individuals immersed in community, in making things. *Film-composition*. Highlighting the value of MODs for
studying and perhaps modeling the rhetorical nature of filmmaking, MODs
are important stories that are

> not just about how a film was made, but about how com-
> munication practices enabled the work of the group. As
> resources for studying collaborative creativity, MODs are
> texts that answer the call for studying creativity in groups, in
> context, and in language. (Gonzaléz, 2008, p. 3)

But so if films are storied as collaborative endeavors, uniquely emerging from
within networks of human and non-human creative energy, we might think
about auteurism as a function of one's immersion in a filmmaking community even as we recognize that a film is *crafted, directed, composed* and
that one name often associates with that effort. So, obviously, the auteur is
immersed in language. It's helpful, here—toward the goal of making all of
this matter very much for our work in rhetoric—to think of this immersion

---

4   See Vreeland, A. V. "Color Theory and Social Structure in the Films of Wes Anderson."
For a more visual-oriented display, see http://www.anothermag.com/art-photography/3586
/wes-andersons-colour-palettes.

in terms of *rhetoricity*. That is to say, we might see any textual output by a director as functionally emergent from culture rather than from a private or somehow hermetically cordoned-off individual. I use the term to signify both concepts—authorship and isolation—the notion that working "by one-self" to compose film, *and* working absent the support of a disciplinary of well-funded power source is both problematic and possible, both cruel and optimistic. To comprehend the auteur as existing in a state of "cruel optimism," I will come to argue, is to also glimpse potential for greater "zones of optimism" in ways that intimate the promises of both personal experience and networked sociality, the promises of rhetoricity.

Performing a sense of rhetoricity is Diane Davis, via transcript from a *Rhetoricity* podcast hosted by Eric N. Detweiler:

> [futuristic space sounds]
>
> Diane Davis [with reverberating, ominous vocal effect]: In the beginning was rhetoricity.
>
> [sound of the needle on a record player dropping, space sounds replaced with record hiss]
>
> [...]

As she puts it, rhetoricity is

> [quoting from p. 2 of Davis' *Inessential Solidarity* with a telephonic vocal effect]
>
> an affectability or persuadability . . . that is the condition for symbolic action.
>
> [percussive shaker joins bass]
>
> I get how this sounds, but I'm not going mystical or even particularly abstract on you here. By definition communication can take place only among existents who are given over to an "outside," exposed, open to the other's affection. [telephone effect and music end]. (2015, p. 1)

More straightforwardly, Detweiler summarizes Davis' (2013) definition as follows:

> So while rhetoric often focuses on persuasive encounters, situations, or strategies, rhetoricity emphasizes the conditions that make persuasion possible—not the rhetorical power or agency of a masterful communicator, but the vulnerability, the openness and feeling of exposure that have to be in place

for any attempt at persuasion to unfold. Rhetoricity empha-
sizes not the individual speaker or writer, but the web of relations that has to be in place before that individual ever has
something to say or someone to talk to. (2015, p. 1)

Cruel Auteurism is in many ways about the cinematic conditions that make
persuasion possible in contemporary terms, within digitally mediated scenes
of rhetorical action. There are many paths we might choose to trace a sense of
support for this claim. That none seem definitive might worry us, but I find
that film's evasive capacity to escape capturation is a virtue that bespeaks its
promising affective intensities as a primary frame for valuing its complex
rhetorical nature. Just as Composition has been understood as complexly
interdisciplinary in ways that contributed to its rhetorical nature as a zone of
optimism that escapes a variety of disciplinary constraints (and affordances
that make the evasion seem cruel), so too does film remain in the dark, affording us both individual and collective pleasure. What I am getting after is that
the interstitial need not suggest a lack of rigor. Regarding film, the interstices
may seem more immediately appropriate as zones for optimistic production.
That is to say, the liminal space of film need not render it a-critical or less than
an ideal object for rhetorical study, and it certainly need not diminish our
efforts to enact rhetorical desires through film as valid and powerful rhetorical work. Many of us working with film have witnessed the affordances of digital media as unavoidably present, moving us to take on work that previously
seemed impossible due to disciplinary constraints, technological limitations,
and personal doubts and fears. Yet, our hopes and desires, along with the
affectively embodied pleasures that rhetorical cinematic activity has moved
us to experience creates immersive "webs of relations" that now want to be
named and illuminated as "film-composition."

Interstitial Sublime

Ideally, this book is a film. For years, though I worked toward the production
of print text that might articulate the value of DIY filmmaking as rhetorical, I
didn't seek to write a book. I crafted films that longed to radiate the rhetorical
value of digital filmmaking. And while I stand behind my cinematic rhetorical output, I've always suspected that while working from within what Jon
McKenzie (2001) calls "the liminal norm," where "[t]he task is . . . to multiply
the models at one's disposal while at the same time opening up these models
to their 'own' alterity" (p. 29), I'd be both expanded and contracted to write
the book. That I was both working in the film ecology associated with independent film (Sundance) and working at a state university created the conditions for the compositional practice. A mid-career shift to a smaller, private

university meant additional interstitial anxiety and trauma. Nevertheless, the book obtains. I'm grateful to be able to maintain my liminal status and to be productive at the same time. The metaphors that associate with this project—*hope, fear, desire,* and *pleasure*—have created the conditions necessary for focusing even as I am generally destabilized by life. *Vertiginous sublime.*

Composing my scholarly filmic entertainments, I've been guided by metaphors that hint at my complexly shifting dispositions, always hoping, fearing, and desiring that my films, with their pleasurable multitrack, multimodal attempts to entertain might in fact entertain audiences. Situating these metaphors on a historical timeline is a fairly cinematic, narrative-driven, compositional practice. In operational terms, any film's timeline—a film's essential structuring tool—would help me to craft a meaningful report on many different vectors of complicated thought (differing depending upon each film's central inquiry and development). Affect theory operates in ways that seem to me to mimic the flexibility of an editing suite's timeline, affording a roomy space for enacting intentional but dynamic curatorial choices, driven by a particular sort of cinematic vision (rhetorical strategy). It seems to me that film, and the editorial timeline (in the case of my work, in Final Cut Pro), seems the perfect medium for tracing affectively intense compositional practices, given film's capacity to capture image, text, audio, and effects, all toward the goal of resonating a precise ambient experience that vibes with the researcher's immersive inquiry and findings. Because I see film as such a remarkable tool for composing an affectively intense and immersive compositional history, it is quaintly amusing that Miles and Huberman (1994) offer as a warning the notion that "reports can go beyond words," explaining that "many qualitative researchers use presentation modes of drawings, still photos, and videotapes," and that these multiple modes may function as obstacles, as they "have issues that transcend compellingness" (p. 302). This reads as an invitation to interpret the extra-lexical report with a terrifically critical eye (perhaps this helps to explain why I am horribly ill just prior to a screening, so aware am I of my audience's critical eye). Yet, despite my parenthetical admission, I always hope that viewers read my films critically. What's more, it seems quite possible that "transcending compellingness" might mean "something more" rather than less, generative rather than constraining.

Whatever the case, my primary hope is that my films entertain, given that the best entertainments are also complexly persuasive and available for clever critical analyses. Similarly, while I might only hope to someday generate *Cruel Auteurism* as a cinematic object, in the meantime I hope that this book moves you to (re)value digital filmmaking as powerful cinematic rhetoric, worthy of your attention, support, and compositional energies. Additionally, I hope that you embrace my claims and the affective frames into which I have cast them. To be sure, my claims have emerged from my experience of the liminal norm, a state of being that attends many aspects of the working lives of many academics in the complicated present. Essentially, despite or perhaps due to my interstitial status, I'm claiming that this book emerges from immersive craftwork in two distinct ecologies, film, and academia. It has thus a kind of hopeful quality that seems to haunt every page. It lives as a kind of extra-institutional fantasy, fantasy as pragmatic theoretical and rhetorical craft.

I've been practicing my craft for some time now. Existing in the form of filmic documentaries and experimental shorts, print articles, and webtexts, I share my findings' in-process inquiries in complex ecologies that integrate short films, contextualizing prose, and a constellation of social media sources that capture and theorize my findings. I use blogs, social media, formal written pages toward publication, conference presentations and conversations, and an editorial timeline in a film editing suite (most often, I use Final Cut Pro). These various textual artifacts coordinate to articulate the rhetorical value of the work. Whether rendered cinematically or as a more conventional print text, my projects are about making. Guided by speculative inquiry, I explore in the role of teacher-scholar who both inhabits and studies digital media, (the teaching of) writing, and the affordances and problematics of screen culture. In my immersive and curatorial role (the role composers ubiquitously enact in digital cultures where making is perpetually happening), I work as researcher. In composing for publication, I take on a curatorial, directorial role, theorizing our shared efforts and textual phenomenon. In many ways, I hope to shine light on our practices as makers in digital cultures.

David Rieder (2015) in his introduction to *Hyperrhiz 13* (an online journal featuring digital scholarship), hopes to explain the scope of maker culture by identifying it in terms of, "modern, Do-It-Yourself (DIY) practices of counter-cultural production [that] combine with new, experimental forms of humanities scholarship" (Introduction). Like the desire to make via film in Composition, Rieder explains that maker culture is not necessarily new but that it is coherent as a critical practice:

> For decades, maker culture has been a set of countervalent practices that define themselves in contrast to modern scientific methods that marginalize the amateur inventor, as well as against an ethos of complacency promoted by brought-to- fᴏ you-by consumerism. (Introduction)

Filmmakers in Composition have worked in DIY, "amateur" mode, and some offer more conventionally professional skills, but most cohere over the concern for rhetorical analysis, production, and critical intervention—critical making.

Cruel Auteurism wants to identify film-composition as a kind of virtual makerspace⁵ that has been assembled by various teacher-scholars working within Composition. I join many creative makers in arguing for film-composition as a vital scene for rhetorical inquiry and practice. Through a judicious use of anecdotal reflection from my experience as rhetorician, compositionist, actor, Sundance volunteer, digital filmmaker, and installation artist, I situate my authorial investment onto a timeline. Soon, the book advances a historical overview of rangier discourses on film in the field of Composition. Eventually forecasting future developments, the book initially looks back in time, to published conversations on film in the classroom (by English professors teaching writing prior to the establishment of Composition as a discipline). The historical overview initiates the timeline across which *Cruel Auteurism* renders its chapters. Because of my readerly attachment to my findings, my reading of this history has been affectively charged, and at the same time, I find such value in thinking with and through the body to infuse this history with cross-epochal theories on affect—it seemed inevitable, based upon the voices populating the narrative. It made sense to me to identify with those who had shared my passion for film (for its potential) as critical rhetorical practice in a writing classroom.

Jenny Edbauer's work attends to affect in ways that align with my desire to trace a history of affects associated with the emergence of film-composition. Tracing a theoretical lineage, she exposes environmental scenes of potential, a zone of optimism for valuing affect. She explains that

> a range of theorists, from Henry Bergson to Mark Hansen, have tacitly suggested that the writing scene can never be reduced to mere signification insofar as the body is the very apparatus that creates meaning. (2005, p. 133)

Through Hansen, Edabuer defines affect as "the capacity of the body to . . . deploy its sensori-motor power to create the unpredictable, the experimental, the new" (2005, p. 133). Note that Hansen's definition hinges (as does Aristotle's definition of "rhetoric") upon a "capacity," an "ability" which may also resonate with a "willingness" or "desire," for rhetoricity. For Edbauer, as for myself, it feels important to recognize how affect motivates the writing body. Hansen notes that the affective experience "comprises a power of the body

---

5   These makerspaces are as yet virtual, as networks of film-compositionists exist mostly online, collaborating through networked rhetoricity. While many programs feature processes for students and faculty to check out digital capturation tools—cameras, mics, and so on—most film-compositionists rarely share physical time and space toward the production of their works. I hope to see this change, toward the emergent existence of makerspaces that honor the physicality of making and a return to film (yes, silver acetate), "resulting in new [old?] ways of enacting rhetoricity" (Sheridan, 2016).

that cannot be assimilated to the habit-driven, associational logic governing perception" (as cited in Edbauer, 2005, p. 133). Nevertheless, we write, and we carry forward our arguments, driven by affective intensity even as we take up various (seemingly static or rule-bound) rhetorical methods for enacting our compositions. Edbauer reasons thus that, "the body-of-sensation is always stubbornly present in scenes of writing," so "there can be no affectless compositions" (2005, p. 133). This insistence represents a persistent track for *Cruel Auteurism,* and in many ways highlights my decision to read with affect theory as I have crafted my narrative. It's only obvious. We are affectively motivated to write, to compose. We are affectively moved by compositions, particularly filmic texts. We have for some time longed to compose more routinely via film. Due to the affordances of digital media and their multimodal, multi-track capacities, we may be better equipped to capture a dynamic range of affective associations (through image, video, sound, and text).

Earlier scholars working in Composition hinted at relationships between emotions, affect, and cognition. Against worries that thinking through affect might mean working from extreme ends of a phantom emotional spectrum (Murray, 2009, p. 99), Murray describes Alice Brand's glimmer of this in her sense of "cool rationality," (2009, p. 103). Cool rationality as a concept refers rather simply to what seems obvious—that affect and emotion matter in our reasoning processes. Thus, they matter for writing, thinking, teaching, and learning. Murray turns to ethicist and political philosopher Michael Stocker, who worked with the psychologist Elizabeth Hegeman to write *Valuing Emotions* (1996). Stocker elaborated something akin to cool rationality when he explained some of the more concrete aspects of thinking with affect and its relation to cognition and learning. Murray summarizes: "concepts such as intellectual excitement and interest, motivation, and the ability to concentrate on a task in order to make observations" (2009, p. 103) are discernible indicators of these connections. Furthermore,

> In the case of intellectual interest and excitement, emotions play a part in helping (1) to select one idea over another, (2) to develop a research interest, and (3) to discover and consequentially follow relevant facts and discard others. (Murray, 2009, p. 103)

Murray works through Stocker, Brand, and McLeod to further articulate a complex network of affects and how they manifest as emotion and shape learning, insisting that, "these emotional states—interest, motivation, and attention—weigh in heavily during 'rational' processes we consider to be so crucial to reasoning" (2009, p. 103). For my purposes, the direct nature of how and to what extent affect functions is less intriguing than *that* it functions in our rational and cognitive processes. Whereas we may frivolously assume that sensory input obviously encourages and motivates our and our students' interests and possibly the value of the work we produce, we also see through Murray's recasting of affect here that a powerful association with affect toward critical reasoning has for some time occupied Composition scholars attempting to find new ways of comprehending creative scholarship and pedagogy. In today's Composition, with the generous range of compositional options open to us for scholarship, teaching, and learning, we are more fully able to act on our capacities for engaging our vibratory affects in ways that delight, provoke, and at the same time articulate rhetorical dispositions and creative vision.

We have not always waved off affect lightly. Troubling the seeming lightness of affect as critical theory, Edbauer offers a detailed review of affect work in Composition, citing laudable works by Kristie Fleckenstein (2003), Lynn Worsham (1998), and many others. Vibing with Fleckenstein's rejection of the idea of images as static but instead affectively infused, as "Information becomes meaningful through relationships" (2003, p. 9), and similar to Worsham's illuminating "Going Postal: Pedagogic Violence and the Schooling of Emotion" (1998), which begins to articulate the value of affect theory by helping distinguish the ideological nature of emotion, Edbauer (2005) highlights concerns over a troubling binary regarding the notion that affect studies privileges affect over signification. Edbauer dismisses this binary as false, arguing instead that affect and signification are pragmatically inseparable: "Indeed, writing is nothing but the proximate operation of affect and signification. In talking about the pedagogical practice of writing, . . . we are already addressing affect's operation" (2005, p. 136). In many ways, this co-existing set of relations is what drives my work in film-composition. That is to say, I have been compelled to write this book because of my own compositional experiences as a filmmaker, through "the proximate operation of affect and signification" (Edbauer, 2005, p. 136). Driven by my awareness of affective intensities as motivational, attendant, coterminous, trans-process, and at times seeming to move beyond the boundaries of rhetorical logic, much of my work as a filmmaker, teacher, writer, and public speaker on the nature of my filmmaking processes has been about articulating the essential vitality of the work as capable in itself, as available for our trust as both teachers and composers. Our affectively intense film compositions reveal their logic over time (throughout composing processes) and even at times especially in performance, at the very moment of a screening, when a certain rhetorical choice that had seemed so necessary "suddenly" reveals its fuller rhetorical logic (as is sometimes evidenced by audience response, it too registering in the moment through laughter, applause, and other forms of receptive approval or enthusiasm). As I read her, Edbauer is attentive to chronos in ways that value the circuitry of affect and meaning. For my purposes, then, I read her as capturing the embodied sensation and processing of affect toward thinking the value of film-composition as rhetorical praxis when she smartly insists that, "rhetoricity itself operates through an active mutuality between signification and affect" (Edbauer, 2005, p. 134). I want to assert that this operation may be experienced, that it happens during a screening, within a time frame that captures how our cinematic arguments render their affects/effects, hopefully in ways that confirm our affective desires to argue cinematically regarding the matters explored in the filmmaking process. That we, as digital scholars, and our students, as students of composition may witness audience effects in real time suggests a tremendously exciting new project on audience that our print work doesn't allow. Film offers a glimmer of hope for seeing and otherwise comprehending audience response in compressed, immediate, and affectively moving ways. Those of you who have screened and/or had students screen their work in classrooms or other venues might recognize this value; if you have not experienced it, I encourage you to seek out such performances as a way of exploring the rhetorical and pedagogical value of film-composition.

Questions about affect and its role in pedagogy remain in various states of evolution, and much of it intimates that rational rhetorical action need not emerge solely from a discrete, strategically crafted plan of action. Planned, or unwittingly experienced and reproduced, affective being and becoming are valuable components of writing processes. That we may capture more sensorially such a wide range of affect through the affordances of digital media has meant that we are now able to vibe with one another through our cinematic and other multimodal works. Obviously, as we are drawn to particular affects and the arguments they seem to inspire or from which they may emerge, we may attune ourselves to a range of specific rhetorical choices. Same as it ever was. Rhetoricity's performative structuration is in many ways a zone of optimism for affective being, becoming, and becoming more finely attuned to artisanal[6] rhetorical sensibilities and kairotically effective choices.

Wherever possible, *Cruel Auteurism* looks to affect theory as it is used by scholars in Composition. However, because this book is about an emergent area only glimmeringly apparent in our scholarly record, I will look mostly to affect theorists, seeking in ways that are guided by my filmmaking and pedagogical experience those provocative or illustrative concepts that help to render clearer a vision of film-composition. Naturally, because film-composition evolves in the context of a wider range of discourses about alternative rhetorics and multimodality, *Cruel Auteurism* contemplates film-

---

6   I know.

composition as somewhat contextualized within scenes effectively articulated by Bump Halbritter (2012) in *Mics, Cameras, Symbolic Action: Audio-Visual Rhetoric for Writing Teachers*; Jason Palmeri (2012) in *Remixing Composition: A History of Multimodal Composition Pedagogy*; Jody Shipka (2011) in *Toward a Composition Made Whole*; and Todd Taylor in *Take 20* (2003), an impressive documentary treatment of Composition history.

Halbritter (2012) concerned himself with pedagogy, asking how we now teach writing, given what he calls "terministic catharsis," a term he borrows from Kenneth Burke to highlight active production as a site of pedagogical possibility. Halbritter agrees with Lawrence Lessig that "audio-visual media making is writing," and he endeavors to expand upon this claim by way of Burke's concept of "symbolic action." In other words, Halbritter seeks to ensure that we see filmmaking (as one instantiation of audio-visual media making) as rhetorical work (2012, pp. x–xi). It seems that even in this contemporary moment, the claim called to Halbritter for validation, despite his experience as a documentarian. He cites as a source of motivation an admonition from one prominent foundress of Composition, Erika Lindemann (pp. x–xi). Lindemann surely recognized the need for disciplinary validation, having herself experienced the emergence of Composition and the challenges such work presented to hopeful writing instructors.

Palmeri (2012) generously covered a range of audio-visual media-making activities through his attempt to articulate the value of remix work and multimodal Composition. Palmeri essentially argued the always alreadiness of multimodality in ways that make clear the complexity of scholarly and pedagogical activity. Arguing against the novel idea that remix and multimodal work is something new to Composition, Palmeri cites cultural vibrations from the timeline of early Composition, recalling that scholars in the early 1960s and 1970s concerned themselves with, "shifts in communication technologies [that] necessitated a rethinking of composition's exclusive focus on linear, alphabetic text" (2012, p. 87). Additionally, Palmeri exposes the seemingly obvious notion that at that time, film, television, and comic books were considered forms of "new media" that might be manifesting new behaviors and shaping how students understood and produced the (then, more routinely conventional) alphabetic texts (2012, p. 88). Palmeri also traces a pivotal time in Composition's history, in the 1970s and early 1980s, when writing teachers began to use cameras in their classrooms for a variety of purposes. Though emphasizing the analytical affordances of film in the classroom, Ira Shor nonetheless argued for the pedagogical value of video production, through which students might acquire critical consciousness (Palmeri, 2012, p. 139). No argument here.

Shipka reveals a devotion to the use of a variety of methods for teaching that matters, including a call to desensitize ourselves not only to the value of film as "beyond words" but to beyond pages and screens, themselves. Shipka seems to have written out of a powerful desire for Composition to reconsider and highlight that and how technologies mediate text. In her terms, this means that in order to help students learn to compose effective texts, we might do more both with print and digital texts, and, importantly, with other types of composed objects, scenes, events, and performances. Shipka shares her own moving and illustrative pedagogical experiences to reveal powerful student responses to various forms of textmaking, including dance performances, drawing, remix work, and more. In other words, Shipka models how compositional activity need not tend solely to the page or even the screen, but that our pedagogies might most effectively be about the activity, the activities, to acts of composing in its various stages and forms.

Taking a more traditional documentary approach, Taylor's filmic rendering of film in composition features interviews with Composition scholars who represent some of the field's most prominent areas and interests. From the Bedford / St. Martin's host site abstract, the project is revealed to be an "hour-long film that captures a corner of an ongoing conversation about current practices, changing conditions, and emerging ideas around the teaching of writing" (Bedford/St. Martin's), and with the other texts mentioned here, the work stands as some of the earliest scholarship of the post digital turn that features a re-appraisal of film in Composition. Thus, *Take 20* offers a powerful sense of a collective affective longing to work with film as both scholarship and pedagogy. I have been drawn to these works for their creative, inventive, and rhetorically sound approaches to rethinking composing and the teaching of writing. *Cruel Auteurism* joins in the project of moving with these laudable and courageous scholars.

Each chapter of *Cruel Auteurism* draws upon theories of affect that engage critically with various scholarly indications of affective intensity (i.e., hope) found in our discipline's scholarly record. However, chapters more elementally operate via two zones. Guided by Berlant's (2011) theory, chapters move on a spectrum from "cruel" to "optimistic," and thus each finds within our discourses, theories, and practices a range of troubling and hopeful potentialities. Additionally, in the hopeful zone, chapters are structured to explore affective registers of meaning associated with early and ongoing scholarship by responding with contemporary discourses that gesture toward fulfillment of or perhaps distancing from the promises made by earlier claims. So, whereas an earlier scholar expressed hope for using film in the classroom, contemporary film-compositionists are doing just that, supported by certain theories of affect (many of which also resonate with prominent theories on film, rhetorical, and composition theories). *Cruel Auteurism* reframes historical hopes with methodologically generous moves to argue for the rhetorically valid creative vision of these earlier scholars. In this way, each chapter articulates both zones of "cruelty," and "optimism."

Coterminous Interstices

More specifically, and in terms of the timeline on which I am working, my use of affect terms (hope, desire, etc.) as structuring agents links past and present. The conceptual affect terms articulate disciplinary trends and practices that have been taken up by scholars working in Composition. Both my current and past curiosity regarding affect—via Alice Brand (1985–1986, 1987, 1989, 1991), Ann Berthoff (1978), Susan McLeod (1987, 1990, 1997), and Sondra Perl (1980)—integrate productively with my affective experiences in film-composition and afford me clarity regarding how affect theory shapes a variety of digital media projects. Essentially, early affect work in Composition hinted that what I was feeling, that my hope, fear, desire, and pleasure mattered. It mattered for cognition, and it mattered for intuitive approaches to compositional choices, to the rhetorical strategies guiding my choices regarding . . . everything—how long to hold a shot, what audio to include, what sorts of overlays or effects to incorporate (or not), when to repeat a shot as a form of emphasis or to move back and forth on a timeline, how long a film should be, when it's "done," and . . . everything. In many ways, my somewhat rebellious moves as a DIY digital filmmaker have been driven by my aesthetic sensibilities, my cinematic history (black & white, foreign and independent, documentary, anti-big budget or mainstream, avant-garde) and this disposition guides my aesthetic, rhetorical, compositional, curatorial, and directorial choices, often beyond or above or in excess of what I know to "work" in print culture, in the dominant mode that confers status and "good life" rewards to scholars in Composition. To be more expansively forthcoming, my choices are also quite often driven by what seem like "hunches," which may once have seemed an embarrassment. However, valuing affect suggests that I need not be ashamed. Experience often confirms the value of hunches in compositional activity. In processes of revision, during screenings, and in re-viewing my films in their situated published webtexts, I often find things that seem clever, though in my recollection these clever clips sometimes seem less like clever rhetorical moves and more like happy accidents.

Toward proceeding with a shared awareness of the range of meanings and forms of clarity I'm seeking by using affect theory, a definition. Affect theorists and editors of *The Affect Theory Reader*, Gregory Seigworth and Melissa Gregg (2010) explain affect as visceral forces beneath, alongside, or generally other than conscious knowing, vital forces insisting beyond emotion—that can serve to drive us toward movement, toward thought and extension, ... Indeed, affect is persistent proof of a body's never less than ongoing immersion in and among the world's obstinacies and rhythms, its refusals as much as its invitations. (p. 1)

Affect—"visceral forces"—structures this book because of our immersive, embodied experiences of shifting literacies, pedagogies, and creative and scholarly dispositions. We are (many of us) digital scholars because of the ubiquity of digital textuality in the present. Thus, the book reasonably draws upon these dynamic affects to characterize film-composition's vital emergence. And while affective intensities resonate throughout the discourses on film in our scholarly record, they also support a great deal of pedagogical effort in the present. Thus, using affect to provide frameworks for exploring the evolution of film-composition makes sense as a tool for surfacing a history and highlighting current practices even as it also enables me to articulate my own hard-earned knowledge and skill, hopefully in ways that suggest a suitable ethos for the work of articulating this vital area in our field. As I see it, in a sense we are critically (re)appropriating "felt-sense" (Perl, 1980), a desire toward production, immersion, critical making, remixing, and remaking. It's about a nearly inarticulable desire toward participatory culture[7] through the production of moving texts. If we continue struggling against our hopes and desires in our efforts to perfect our technical knowledge, our abilities to frame and assess assignments, and generally to bypass or transcend them (because they are, as we imagine—wrongfully, as Deleuze would have it—a-critical), we foreclose opportunities for rhetorical ethics and sensitivity that may more appropriately guide us in film-composition. If we elide film-composition because of our fears regarding mastery, then we miss creative and critical pedagogical and scholarly opportunities. Thus, this book is essential, now.

Toward a structural narrative for the emergence of film-composition, I trace my own affective experiences as a filmmaker and rhetorician and at the same time situate the concepts both historically and contemporarily. These vectors of experientially derived thought and action integrate importantly with a range of prominent theorists and practitioners shaping the field both historically and in the present moment. Within *Cruel Auteurism*, I am inspired by many works that resonate their affects on the contem-

---

7   See Arroyo, Sarah J. (2015). *Video and Participatory Culture: Video Culture, Writing, and Electracy.*

porary spectrum, many of which may be situated as forces of attunement within the cultural moment. I am awed by Shipka's (2011) vibrant narrative account of various efforts to provide students with diverse compositional opportunities. I am joltingly motivated and at the same time undulatingly calmed by Thomas Rickert's (2013) smart and affectively vibratory attentiveness to "ambience," a kind of radically open network for rhetorical work:

> What is ambient is immersive, osmotic, peripheral. Ambience is not so link driven, for it suggests many tactile forms besides connections among already established points or nodes. The link gives us little leeway with the more ephemeral, auratic modalities of everyday life . . . The richly osmotic character of ambience includes choric engagement and interaction beyond the link . . . [and] this includes affect; affect certainly circulates in and gives rise to networks, but we need to augment this understanding of affect as more fundamental, being the mood, or affective comportment, from which our attitudes, decisions, and actions emerge. (p. 122)

Toward thinking "ambient" through film-compositionist lenses, I imagine Rickert's ambient rhetoric as a zone of optimistic aesthetic sensibility that shapes compositional potential and desire, being and becoming. This zone of optimism is radically open, potentially disruptive, and in many ways reflective of our immersive experience sufficient to articulate ambient rhetoric as vibing with Davis' (2010) "rhetoricity" (p. 2). Whatever the "link" or particular case—regarding which theory/theorist to read with—the value is in comprehending that the present moment is open to valuing our affectively-derived arguments, even to the fine-grained level of, say, a film about feelings as rhetorically valid work. As I see it, an important aspect of the work of film-composition is to ensure that films about feelings are rhetorically powerful and effective as they are situated within their particular networks, that their beat is correct. But first, ambience. Experientially speaking, whereas I (2005) have written of and still find value in chaos theory and metaphors intimating at the affective experience of complexity and/in writing, my 14 years of service as a Theater Manager at the Sundance Film Festival has attuned me to the more genuinely pleasing value of thinking about chaotic complexity as it is refined through the concept of ambience. So too does Rickert move from Mark Taylor's use of a complexity metaphor toward ambient rhetoric. I have been affectively moved in a profoundly felt way by Rickert's choice regarding the ambient frame for rhetoric, and its linkage to my own work in the Sundance ecology somehow feels right—it seems to confirm that what I have been doing, reading, and taking in, both in film and in Composition ecologies. Thinking ambience, with its networked associations to design, to performance, I contemplate and practice writing, rhetoric, filmmaking, and being. The ambient metaphor has been productively moving me toward this moment, toward this book, toward this sublimely perceivable intertextual state of interstitial being and becoming. Here, these glances—affective shimmers of hope and desire—articulate the seemingly inarticulable nature of hopeful alternatives, validating and compelling me/us (I hope) toward dynamic moving texts and inspiring cinematic rhetorics. Soberingly and ongoingly, however, I enthusiastically respond to the refrain; I contemplate Lauren Berlant's (2011) affect theory of "cruel optimism," which involves motivation to participate in some particular cultural activity, quite probably at the expense of a kind of critical failure. Berlant's frame maps some of the earliest hopes for film in writing classrooms; later, cruel optimism considers the limits of DIY digital filmmaking and the return to film. Further animating film-composition, I argue that the work of digital filmmaking as pedagogy and scholarship is both robust and crafty. By exploring DIY digital filmmaking as a kind of improvisational invention activity that is pedagogically available and instructive, I validate its essential necessity in the moment. Digital filmmaking enables multiple takes, endless editorial revision potential, and limitless possibilities (through iterative processes) for refining filmic text toward eliciting certain affective intensities and assuring rhetorical efficacy.

Looking ahead, DIY digital productivity may return us affectionately and in critically vital ways to the production of filmic objects through networks of technically skilled maker-agents who participate in the emergence of the film (analog film, with sprockets, silver acetate). In this way, film-composition participates in a "calling" to revalue film as special and worth retaining, particularly in light of digital's powerful reign. This vector of the argument is guided by works that draw upon affect theory and have emerged in Composition as particular areas of study and production, including the Maker Movement (Sayers, 2015; Sheridan, 2016), New Materialisms (Gries, 2015), Object Oriented Ontology (Bogost, 2009), Vitalism (Hawk, 2007) and the project of "making composition whole" (Shipka, 2011).

We begin with hope . . .

Chapter 1: Hope

> The Woodstock Nation, as the young counter-culture has been called, receives its information largely from underground radio stations, from television, and from the cinema. And since English teachers agree that we learn to communicate by imitation . . . why not ask the student to express himself in the way he is most often communicated to? By the time he reaches college composition class, he has already learned the language and the techniques of visual communication. Therefore, an alternative to written composition classes . . . is obviously the filmmaking class. (Richard Williamson, 1971, "The Uses for Filmmaking as English Composition")

> Professor Bond introduced the workshop by stating that he found the first twenty years of CCCC boring, though he had attended faithfully and had wanted to enjoy the meetings. Now he feels that a workshop on film promises that we are on the threshold of something big and important and different. (Martha Heasley Cox, 1969, Recorder, *CCCC Workshop Reports*)

We research a question, hoping to support our hunches, the graspy sense of value we attach to our work. Often, we struggle. Sometimes, we find leads that trace a coherent line through vibratory invention fields. Sometimes, we find that someone has been there before, not in a vague whispery way, but in a way that says, "I've always been after what you are now about." In this latter scenario, one might be disappointed, move on to new ideas, seeking the hot young thing that will leave its shiny mark. Alternatively, in this "been there" scenario, we might also find that the earlier gesture was—while charmingly affect-laden and hopeful—somewhat less than ideally complete in its rhetorical validity, less than fully supported but nonetheless worthy of publication because of its passion and hope and desire. Emergent sublime. I find that much early Composition scholarship reads in this way, but I don't deride this tendency. Instead, this early passion, underwriting so many arguments about film in Composition is fairly enchanting, and in its tacit rhetorical attunement and interdisciplinary vision, this early work is also highly rational. *Cruel Auteurism* wants to honor these earlier hopes by integrating works from affect, rhetoric, film, and both historical and contemporary "film-composition" scholars. The latter, through their willingness to take up their cameras and begin making films as scholarship, have begun the work of fulfilling the earlier hopes of those contemplating the roles of film in writing classrooms and highlighting their shimmering rhetorical promises. The "fulfillment" takes place in Composition classrooms and in digital scholarship that is often best (in my arguably biased view) performed "live." As for the promises of early film-composition's rhetorical articulation, I'll gesture toward elaborating and in many ways providing the validity of many early arguments with a variety of contemporary sources that support the hopeful claims they've made. That is to say, I am attempting to create a sense of the ambient scenes surrounding the emergence of film-composition, scenes that are more clearly coming into view via scholarly works that now appear to support earlier claims. To be sure, there is much work to be done in order to fully capture the fine-grained detail of these scenes. The film version will perhaps provide a more fitting venue for the fuller drama, while this book seeks to create a sense of the affective contours shaping film-composition.

Today, we're making films in composition classrooms. Composing with playful joy and passion, we craft rhetorically sophisticated works that radiate far beyond the contours of an 8.5 x 11-inch page (or screen approximation of the same). Beyond watching, or drawing from content to generate topics, and practice summary writing, or highlighting cultural rhetorics for analysis and critical intervention (all good moves), we're making films. I've been making films as my primary form of scholarship since around 2004 (publications surfacing in 2008, unspooling into the present). As I have conceptualized, shot, and edited my films and their contextualizing webtexts, I have been writing this book. I've been writing with a view toward capturing "How We Have Talked About Film in Composition," interested in illuminating obvious rhetorical trends, mapping developments in the field and in culture at large, and hoping to discover support for what I had been finding in my DIY digital filmmaking activities, that filmmaking is powerful, affectively charged, and critically revitalizing rhetorical training. This is a bold claim, and I hope you will indulge me as I tell you what you already know about film-composition.

"Film-composition" is a term I've been using throughout my filmmaking career in academia. It attempts to capture an area within Composition, an area of appreciable momentum and an area that is both generating films and rethinking the construction of "things" and "thinginess" toward (re)animation of the critical value of production, of making—a paper, a book, a collage, a craft beer, a working computer, a film. The book's title suggests evolution "toward" film-composition. This "toward" illuminates a historical tradition and an emergent area of scholarly inquiry (the forces of which sufficiently hint at a cinematic turn). That is to say, this, "toward" hovers dynamically, moving in both directions—back, toward the history I'm tracing, and forward, toward increasing work in film production in writing classrooms. Both moves make clear the breadth of what it means to study writing and those theories and practices that are central to our always evolving, persistently dynamic field, within which film-composition shines ever more brightly. *Cruel Auteurism* projects film-composition across a timeline of scholarship, theory, and practice.

Though film-composition is illuminating a great deal of rhetorical work in our field, we need to continue rolling with the question of this term in order to render it effectively. With "film-composition," I describe filmmaking itself as valid rhetorical work for Composition. The hyphenated term recalls Robert Connor's (1997) linkage of "Composition" and "Rhetoric," (see *Composition-Rhetoric: Backgrounds, Theory, and Pedagogy*). Among many laudable desires for advancing the field and its work, Connors' gesture wanted to infuse college and university-level writing instruction (Composition) with an appreciably sophisticated historical body of knowledge that might elevate the work of Composition and its academic profile. So promoted, the field could evolve with a more rigorous disciplinary history and coherent identity as it took up the linkage and its implied emphasis on rhetorical knowledge and skill rather than merely imitation, forms, and repetition of normative ideas associated with the prevailing academic climate. And while Connors subordinated "Rhetoric" to "Composition," "film-composition" playfully nods to the production of films ("film composition" as "the making of") rather than worrying a precisely appropriate order throughout the process of generating new hierarchies with our defining terms.

As you might imagine, film-composition moves beyond simple awareness of Composition's continuing emergence as a field devoted to more than conventional academic writing.[8] I emphasize the "more than" because film-composition[9] plainly enjoys its association with the notion of composing that emerges from an aesthetic sensibility rendered in the context of a particular métier (in this case, film), or, as is increasingly common, as an interdisciplinary assemblage mediated by rhetorical and other theoretical discourses and practices. "Rhetoric" is not absent from nor is it subordinated to the conceptualization of film-composition (for Composition as a field today is

---

8   For a brief sampling of film-composition scholars working with an extra-academic, multimodal perspective, see some of the works of Jonathon Alexander, Dan Anderson, Geoffrey Carter, Sarah J. Arroyo & Bahareh Alaei, Alexandra Hidalgo, bonnie lenore kyburz, Robert Lestón, Jacqueline Rhodes, Jody Shipka, and Todd Taylor.

9   You may wonder why I do not capitalize "film-composition," especially given its association with Connor's validating and thus capital-worthy term. First, I am no fan of capital letters, but more importantly, I see film-composition not as an entire field but as a subspecialty or series of potential practices within Composition.

clearly mediated by a primary concern for rhetorical knowledge and skill[10]), but in referencing the larger field from within which *Cruel Auteurism* traces the emergence of film-composition, I will abbreviate to "Composition," in the long tradition of remixing our terms (and to feature the notion of production inherent in "composition").

As I have looked back into the history of scholarship on film in Composition, I have seen that many of the works falling under my improvised "How We Have Talked About . . ." heading seem to articulate through affectively charged rhetorics of desire (and the attendant affects of hope, fear, and pleasure). This did not surprise me, given my own love of film, filmmaking, and the heightened rhetorical sensitivities that are activated in processes of spectation and production. My findings were additionally unsurprising because as a "film person" I am inclined to think through desire, along with the powerfully resonant works of Gilles Deleuze (1983, 1985), who has so famously shaped film theory, cinematic rhetorics, computers and writing, digital humanities, digital rhetorics, discourses on multimodality, and postmodern Composition. Naturally, teacher-scholars in English departments have long been invested in narrative structure, which has at its heart an investment in character motivation (desire), a conceptual frame uptaken widely and persistently by rhetorical theorist extraordinaire, Kenneth Burke (1931, 1950). From his earliest writings to his more overt references to "motive" as a titular concept capable of encompassing the drives of rhetorical action, motive enacts via form—"as the psychology of the audience," or "the creation of appetite in the mind of the author and the adequate satisfying of that appetite" (1950, p. 31), all of which aims at the "arousing and fulfilling of desires" (1950, p. 124). So much desire must necessarily attend so many affects. As far back as I read, the affective intensities obtained. Shimmering to the surface of my readings were memories of critical explorations into affect or "the affective domain" in the history of Composition (then, primarily through Berthoff, 1978, 1982; Brand, 1980, 1985–1986, 1987, 1989; McLeod, 1996, 1980). Though the nomenclature likely has more to do with its roots in Psychology, the oft-quoted "affective domain" was perhaps provisionally meaningful only if constrained to a certain range of conscientious pedagogies and compositional moves. I had long been drawn to thinking about affect; an early dream job in Psychology obtained in my memory, and I was emo before emo, so this did not surprise me. I began to see that this book might do more than provide a historical record of conversations on film in the history of Composition but that instead it might also enable me to theorize my own experientially derived knowledge of the affectively intense power of filmmaking to enhance rhetorical knowledge

10   See the first Learning Objective, "Rhetorical Knowledge," listed in The National Council of Writing Program Administrator's Outcomes Statement.

and skill. And, because so many of my contemporaries have been working in film-composition, the book might also afford me space on a timeline with them, locating my own work within an emerging tradition in the field.

Toward articulating the value and meaning of this book's primary title, I note that by exploring the emergence of film-composition with critical attentiveness to affect, I came to recognize that my experience registered as a form of what Lauren Berlant (2011) calls "cruel optimism," a situation that "exists when something you desire is actually an obstacle to your flourishing" (p. 1). The formula goes like this: The work that gains "conventional" rewards (publication, grants, tenure, promotion) is the work that matters, and that work is disproportionately about convention, correctness, surveillance, and normative mapping that forms the very contours of our success. So, my DIY digital filmmaking, while capable of igniting intense and increasingly effective rhetorical velocity[11] for my arguments was perhaps also standing in the way of more conventional kinds of academic arrival. My film work's disruptive critical attunements, which had derived from creative indwelling, existed as optimistic attachments even as they denied me traditional success (the R1 job, the Big Gigs, a Full Professorship). Importantly, my work also proffered gratifying forms of transformative success. Within cruel optimism, Berlant explains the potential for such outcomes, noting

> the magnetic attraction to cruel optimism. Any object of optimism promises to guarantee the endurance of something, the survival of something, the flourishing of something, and above all, the protection of the desire that made this object or scene powerful enough to have magnetized an attachment to it. (2011, p. 48)

Making films wasn't writing books, and books were what mattered as currency underwriting the normative academic good life. Making films on my own (DIY) was thrilling, instructive, and capable of fulfilling innumerable forms of aesthetic, intellectual, rhetorical, and technical desire, but its role as currency toward my flourishing was incapable of catching up with the normative value of the academic monograph. At the same time, the pleasures of digital filmmaking delimited my primary field of scholarly intention, so I continued making what I hoped were rhetorically and aesthetically interesting films and arguing for their validity. Though we might today value a filmic text on terms equal to those of a conventional academic manuscript . . . no. No, I don't think we are quite there yet, though I am hopeful. Berlant might call my hope "cruel," and I see tremendous value in this conceptualization, for

11   More audiences have seen my films than have ever read my print articles, if access records are to be trusted.

it clearly articulates the stakes in these institutional scenes of the everyday. I am hopeful that this book helps clarify our vision regarding what is at stake when we decide to take on alternative forms of textmaking as our validating academic . . . *no*. No, I don't even see film-composition as "alternative" at this point in our evolution in digital textmaking. And yet, the book is entitled *Cruel Auteurism* with a clear nod to Berlant's clever, somber, circuitously optimistic concept. I simply transpose the term "auteur" for "optimist" as a way of suggesting that within DIY digital filmmaking, driven by a particular creative vision that seems to call for what now seems like foolishly individual control, I discovered the rhetorical affordances of digital media in a way more profound than any other in my history of engagement with the tools. I found voice, pleasure and gratification, audiences and accolades, but maybe most importantly, I found hope. I found that in its transfigured form, my writing—my thoughts and arguments—might find expression, and that I need not remain silent simply because of my discomfort with the constraints of print scholarship as I had experienced it.

Cruel Auteurism is inspired by my experiences as a scholar and practitioner in the field of Composition, and it performs a take on the emergence and state of film-composition as a vital scene for rhetorical inquiry and practice. Eventually forecasting future developments, the work initially extends back in time, to published conversations on film in the classroom by English professors teaching writing prior to the establishment of Composition as a discipline. Early mapping draws from publications of the National Council of Teachers of English (NCTE), its readership sufficient to imply an emergent area of study. The history surfaced throughout *Cruel Auteurism* is infused with cross-epochal theories on affect, reaching back to Spinoza's 1677 *Ethics* but more profoundly shaped by Brian Massumi's (2002) conceptualizations on the impact of images and filmic reception as marked by "affective intensities" that are highlighted in current scholarship, most significantly by Joddy Murray (2009), Daniel W. Smith (2007), and Jenny Edbauer (2005). While affect theory helps articulate the history of this emergent area, *Cruel Auteurism* renders partly, or maybe initially through anecdotal elements, as I attempt to situate my claim in experience—mine, and, increasingly that of other film-compositionists working today. To begin, I'll tell you how I became compelled as a filmmaker.

It would be too long a story to describe my early fascination with film, so for a shorthand version, suffice it to say that my early exposure to films on TV made a big impact. I see this now through a rhetorical lens, recognizing how black and white film seemed so magical perhaps because rhetorical effects were somewhat simplistically drawn, but simple in terms of compositional constraints, which often lead to masterful discoveries via rigorous invention and striving. Later, it was through foreign and independent films that I found a more powerful sense of a calling, as the characters, actors, and stories seemed to vibrate somewhat familiarly but were at the same time just off, just slightly more available for attachment through identification with difference. Still later, as a young graduate student (kinda goth), I was drawn to using film in composition classrooms by hearing that others were doing so. This was around 1990, or so. I was shocked and secretly thrilled (!), but I didn't think it was something I could do; I didn't feel it would be "allowed" because it didn't seem "texty" enough, sufficiently sophisticated, or well-theorized. Only after post-graduate school pedagogical training did I find ways of integrating film that seemed theoretically and rhetorically defensible. Later, in 2004, when I started making digital films, I began to sense that this book might emerge as a way of articulating the logical notion that filmmaking and composition are disposed to share classroom space and time. This is when I began my historical research. My reading in the archives confirmed my suspicion that others had similarly desired this potential. Now, with the affordances of digital tools, we have a thrilling array of composing options, and many are working with digital video in ways that honor the desire for film spectation, analysis, and production as pedagogical activity (Alaei & Arroyo, 2013; Alexander & Rhodes, 2012; Carter, 2008, 2016; Hawk, 2008; Hidalgo, 2014; Kuhn, 2011; kyburz, 2008, 2010; 2011; Lestón, 2013, 2015). Tracing this history is thus inspired by experience and a disciplinarily shared desire to engage students in the affectively intense and rhetorically complex work of film-composition.

Film-composition advances as an area within the larger field, one that invests in broad rhetorical knowledge and skill while vibing insistently with what Kevin Michael DeLuca and Joe Wilferth (2009) identify as the rhetorical nature of the "image-event." DeLuca and Wilferth assert the value of the image-event in the context of studies on visual rhetoric, and so the alignment with my interest in dynamic images such as films may seem, for now, slightly unfocused (I hope to elaborate, going forward). Nevertheless, their conceptual frame colludes with what film-composition wants, to promote a rigorously optimistic trust in "speed, distraction, and glances as immanent concepts, not [necessarily] transcendent categories . . . but modes of orientation, modes of intensities" (2009, para. 13) (foreword), all of which seems procedurally and ideationally resonant with a willful investment in what digital media tools enable for film-composition. So, as with Composition-Rhetoric, the term film-composition is designed similarly to link our longstanding desires to validate working with film in composition classrooms but at the same time to avoid the compulsion to see such work as a "will to tame images with meanings," a project that "rarely captures rhetorical force" (DeLuca & Wilferth, 2009, para. 11). I dare imagine that many early film-compositionists worked toward the capturation,[12] toward the simple will and ability to bring filmic content into the classroom for exploration (likely through analysis, exclusively). However, today's film-compositionists seem confident about the project of revitalizing our thinking about film in Composition. They advance a more dynamic engagement, one that is inclusive of both analysis and production, activities rendered possible via the affordances of digital media, a generously reframed conceptualization of "composing," and innovative new projects in deconstructing analog film tools for rethinking their purposes and the processes they might serve.

Aligned with the desires of contemporary film-composition, I am shooting for rhetorical force. Thus, *Cruel Auteurism* materializes as a kind of cinematic timeline, as directed by Christopher Nolan. That is to say, the timeline moves in both directions, and my compositional strategy has been about capturing key affective intensities I have both experienced and discovered vicariously through the scholarly works that trace the emergence of film-composition. Motivated by hope, like so many early and contemporary film-compositionists, I want to honor these scholarly works and the rhetorically visionary teacher-scholars who have composed them. Within these scenes, this may mean a kind of direct exposure that seems less-than-ordinarily scripted. The timeline wants to move us, to evade a taming and instead to invite glances as immanent concepts capable of entertaining and revitalizing recognition of our shared desires. If I had to write the script, I might begin in the present:

INT LAB—DAY

Here, in some hip, blisteringly active makerspace, someone is deconstructing an old Rolleiflex, film-compositionists manipulate files on sleek silver timelines, and the

VOICEOVER

(intones)

"Film-composition as right and necessary, in many ways due to the fact of digital filmmaking as ubiquitous 21st century communication" ("the available means of persuasion") (Aristotle, trans. 1924, Bk 1; Ch 2).

END SCENE.

This possibility has by now established itself within Composition, largely due to the New London Group's (NLG), "Multiliteracies" (1996) and the up-

---

12   I borrow this term, "capturation" from the maniacally devoted filmmaker, Thierry Guetta (aka "Mr. Brainwash"). See the Banksy film *Exit Through the Gift Shop* (2010).

take of that work. The NLG's multiliteracies concept has wanted to move us beyond the "restricted project"—"page-bound, official forms of the national language . . . formalized, monolingual, and rule-governed"—that has conventionally characterized "literacy pedagogy." The NLG wants us moving toward an ongoing negotiation amongst "a multiplicity of discourses" (p. 61), particularly diverse and digitally generated, digitally mediated ones. While James Gee (1996), and the impressive ensemble of digital scholars invested in the work of the NLG helped manifest and shiny up existing literacy pedagogies with which many compositionists were well aware (think "CAI," or "CMC"[13]), Anne Frances Wysocki (1998) was busy reanimating Composition with a desire to design better texts, better assignments, better pedagogies that more closely approximated "the available means of persuasion" in the digital and design-savvy present,[14] and she was not only concerned with pedagogy but with raising the stakes for what might count as academic scholarship and rhetorical pedagogy. Wysocki's "A Bookling Monument" (2002) has obtained canonical status in New Media Studies and within Composition, where, now no longer "New," Digital Media Studies, Digital Rhetorics, and Digital Humanities projects all enjoy the lively camaraderie of a network of teacher-scholars devoted to advancing rhetorical knowledge and skill in ways that register as affective intensities[15] rather than merely as schoolbook exercises. For me, it was Wysocki's (1998) "Monitoring Order: Visual Desire, Organization of Web Pages, and Teaching the Rules of Design" that illuminated the right thinking of my hunches about the value of good design, that it mattered as rhetoric and not "merely" as style or personal inclination. Soon, Wysocki, along with Johndan Johnson-Eilola, Cynthia Selfe, and Geoffrey Sirc (2004) generated a sort of handbook for new media work in Composition, *Writing New Media: Theory and Applications for Expanding the Teaching of Composition*, and something of a subculture began to coalesce with greater momentum; the digital turn mattered in Composition.

So all these things were happening. At the same time, I was taking on my volunteer role with the Sundance Film Festival, screening films for rhetorical analysis in my college writing classrooms, and making films for my personal and professional pleasure and/as inquiry in the context of the buildup to Operation Desert Storm. The digital film I made in that moment (*proposition 1984*, 2004) became my primary form of interaction with news of the war and public discourses of doublespeak and political lies from which I

---

13   Computer-Assisted Instruction, and Computer-Mediated Communication, respectively. This goes back to Deb Holdstein's early work in the late 1980s.

14   See Gary Hustwit's filmic argument regarding the ubiquitous and culturally powerful nature of design in both *Helvetica* (2007) and *Objectified* (2010).

15   See Massumi, Brian (2002). *Parables for the Virtual: Movement, Affect, Sensation.*

recoiled, silent and heartshakingly angry, the camera and my editing tasks providing me with any sense of a mattering voice at all. Though I screened the film at the 2005 Modern Language Association (MLA) Convention, the 2004 National Council of Teachers of English (NCTE) Conference, the 2005 Conference on College Composition and Communication, and at a special campus screening (2005), I may not have shared this work at all, publicly, but for the motivation I'd often felt from certain scholars working in Composition. Years prior to but ideationally sharing a vibratory field with the evolution of my evolving digital practices, I encountered Geoffrey Sirc's (1997) *College Composition and Communication* (CCC) article, "Never Mind the Tagmemics, Where's the Sex Pistols," and it read like a revelation, not only because of my longstanding devotion to the Sex Pistols and the critical edge they brought to my lingering 1980s, Sex Pistols–loving sensibility, but also because of Sirc's seemingly retro approach to thinking about the value of pedagogy and scholarship for an individual writer, value that moved beyond the conventional script regarding "the writing process," world-changing, correctness, and strict documentation formats. There was the seamless sampling of lyrics from The Clash, not quoted or cited but simply integrated into Sirc's clever syntax. I recall reading this and audibly gasping! I immediately (no lie) called the journal's editor, then, Joseph D. Harris, to applaud him for publishing the piece as it was, and he graciously relayed a story of negotiating citation practices in order to accommodate Sirc's creative rhetorical vision ("WE COULD DO THAT?!"). Next, I ran to share "my finding" with my colleague, Duane Roen, then Director of Composition at my institution, Arizona State University. He had been in a meeting with another colleague, but his door was open, so I rushed in, unstoppable, to ask, "HAVE YOU SEEN THIS?!!" Duane was polite but indicated that he'd not yet read the latest issue of the journal, *College Composition and Communication*. Despite the missed affective connection, I knew I'd shared something important. I left feeling as though I MYSELF HAD WRITTEN THE THING, so thrilled to be able to share such pulsatingly thrilling prose with my colleagues, so proud to associate with it at all. Later, controversies over the boundaries of Fair Use in my digital filmmaking career would compel me to recall this anecdote again and again, recirculating its images and affects in ways that seemed to validate the loopy sampling efforts some of us in Composition (especially in film-composition) have felt emboldened to make. At the time, I wasn't thinking about filmmaking, but the learning about rhetorically bold moves to support creative vision began to shimmer brightly in my ongoing practice. Importantly, "Never Mind" at the same time reanimated a general concern for something like "truth" and personal proclivities, a willingness to honor what actually engages us and our students but also invites us to share the affective intensities that have shaped our own critical dispositions.[16] All of this—affect, emotion, and "authenticity," even in postmodern Composition (!). I was thrilled and motivated, but my abilities to articulate my shared vision eluded me. That is, I felt I couldn't work with these contentious ideas in print (Sirc is a wizard; I can't compete). Years later, DIY filmmaking made much more sense.

Cut just so, these various related texts and their conceptual orbits eventually emboldened me (and many others) to take on new forms of composing, even forms that might not have been ideally valuable in a conventional academic sense. Still, film-composition registers unevenly. My film projects seem to rate on a love-it-or-hate-it scale, with seemingly little room for serious reflective contemplation, which has been a somewhat desirable state of affairs, not because I don't want to matter but because of my desire to generate (or value emergent) DeLuca and Wilferth's "modes of intensities" (foreword), and there is little regulating these sorts of events. This indeterminacy animates the extremes, lighting up the critical potential and rhetorical edginess of film-composition. Perhaps because of the vibratory sense of potential in this work, film-composition both as scholarship and pedagogy promises affective intensity that may not happen in scenes of conventional composition. In a hopeful light, my work in film-composition both emboldens and delights me, and I hope that it aids you similarly in your projects. And while my personal story of engagement with high profile publications that have encouraged me may be useful, most academic projects need to demonstrate also that they are more than simple[17] home movies; they must emerge as feature-length documentaries (i.e., have a long and complex history). So, with a promising kind of hope, I imagine that, just as I have been, you too will be fascinated to know that film-composition has been decades in production.

Earlier calls for film-composition emerged in the pages of *English Journal*, where Peter Dart (1968) proclaimed that

> Teachers are encouraged to use films in their classes. Films,
> they are told, should be used to provide vicarious experiences,
> to provide focal points for discussion, and to provide compar-

---

16   Throughout my filmmaking career, I have found that one of the primary concerns from audiences is about copyright. As a strong advocate for rhetorical strategic uptake via Fair Use, I often find a way of answering and redirecting to explore a film's content. Sometimes, we run out of time. Sometimes, I say simply that, "That's a matter of Fair Use, and I agree that we need to study the law but also to argue effectively for our rhetorical purposes."

17   In a 1973 issue of *Cinéma Pratique*, Jean-Luc Godard reveals his desire to turn from the political to the personal. Godard implies, however, that the political obtains, arguing that "the true political film" would be, in essence, "a family film" (as quoted in Brody, 2008, p. 368).

isons of media and communication. But the film's most effective and profitable use is probably its most neglected function: students need to produce their own films. (p. 96)

And then there is Richard Williamson's (1971) "The Case for Filmmaking as English Composition," which is the article I would have liked to write, as a first, a heartfreakingly joyful and liberatory move capable of inspiring Composition teachers to move on, to accept that "the available means of persuasion" do not begin and end with words. But I'm not the first. Williamson is not the first. Even Dart is not the first. In fact, we have been talking about film in our various iterations of academic instruction (i.e., Composition) since at least 1911. Through his detailed archival research, Ben Wetherbee (2011) traces these conversations to the birth of the National Council of Teachers of English. Using a 1987 NCTE-commissioned report, Dale Adams notes that film in English department course work had long been a staple due to the relationship between film's form and content, and its narrative structuration, which made it an easy fit for departments devoted to studies in "narrative literature":

> By 1911, when the [NCTE] was formed, the motion picture, both as an art and an industry, was already recognized as a medium of tremendous sociological, educational, and artistic possibilities. As such, motion pictures[,] primarily because of their affinity with other narrative literature, came under the varying degrees of purview of teachers of English and [have] remained so until the present time. (as quoted in Wetherbee, 2011, p. 8)

Wetherbee's careful emplotment continues by noting what may seem like an obvious trend, in hindsight—the subordination of film production to film analysis. Wetherbee characterizes the nature of these hermeneutic practices by noting their primary attentiveness to reading for literary value as well as for moral training: "The earliest years of film studies (1911–1920), saw English departments employing films as stimulants for student writing, but subordinating both films and student compositions to the study of 'legitimate' literature" (Wetherbee, 2011, p. 8). Adams explains that "[w]here film study was given any positive artistic consideration, it was done by energetic but maverick teachers of English" ("Historical," p. 4). Wetherbee notes that consideration of film in secondary English curricula swelled in '20s and '30s, though chiefly motivated by a concern that film was, according to Adams, "having negative effects on students." Thus, moving pictures found their way into the classroom, ironically, in order to "keep children from attending movies and to raise standards in film appreciation" (Adams, "Historical" 4–5). An enterprise known as The Payne Fund, which between 1929 and 1932 sponsored this moralizing inquiry into the effects of cinema on youths, sought, like Hugh Blair a century and half before it, to cultivate good taste (Wetherbee, 2011, p. 8).

As noted, Wetherbee's work valiantly takes on the attempt to trace "A Rhetoric of Film" that might tease out various rhetorical approaches to considering film within the field. Our projects thus seem to emerge from a shared hope. In my own reading, I have sought to discover discussions of film for its pedagogical roles. If I am honest, I have specifically attempted to find arguments invested in identifying the sort of rhetorical value I associate with film-composition. So whereas the early history will yield mostly hopeful (and some fearful—see chapter 2) discussion on film in Composition, the discussions center primarily upon film as it is used to explore narrative structure, and, later, as it is used to examine complex cultural content ("issues"). For my part, I want to share what DIY filmmaking has taught me and like-minded film-compositionists. I want to articulate some of the ways I see this emergent area of study happening across a timeline of my own emergence as a teacher-scholar who promotes film production as rhetorical pedagogy and scholarship. And this means that the story finds room to unspool within the interdisciplinary multiplex, Composition.

My foraging begins with a work from 1939, when, J. Hooper Wise published "A Comprehensive Freshman English Course in Operation" in *English Journal* (volume 28, issue 6). In it, Wise describes the University of Florida's Freshman English course, where lectures featured work on both writing and, importantly, listening skills via "[c]onversation, . . . stage plays, music, all radio programs, and, in part, TV programs and motion picture productions" (1939, p. 131). Wise also lists the course objectives, which are guided by several assumptions that have currency in today's Composition, including the by-now common sense notion that teaching well involves working not only with ideas and texts that teachers consider to be "ideal" but also by integrating material that fascinates students.[18] For example, among UF's central assumptions for their FYC course is this: "ideas are of prime importance, and teaching the communication arts is fruitless when attempted apart from ideas meaningful to the student" (Wise, 1939, p. 131). A related assumption is as follows: "the communication arts are so closely inter-related that progress in one makes progress in each of the others surer and easier—in fact, that they operate in a complementary manner" (Wise, 1939, p. 131). While we might have to forgive

---

18   It will be impossible to place into a note the number of scholars who argue for pedagogies that engage students by encouraging them to write from what they like, enjoy, or know. A small sampling includes: Peter Elbow, 1973; Ellen Cushman, Jenny Edbauer, Krista Fleckenstein, Jeff Rice, Geoffrey Sirc, 2002; Kurt Spellmeyer, John Trimbur, Victor Vitanza, and many, many more.

UF for the assumptions they make about causality,[19] many of us also realize that Composition, especially when viewed as Composition-Rhetoric, has always been an interdisciplinary endeavor. As well, we recognize that when students are interested in what they are writing, they seem to perform more joyfully and effectively. Finally, we might usefully take note of the ways in which Wise's informed but generally unsupported claims shape a loose but hopeful rationality that begins to radiate the rhetorical scenes within which film discourses emerge in Composition.

Cruel Auteurism begins to identify and examine various discourses mediating, remediating, animating, and revitalizing our notions of film in Composition. Several guiding questions animate my inquiry and shape the story I am seeking to tell. How have we talked about film? How have our discourses promoted, discouraged, tested out, and authoritatively endorsed or rejected various uses of film in Composition? What sorts of discourse seem more or less effective at creating validity for our studies in film within our broader field(s) of interest? What is the nature of film discourses in Composition, and how can those interested in film make use of these discourses?

As we have talked about, explored, used, and produced film in Composition; we have been creating webs of discourse that provide access to ways of thinking about film and/as textuality today. It seems especially important to think about film in this moment, as digital media practices evolve into prominent[20] areas of scholarly inquiry and as coursework in film becomes more common in Composition classrooms. Clearly, this recasting of film in Composition may help us rethink composing writing instruction in what Douglas Kellner (1994) calls a "media culture" (a term that by now need not render as a quote, but as I am tracing discourses sufficient to theorize a history, they remain). And, as "the future of text" is in question—Todd Taylor (2005) has called film "the end of Composition"—such a review of our history with film seems capable of providing us with discourses of hope, those that make available various kinds of pedagogical, rhetorical, and theoretical possibility for the increasingly diverse literacy scenes in which we live, work, and play. *Multipass.*[21]

---

19   . . . or not. Consider Julie Thompson Klein's work on interdisciplinarity, or N. Katherine Hayles' "matrix" of interdisciplinary influence that enables work in one area to resonate with others that are enmeshed in the matrix via a particular paradigm or cultural moment.

20   As of an earlier draft of a revision of this chapter (in 2009), consider the rapid rise of Digital Humanities conversation at the MLA. For a listing of the number of Digital Humanities (DH) sessions at The 2009 Annual Convention of the Modern Language Association, or MLA 2009, see Mark Sample's Sample Reality entry. For a discussion of the DH as "next big thing" see William Pannapacker's Chronicle column, entitled "MLA and The Digital Humanities." For a detailed synthesis of information on DH and especially social networking, see George H. Williams' ProfHacker posts.

21   See *The Fifth Element*. And be sure to read Byron Hawk's (2003) rhetorical treatment

Cruel Auteurism is arranged according to prominent concepts that I have discovered in the process of analyzing film discourses found primarily in two academic journals with very wide National Council of Teachers of English readership, *College Composition and Communication*, and *College English*. Taken together, these two journals enjoy circulation wide enough to support the claim that the film discourses within them rise to the level of operational discourses in Composition. Within my work, I hope to enable these discourses to articulate their vibratory power via the terms I have ascribed to them, *hope, fear, desire I, desire II*, and *pleasure*. I use these concepts to give shape to this work. I look at early discourses that render as tentative questions,[22] as resistance, as theories of desire (*desire*), as acceptable pedagogy, and as forms of critical pleasure. This work only begins to script how we have talked about and are currently discussing, using, and producing films. However, by creating a conceptual schema that accounts for our historical and present engagements with film, we may begin to get a sense of coherence for film work in Composition. I begin with references to the faint "hopes" of early film-compositionists, "faint" because they are rendered without much concern for the value of conventional academic evidence or even very careful theoretical frames. I intend to boost the production value of these early attempts even as I consume them on their own terms.

I begin with "hope" because early Composition scholarship is marked rhetorically by affective registers of hope. These hopeful pleas articulate shared desires for workable pedagogy. They come from writing teachers who seem to be well aware of the quaintly suspicious nature of their claims (I refer to these early authors as "writing teachers" because these earliest discourses emerge from English department writing teachers who may or may not identify as "compositionists"). Many early claims for film work in Composition reflect a quiet approach, and in this silence, the arguments render as tentative, under-theorized, and not well supported by any form of factual evidence. Nevertheless, they unspool freely, mediated by a sanguine disposition, an uncertain longing writing the hope that whispers its intensely seductive nature even in the crisp, clean light of its rhetorically shaky status and potential to screen as less-than-ideally "academic." Addressing this gap in the seriousness of hope, I turn to contemporary affect theorists, who articulate the experience of hope in empathetic and quasi-poetic fashion. My use of the term "hope" is mediated first by contemporary affect theorist Lauren Berlant (2011) and her categorization of hope as a "cluster of promises" (p. 93), a concept echoed by Seigworth

---

of the film, "Hyperrhetoric and the Inventive Spectator: Remotivating The Fifth Element" in Blakesley's collection, *Terministic Screens*.

22   For an example of a "tentative question" via discourse analysis, see Wise's "in part," emphasized, above.

and Gregg's (2010) characterization of desiring, emergent "bloom-spaces," which they explain as

> excess, as autonomous, as impersonal, as the ineffable, as the ongoingness of process, as pedagogico-aesthetic, as virtual, as shareable (mimetic), as sticky, as collective, as contingency, as threshold or conversion point, as immanence of potential (futurity), as the open, as a vibrant incoherence that circulates above zones of cliché and convention, as a gathering place of accumulative dispositions. (p. 9)

The earliest bloom-spaces of film-composition I found of particular value are located within the writing of J. Hooper Wise (1939), whose piece gets at one of the central concerns among film-compositionists working in Composition today. Wise helps us worry the analysis/production dichotomy even as his work surfaces early suggestions regarding the value of teaching toward the critical consumption of cultural texts that is assisted by studies in "motion picture productions" (1939, p. 132). Wise was apparently hopeful about the nature of lectures offered by the University of Florida's 1939 course in "Freshman English." Wise intrigues with his interest in both rhetorical listening and the value of film for teaching this critical skill. While it is true that he begins by stating that the value of the lecture itself is "to engender in the student the ability to listen" (1939, p. 132), which might feel like an invitation to reify crusty pedagogical conventions and an emphasis on analysis, he goes on to imagine "listening" as "the complement of speaking," (1939, p. 132) and in this way Wise generates a gentile synthesis rather than the conventional schism between hermeneutic and generative pedagogical practices. Contemporary film-compositionists and other digital media scholars working Composition have been wearing away at this faded distinction for quite some time (Arroyo, Ball, Carter, Deluca & Wilferth, Kuhn, kyburz, Lestón, Vitanza, and more).

Wise was surely limited in his articulated vision (note the emphasis on the lecture), but it is noteworthy that as he thought about the relationships between the value of listening and the act of conventionally privileged speaking (as pedagogical ends), he did so by intimating a point that many filmmakers have famously argued, that *sound matters*. This immense claim finds early expression within film discourses in Composition, yet it is rendered without access to much evidence or the rhetorical flourishes of grounded affect theory. Framed today, Wise might have introduced the value of rhetorical listening via famed sound editor Walter Murch and sound theorist Michel Chion. For Murch, and Chion, sound matters a lot. For Murch, its power equates to our first experience of a fusion between "I" and "(m)other," clearly a momentous occasion in the evolution of our rhetorical knowledge and skill as well as for our attentiveness to an other, an audience, and a vehicle for sharing hopes and desires and other affective intensities:

> We begin to hear before we are born, four and a half months after conception. From then on, we develop in a continuous and luxurious bath of sounds: the song of our mother's voice, the swash of her breathing, the trumpeting of her intestines, the timpaní of her heart. Throughout the second four-and-a-half months, Sound rules as solitary Queen of our senses: the close and liquid world of uterine darkness makes Sight and Smell impossible; Taste monochromatic, and Touch a dim and generalized hint of what is to come. Birth brings with it the sudden and simultaneous ignition of the other four senses, and an intense competition for the throne that Sound claimed as hers. The most notable pretender is the darting and insistent Sight, who dubs himself King as if the throne has been standing vacant waiting for him. Ever discreet, Sound pulls a veil of oblivion across her reign and withdraws to the shadows, keeping a watchful eye on the braggart Sight. If she gives up her throne, it is doubtful that she gives up her crown. (as quoted in Chion, 1994, p. vii–viii)

For hopeful, early film-compositionists, Sound provided a means of theorizing the value of film for writing pedagogies and a range of associated rhetorical skills. Among these early film-compositionists are many digital humanists, digital rhetoricians, and technorhetoricians currently enjoying wide audiences and support (Steph Ceraso, Eric Detweiler, Brian Harmon, Byron Hawk, and David Rieder, to name only a few). These contemporary teacher-scholars seem to know what Wise intuited, that an emphasis on listening is critical to pedagogy. Wise explains that "[c]onversation, lectures, stage plays, music, all radio programs, and, in part, TV and motion picture productions are transmitted through the ear" (1939, p. 132). The ear! Not the eye?? Yes. (Murch would be pleased). As Wise explains his version of listening as critical work, he never uses the term "rhetorical" or "critical listening," yet he moves in that direction when he asserts that

> A poor and untrained listener is hampered in modern society and may even become a menace by acting on the half truth or by being prayed upon by emotionally toned propaganda. A sign of maturity is the ability to listen actively and accurately. (1939, p. 132)

So, for Wise, writing pedagogy possesses potential to teach critical listening, but one might also imagine that he intends—with his concern that a poorly trained student become a "menace"—that we are also teaching rhetorical skills in production (presumably, the "menace" acts, producing rhetorically sloppy, inflammatory or otherwise hateful text/actions). Here too, it is useful to read from within Wise's prose, to discern his understanding of pedagogy's role and its primary value as associated with ostensibly unproblematic media: "[c]onversation, lectures, stage plays, [and] all radio programs," (1939, p. 132) which was for so long just fine with English Studies. Note that Wise assigns the power of "TV and motion picture productions" to the realm of the "in part" (1939, p. 132), which hints that while Wise seems sure of the urgency of his claims, he is nevertheless aware of the secondary or potentially suspicious nature of film as pedagogy in English classrooms of his time. Perhaps it was merely about The New, but I suspect that Wise (and others thinking along these lines in the late 1930s) was both intrigued by and worried over the affective intensities of the (then) new media. And, given his concern for critical listening, I imagine that Wise worried the stimulating potential of "synchresis, the forging of an immediate and necessary relationship between something one sees and something one hears" (Chion, 1994, p. 5). That is to say, highly mediated texts, grinding out several tracks at once (not merely words, not merely sound, not merely image) seemed perhaps overfull of meaning, controversy, and provocative value. Notably, in Composition today, we amp up such affects. We are currently invested in grounding rhetorical theories,[23] productive theories on affect,[24] and (new) media theories and pedagogies that consider film as a primary form of cultural currency, both outside the academy and within.[25] Having dispensed with the minimalist philosophies of current-traditionalism and embraced postmodern pluralism, uncertainty, and ambiguity, along with posthumanist cyborg sensibilities and digitally mediated identities, Composition no longer fears but desires the critical, experiential, problematic, and sensual multimodal.

Like Wise, hoping and suspecting value in film-composition, Herbert Weisinger (1948) "plead[s]" for us to see that it is up to English to provide serious study in film (p. 270). It is not difficult to read Wise and Weisinger's pleas as emblematic of what contemporary affect theorist Lauren Berlant (2011) calls "cruel optimism," . . .

> the force that moves you out of yourself and into the world in
> order to bring closer the satisfying something that you can-

---

23   See The Usual Suspects in Composition: from Aristotle to Burke.

24   See Brand, Edbauer, Fleckenstein, Jarratt, Massumi, McLeod, and Worsham, to name only a few.

25   See David Blakesley, Karen Foss, ...

not generate on your own but sense in the wake of a person,
a way of life, an object, project, concept, or scene. (pp. 1–2)

Wise was especially attracted to taking up film work in English classrooms and he worried the culturally underprepared "menace." His attachments to culturally and rhetorically powerful modes, along with his belief in the moral obligations of the professoriate seem to have motivated his desire, yet he was in many ways unable to act, constrained by the hopeful yet unsupported desire to participate in film analysis as pedagogy (production was unthinkable, at the time).

Weisinger's emphatic "plead" is both enchanting and urgent. Weisinger worried that the sorts of exciting film work he might have enjoyed teaching would be taken up by others "less qualified," and he claimed that it was the "social responsibility" of the English teacher to begin teaching film "as an art" (1948, p. 270). Again, here, cruel optimism in the form of hope that English professors might use film for casting, analyzing, possibly guiding and maybe even very hopefully disrupting "the ambiance of the classic public sphere," where normative politics may be "cast as a feedback loop" beyond which new methods and forms may emerge. Perhaps Weisinger imagined his social responsibility as "radical in the traditional sense, taking up the position of the interfering intellectual, the counterconceptual aesthetic activist reorganizing the senses along with common sense" (Berlant, 2011, p. 249). Likely, this was not the case, though it is possible and points to merely one example of cruel optimism that will appear in this book.

So although there is a hopeful and possibly critical urgency in Weisinger's "plea," we also find that the classic "English" privileging of hermeneutic practice is used to support the cause. In fact, instead of simply arguing that it is the English teacher's job to teach a certain kind of text for its artistic merits, Weisinger's arrangement belies his suspicions regarding the less-than-nuanced nature of his claims. He argues via negation, assuring that he will "refrain from using the specious argument that, if we will not do the job, someone less qualified will, nor shall I even say that it is our social responsibility to do so (though I honestly think it is)" (1948, p. 270). No arrogantly detached academic, he (some might refer to him as a rhetorician invested in civic participation? a sophist?!). Instead, Weisinger poses as the high-minded but humble ("I honestly think") academic, perhaps tilting his chin ever-so-slightly-skyward as he insists, "I base my appeal on the grounds that the study of the motion picture is on an aesthetic plane equal to that of the study of literature" (1948, p. 270). Weisinger offers no initial evidence in support of this claim (although later in the piece, he catalogs a list of references). Rather, he refers to films as "significant art form[s]," and offers his opinion-rendered-as-truth when he suggests "I believe, in fact" (n.b., belief does not equal fact) that film's emergent value places it on track to "equal, within its own aesthetic terms, of course, the artistic achievement of the Greek drama and the Elizabethan theatre" (1948, p. 271). So Weisinger's attachments to the texts of high culture and his pedagogical hopes for morality instruction converge in the form of his opinions and beliefs, along with a brief nod to a supporting argument, the latter in the form of reference to a book entitled *Film and Theatre*, by "Professor Allardyce Nicoll" (1948, p. 271) (note the identifying title, which we no longer include as a way of conferring authority). He sought—for himself and his students—to travel intellectually "in the wake of a person, a way of life, an object, project, concept, or scene," (Berlant, 2011, pp. 1–2) namely, on the whispery trails of affective intensity vectoring outward from visceral encounters with Great Literary Texts and Theater.

The argument continues to evolve in its name-dropping manner, Weisinger persistently posturing with his urgent beliefs and "I think[s]" (1948, pp. 270, 271, 275) and linking film to "Greek drama and the Elizabethan theatre" ("re") (1948, p. 271). A sign of the times, as Wetherbee's history makes clear, literary study trumped all. Thus, while Weisinger seems convinced of the value of film—"the motion picture is the most distinctive form of expression of the culture of the twentieth century on quite valid technological, aesthetic, and ideological grounds" (1948, p. 271) his assertions on the value of film are rendered so hopefully as to seem, at times, desperate or irrational. Absent arguments on the rhetorical and pedagogical value of film that extend beyond association, Weisinger's argument instead relies far more on his established ethos than upon a missing (because as-yet-undertheorized) logos. To be sure, Weisinger's argument eventually offers meaningful references to support his claims. Notably, however, his references are all charmingly and—as if cast as THE PROFESSOR by Wes Anderson himself—glowingly revealed: "The finest Russian directors; . . . a number of notable books . . . the learning of a great art historian" [Panofsky] (1948, p. 271). These rhetorical flourishes are valuable tools for understanding the emergent struggle of film discourses in Composition. They reveal the (cruel) hopes and suspicions (the latter, regarding just how much sweetening, flattery, or posturing an audience requires) of writing teachers situated in English departments who wanted to invite film analysis but were a.) not film experts, and b.) not much invested in emphasizing rhetorical production via film-composition.

Today, no longer so clearly grasping for disciplinary status (thereby routinely defaulting to analysis and imitation), but instead as Composition embraces its interdisciplinary nature and privileges production, we see potential to register arguments in support of film-composition through a variety of theoretical discourses. Today's film-composition is more readily supported through theories on affect, composition, design, film, and rhetoric. And through both conventional and digital media publications, we seem less clearly beholden to flattery and more obviously able and willing to share—via informal (social networking, microblogging) venues—our experiences in film-composition, many converging on the value of critical making and doing.[26] Tracing these shifts in affect and rhetoric may seem to be merely nostalgic, but they represent an emergent series of discourses and practices, and I have found pleasure and hope—perhaps in their humanizing intimacy—in spending time with them. It is my hope that we may at times benefit from exploring these earlier iterations of film-composition as we move more confidently ahead with our contemporary version(s).

Sharing vibratory space with my own project (I humbly submit) is one of the boldest and most clearly articulated visions for the value of unconventional, non-discursive, multimodal work like film-composition, *Nondiscursive Rhetoric: Image and Affect in Multimodal Composition*. Here, Joddy Murray (2009) brilliantly reconsiders the value of affect for Composition, arguing that "it is even more important than ever for writers/composers to become aware of the affective domain: both its history in rhetoric and its place in the everyday classroom" (p. 83). Murray evolves a careful and critical synthesis of affect studies in Composition, reviewing earlier scholarship from the field (notably, Alice Brand and Susan McLeod) in ways that help us to more fully engage in interdisciplinary scholarship that explores cognition and affect. We have often been timid in our approaches to such scholarship. Murray notes the works of Brand and McLeod as exemplary models of our neglect:

> Brand and McLeod's theories were largely ignored because they seemed to be investigating areas of composition deemed irrelevant or otherwise hostile to a social-epistemic, postmodern conception of writing. Such a reaction was due invariably to the fact that any mention of the emotions evoked several binaries: intellect/emotion, cognitive/noncognitive, rationality/irrationality, mind/brain, mind/body, individual/social, et cetera. Any conversation in the field on the emotions was seen as a return to favoring the individual over the social or cultural, and though the work attempted at times to refute such charges, research on the affective domain continued to be branded as "expressivist," leaving much of the work done by Brand and McLeod underappreciated. (2009, p. 87)

Against the trend to see affect work in binary opposition to rationality, Murray's work is perhaps the most progressive in asserting that not only does

---

26   See Clemson's Program in Rhetoric, Communication, and Information Design; the University of Texas at Austin's Digital Writing and Research Lab, for only two of many examples.

affect matter for composing and especially for multimodal composing but that it marks a sophisticated and highly evolved form of rational thought. Murray's promising aims are especially intuitive and resonate powerfully with established arguments that routinely mediate affect studies. For Murray, we may presently find it substantially relevant to accept that "the non-discursive in general and image in particular most directly carries meaning through its connection to our emotions and the affective" (2009, p. 83), and this quickly resonates for me with Brian Massumi's (2002) well-known assertion (gleaned from studies in psychology) regarding "the primacy of the affective in image reception" (24).[27] Murray insists that, "other fields (such as neuroscience and philosophy) have come to similar conclusions," that we might with greater confidence draw from a grounded understanding of the "far-reaching consequence of image to cognition" (2009, p. 83). Murray is sure to note prior attempts at evolving such a grounded understanding, but he is presently most invested in exploring "new research being done in fields such as neuroscience and psychology [that] have made it possible to see to what extent emotions and feelings inform our images" (2009, p. 83). He concludes therefore that we must attend to such convergences in ways that will "reinvigorate the debate on emotion in composition primarily because image cannot function without emotion and composing cannot function without image"(2009, p. 83). Even more elementally, Murray insists, we must "investigate how the debate between reason and emotion and between body and mind inform the way our field has largely overlooked these connections in the past" because "this connection between emotions and image offers yet another justification for the importance and power of non-discursive text in our composing and inventing processes and theories" (2009, p. 83).

The contemporary "Neural Turn" seems capable of moving us as Murray desires. Brett Ingram lights up a sense of the "connection" to which Murray alludes, and though indeterminacy prevails, Ingram curates a vision of the neural turn that incorporates ancient rhetorics, through twentieth century philosophy, rhetoric, and, as I see it, multimodality, and film-composition. Especially hopeful is the staging of this vision, for Ingram projects a sense of value for states of being, states of mind—conditions we might seek, rather than overdetermined practices and rules we might enact in our hopes for creative intellectual projects. Ingram argues that in *Phaedrus*, Plato's worries over how rhetoric might "incite unruly behavior" (see DJT, 2016) "promote[d] the ethical use of rhetoric," through his invention of "a tripartite ontological narrative that separated the mind, body, and soul," urging "his students to suppress their physical desires with rigorous mental discipline for the bet-

---

27   Don't worry. I will be taking up the worries over the validity of Massumi's free-flowing affect concept in the "fear" chapter.

terment of their souls" (2013, p. 6). This hopeful move carried into twentieth century philosophy and its central debates, many of which return in the present moment through affect theory and "new materialisms" that attend to the body and the mind. These conceptual provocations flicker ongoingly into various rhetorical studies, composition theory, and for our purposes, as central concerns of multimodality and film-composition. The hopes associated with thinking affect, experience, and information processing shape many discourses on film-composition. The neural turn highlights the complexity of how we process information:

> While cognitive and corporeal knowledge may arrive to us via different orders of experience, in neurological terms, they are born and nurtured by the same physiological processes and systems. (Ingram, 2013, p. 12)

As such, the neural turn will shimmer into and out of focus in *Cruel Auteurism*, more notably in chapter 4, *desire, (II)*, and in chapter 5, *pleasure*. Thinking the plasticity of brain processing and embodiment as conditions of being that incite potentially trance-like states of receptivity and performativity, we find a contemporary maker, a fleshly being with rhetorical insight and hopes for complexly ongoing intake, uptake, remix, and performance-based beingness. In an of-the-moment reference to zombie culture and hopeful makers remixing their relationship to things, consumerism, consumption, and being, Ingram cleverly explains:

> Indeed, evacuating the Cartesian ghost from the machine does not turn the human into a mindless computer made of flesh, an amoral and self-serving zombie, or any other metaphorical expression of sublimated existential dread. We may instead think of the mind-as-matter as raw material fashioned into a work of art by the cooperative, intertwined hands of nature, society, and the self. (2013, p. 8)

Similarly rebooting our disciplinary disposition to streamlined clarity, Murray's argument confidently remixes several contentious theories that have circulated, often unsuccessfully, in Composition. His logical alignment of rational thinking, emotion, affect, and image work echoes work that has in the recent past animated many Digital Media arguments in Composition (Edbauer on affective intensities and pleasure; kyburz on the pleasures of DIY filmmaking and "image-pleasure"; Shipka on multimodality and engagement; Wysocki on design pleasure—to name only a few). Most successful is the work Murray does to compel us to see that

> [v]aluing the non-discursive necessitates valuing the emotions and intuitive reasoning because the two are interconnected. Image, as a vessel full of relationships, carries with it the emotional import that belongs to our understanding of that same image: the two complete each other. Without the emotional connection, there cannot be a full and appropriate understanding of the images we encounter, and this has everything to do with the way we generate text in the first place. (2009, p. 83–84)

Not only does Murray's work recover a detailed history of affect work in Composition, but it imbues our understanding of that history with a sense of how current theories and their interdisciplinary uptake in Composition further validate these earlier assertions regarding the valuable roles of affect and emotion—especially for production.

My experience of this history recalls a story of conflict regarding distinctions between affect and emotion (Jarratt, 2003; Massumi, 2002; Metzger, 2004; Worsham, 1988) because of a concern to create a productive distance between the weighty and complicated domain of emotion and the seemingly more clinical nature of studying affect. David Metzger (2004) briefly summarizes this troubled reading by considering Susan Jarratt's (2003) "Rhetoric in Crisis: The View From Here," and while Jarratt's piece never uses the term "affect" or "emotion," Metzger infers a rhetorical sensitivity to certain institutional trends in Jarratt's reference to the alleged "crisis" in which rhetoric purportedly finds itself and toward which a 2003 issue of *Enculturation*, "Rhetoric/Composition: Intersections/Impasses/Differends," devoted its bandwidth. In particular, Metzger sees Jarratt intimating a "possible distinction between feelings and emotions," which has it that "emotions tell us and others what to do; feelings do not" (Metzger, 2004). Metzger's critical reading surfaces the potential to see that we are not so much given to marginalizing feelings but, taking Jarratt's comment about "unproductive breast-beating" (Metzger, 2004) to task, we are perhaps invested in distinguishing "the unproductivity of some feelings" (Metzger, 2004). Surely, we can read with Metzger here, agreeing easily with the potential for "some feelings" to register as "unproductive," but I appreciate his attention to further movement within these fine lines. He explains:

> My concern is not that unproductivity has been shown the door; rather, by assuming that unproductivity is bad, we may have scripted an under-theorized distinction between feelings and emotions as the difference between good (aka productive) emotions/feelings and bad (aka unproductive) emotions/feelings. (Metzger, 2004). [sic]

The narrative uptake of these delineations reveals an important but problematic set of categories. As Metzger explains, "And what is that difference, again? Simply put, feelings are unproductive; emotions are productive" (Metzger, 2004). Metzger does not go on to categorize feelings or emotion with regard to affect, and these sorts of projects have historically comprised a good deal of rhetorical scholarship that may be of value to Composition and especially film-composition. The value I see involves potential for creating useful distinctions that further our academic discourses and pedagogies and advancing disciplinary status (which matters not only in terms of the political but also in terms of how our knowledge is valued). Nevertheless, I persistently find myself resisting the polarizing nature of the narrative, particularly given our awareness of the materiality of rhetoric that has feelings and emotions converging through an always already flow of rhetorical being and what Thomas Rickert (2013) award-winningly lauds as rhetorical attunement[28] and both Davis and Edbauer laud as a productive and generous rhetoricity.

Much earlier. My early desires to engage with affect, through the work of Ann Berthoff (1982), Alice Brand (1985–1986), Lil Brannon (1985), and Sondra Perl (1980), were somewhat muted by admonitions to give that complicated territory wide berth; thus, I was pleased to see such matters taken up again in recent years. Today, with Murray's careful history and its powerful claims, along with a growing number of serious academic explorations into the value of affect for composing as well as for teaching writing, I see no reason to guide anyone away from studies in affect, particularly if such studies coincide with image work and various forms of multimodal composing. Neither does Murray, and the results of his studies are not shy. No tentative Wise moves, no "in part" hoping, absent distinctively rational support for his assertions, Murray argues that while affect work in Composition has been careful to avoid the (false) dichotomy between feelings and emotion vs. reason and rationality, we are presently poised to proclaim and practice an understanding of a different set of relations. That is to say, for Murray, we may now argue that "because of the way the brain functions through image," we no longer need cast rationality as separate from densely affective image work but see instead that "reason, critical thinking, and rational discourse are also affective" (2009, p. 84) (emphasis in original). Not "in part," but non-discursive rhetorics as wholly appropriate for our rhetorical work and pedagogical efforts.

Murray's impressive efforts to reanimate Composition with rational discourses on affect and non-discursive symbolization resonate with my own desires to advance Composition as, as Connors would have had it, rhetorically grounded. However, rather than seeing "rhetorically grounded" as

---

28   See Thomas Rickert's (2013) *Ambient Rhetoric: Attunements of Rhetorical Being*, which won The 2014 CCCC Outstanding Book Award.

monomodal and free from "messy" affect (another narrative), I have for years now been resistant to such formulations. Even within social networking venues, which might seem to exist exclusively as venues for non-discursive, affect-laden, and extra-academic play, we find admonitions to skew toward the unemotional, toward the ostensibly disaffected rational, which in many of these venues = just play "nice" . . . just "be happy" (irony alert). So whereas "playing" in Twitter or Facebook has been non-discursive fun, at times, the limitations still seem to default to the older dichotomy against which Murray and others work (feelings vs. rationality). In recent years, the emphasis has been on discouraging any negative associations with our work, our institutions, our professional hopes and perhaps disappointments, our sense of "what's happening," and the like. Ostensibly, silencing one's affective association to our work is more "professional," more "rational," which is actually quite irrational if you ask me, or at least achingly counterintuitive. Pulling a cruelly optimistic Weisinger here, it seems to me that film-composition affords me play even as I register complex affective associations to my work, the nature and status of my work, in particular, and institutional life, in general. Situated as critical scholarship and not bound by the venue associations with frivolity afforded many digital texts circulating via social media, film-composition enables me to transgress rhetorical conventions (i.e., cope) even as the work is itself rhetorically grounded, guided by keen considerations of purpose, audience, and the integration of multiple appropriate ("my beat is correct"[29]) modes of articulation. Perhaps film-composition may build on the work of Wise, Weisinger, myself, Murray, and others who want to ensure cultural and rhetorical power, and the infusion of affective intensity in our work even as we hope to clear the set for more rigorously integrative performances that move ourselves, our student filmmakers and the audiences for whom we strategically overspill. We may hope.

---

29 See Beck. (2005). "Hell Yes." *Guero*. Written by Beck Hansen and The Dust Brothers. Performers Beck Hansen, The Dust Brothers, Christina Ricci. Interscope.

Chapter 2: Fear

> The freshman students were given the option of either writ-
> ing a composition or making a film. The instructor gave nei-
> ther criticism nor supervision for the film. . . . Immediately
> the question was raised as to how an instructor gets approv-
> al and support for film-making [sic], especially when the
> film will be considered equivalent to a written composition.
> (Martha Heasley Cox, Recorder, *CCCC Workshop Reports*,
> 1969)

> [S]ome brave souls will investigate film as a separate and
> distinct form of statement. (Robert Dye, 1964, "The Film:
> Sacred and Profane")

Robert Dye's 1964 casting of phantom film-compositionists as "brave souls" is
both hopeful and inspired. It may have wanted to serve as a warning, but from
the perspective of today's film-compositionist, it's a shiny rhetorical trophy.
We like to think of ourselves as courageous, so the recognition of bravery for
curious, compelling, rhetorical and intellectual work is honorific. However,
bravery is rarely easy, and the stakes of non-conforming disciplinary behavior
are high, so Dye's terms make sense, particularly in the context of its chrono-
logic utterance. More philosophically, to invoke a "soul" in contemporary
rhetorical terms is a questionable move, one worth considering as a preface to
discussing the defining affect of this chapter, fear.

Today's "soul" is perhaps more routinely configured in the context of an environmental rhetoricity, as the postmodern self performs through sociality—
the unwitting response to existence within the rhetorical scenes of our lives.
But in 1964, "souls" obtained primarily as the agentially crafted, surveilled, and
worryingly maintained morality-testifying entities toward which pedagogies
aimed their highest energies. Advancing a more critical disposition, we recall
the social unrest then blooming into a widespread cultural anti-establishment
shift, and we witness various creative and collective stagings toward the articulation of emergent and increasingly liberated "souls" and their role in intellectual work and pedagogical practice. For this and many other reasons, (including the oft-cited chronostamp of "1963" as the "birth of composition"[30]) it's
clear that 1964 may seem a threshold moment for change, certainly for bravery
in new forms of storytelling and public disputes over the nature of our souls/

---

30   See kyburz, b., Sirc, G & Wysocki, A. F. (2007). "The Origins of Modern Composition,
Part I." *Conference on College Composition and Communication*. New York.

ourselves (I see you, New Hollywood! I see you, French New Wave!). I want to argue that via affect theory, particularly through its emphasis on the body, and through contemporary discourses on ambient rhetorics, we find room to theorize the affective sensations and ideational potential of "souls." Initially, however, the more salient feature of Dye's epigrammatic comment is his reference to bravery. To designate as "brave" a creative act that is initiated through a vital creative vision of difference implies that the creator might have most certainly labored to transcend bravery's affective scene partner, fear. There's something to this notion in the history of film-composition. In this chapter, I will read a variety of fears and offer contemporary views that help to resolve them through the identification of Berlantian zones of optimism. In this way, I hope to advance an understanding of film-composition and testify to its critical value— the emergence of new bloomspaces for critical and affective intensities that render as rhetorical potential.

My own fears as a DIY digital filmmaker have been many. For the most part, when I decided to begin making films as rhetorical artifacts that might trace my experiences of the present moment and hopefully say something about cultural dispositions to textuality, I decided that fear had to go. Yet, this decision is a version of delusion and obviously a form of cruel optimism in the sense that such scholarship had at the time yet to be ideally valued. I had received tenure, but my filmmaking work defined my post-tenure output and, in the end, did indeed influence the decision against my promotion to full professor. The letter said something to the effect of, "The committee didn't get your scholarship." This rejection was sorely met, especially in light of my evolving rhetorical skill and sense of purpose. My attachment to this vital form of inquiry, expression, and rhetorical attunement flickered ambiently, lovingly. Yet, my auteurist practices also glimmered obstructively, the twitching eye out of sync with the sight lines of normative academic success.

My fears were comforted not only in the doing, in the process of making films, but also through reading film history, and I have often been especially inspired by André Bazin (1967). Hugh Gray (2005) introduces Bazin's impressive history in a narrative that resonates with composition's sense of disciplinary exigence, as a counterhegemonic force that emerged in response to war's disruptive impact. Gray recalls that Bazin

> founded a ciné-club which developed out of meetings at which he defied the Nazi forces of occupation and the Vichy government by showing films they had banned for political reasons. (2005, p. 3)

Bazin was passionate about cinema as a tool for contemplating "culture and truth," and he has been regarded as "something of a mystic" (Gray, 2005, p.

3). Due to the force of his convictions regarding the cultural value of cinema for intellectual and cultural life, Bazin possessed a "Socratic capacity to make those who talked to him seem intelligent to themselves" (Touchard, as quoted in Gray, 2005, p. 3). Gray goes on to note Bazin's singular importance to the history of cinema: "Indeed one might call him the Aristotle of cinema and his writings it Poetics" (2005, p. 3). Sound inspiration.

I was drawn to read Bazin more precisely because of his role as founder of the infamously first and most widely valued cinema journal, *Les Cahiers du Cinéma*, "which under his direction became one of the world's most distinguished film publications" (Gray, 2005, p. 3). As a DIY filmmaker working apparently against my own conventional academic success by making films rather than writing books, I admired Bazin's powerful self-determination. I identified with what Bazin saw in film; I had seen in film and filmmaking the potential to discover critical ways of seeing and coming to voice regarding complex phenomenon (see *proposition 1984*). I saw Bazin resisting the kinds of turf wars—political demarcations far more powerful and materially consequential than those we draw upon academia—that might have discouraged him from writing. Instead, Bazin saw cinema as cross-disciplinary and culturally integrated in an infinite number of possible ideological arrangements. He proposed a sense of cinema's objectivity that did not reject ideology but instead saw that cinema could objectively project reality in ways that rendered ideology transparent and available for intellectual work (chronicled in the pages of *Les Cahiers du Cinéma*). In this sense, Bazin rejects efforts to align obediently with prior principles:

> The fact that the cinema appeared after the novel and the theater does not mean that it falls into line behind them and on the same plane. Cinema developed under sociological conditions very different from those in which the traditional arts exist. (Bazin, 1967, p. 57)

Gray explains that critics prior to Bazin would "start with a definition of art and then try to see how film fitted into it. Bazin rejects all the commonly accepted notions and proposes a radical change of perspective" (1967, p. 3). To be clear, I am by no means claiming to possess the boldness or visionary status of André Bazin. I am instead attempting to articulate my experience of having had a historical ally with whom I could identify as I began to work in ways not ordinarily scripted. Reading Bazin in the context of my developing role as a DIY digital filmmaker, I found courage in the face of my fears regarding my films as scholarship toward any kind of ongoing success in academia. I had struggled, but I had "made it," with tenure. Fearful as I struck out to develop a new scholarly ethos and method, Bazin lovingly shoulder-patted my fears, assuring them that they might, just for a while, rest quietly on set. In reading of Bazin and through his writings, I had discovered a Berlantian zone of optimism, a filter for my emergent rhetorical attunements that made them appear Instagramagically of-the-moment, and thus perhaps relevant to rhetorical studies on the cultural texts circulating ambiently as (as yet) a kind of noise and increasingly as a form of rhetoricity. Powerfully linked to identification, an immersive experience of rhetoricity is ongoing. It seems likely that we might attempt to invoke, create optimal conditions for, or stage a willful rejection of fear that might enable more powerful identifcations that motivate critical and creative rhetorical practice. As Brett Ingram explains, Burkean versions of this notion exceed his more famous articulation of rhetorical "identification." Instead, Burke:

> intuited a connection between the brain, rhetorical practices, and agency, and understood that this was compatible with the sophistic/mystic tradition. For illustration, we can look to his speculations concerning the mystic trance, a neurological state that seems to suggest neither fully passive nor active decision-making faculties (Burke 1969a: 294). In the mystic trance, the subject "loses the self" to substantive external forces which blur the line between symbolic and material inputs (visual images, verbal incantation, music, drugs), and which subsequently call into question distinctions between autonomy and possession, agency and obedience. (Ingram, 2013, pp. 6–7)

Sign me up for a "mystic trance"! Along with David Lynch, famously auteurist in rhetorical disposition, I'm on board for rejecting fear and entering a dreamy maker's state. Not so, for many early film-compositionists.

Discourses regarding film and its various roles in writing pedagogies range from quite hopeful, desiring, and pleasurable, to less thrilling, historically overdetermined, and affectively charged discourses of fear. Berlant's (2011) concept of cruel optimism articulates this reality more broadly, as she is concerned with a range of desires and attachments. She worries how sustaining these affects may stand in the way of conventional success—that's the cruel part. More hopefully, Berlant enables a "compromised endurance" option by illuminating what she calls "zones of optimism" (2011, p. 48). Here, we are able to retain our attachments, even nurture them, and at the same time flirt with forms of success and pleasure. From my experience as a film composer working in composition, I can say that this unconventional success does indeed feel like a compromise, and it's one I've been unavoidably (entranced!), passionately willing to make. Yet, cruelty. Reading in the archives, I see that many have feared moving beyond convention, despite the articulate hopes shared by so many who dared desire fuller participation in film discourses (to say nothing of film production). Today, film-composition enjoys a vital presence, and I intend to spend far more time on the optimism of auteurism. Nevertheless, cruelty obtains, for despite the hopes, desires, and pleasures of film-composition, remaining doubts, perceived threats, fear-of-missing-out (FOMO), and other obstacles keep the fear alive.

Optimistically emerging from the fear-filled discourses, film-composition has been lit with the vital force of contemporary techné, with its conscious disposition to explore structure, function, and ethics—digital media afford film-compositionists the tools to inquire of each. The affordances of contemporary digital image and video capturation tools have been central to the Postmodern, Social, Visual, Virtual, and Digital turns. Mark Poster argues that central to understanding and critique of these turns is attentiveness to the subject—identity (1995, p. 23), (including individual ethics), and identification. Ethics and identification are bound up in our studies and practices of techné, and both hermeneutic and generative practices are central to film-composition. Against fears of frivolity, this is serious play.

Often, earlier scholars worried the forms of identification their students took on (the focus was rarely on the professoriate). Ostensibly, English writing classrooms were capable of moving students to see differently. This vision would offer a transformative sort of enlightenment, and film might detract from this laudable cause. From a 1973 *Conference on College Composition and Communication Workshop Report*, we learn of early hopes for film in Composition, however painfully constrained and pointing to a sense that the affective intensity of film might foster frivolousness and dumb down course content:

> Chairman Thomas Erskine outlined the direction of the session by raising questions concerning the place of film in English departments: Should film be tied to composition courses by cinema-writing equations? [whatever those are] Should film be used as an attempt to stimulate writing by providing a vague "visceral goose"? (p. 311)

Let's just replay that for a moment, here. "*Visceral goose.*" Okay, so points for recognizing affect ("visceral"), but so. Here, we see a very English Professorish attempt to say that film provokes affect in ways that may seem silly, in ways that may detract from a more mechanical version of film and its constituent parts ("cinema-writing equations"). This fear may not seem like fear; it might more readily be read as contempt, yet it seems to emerge from a more generalized worry over the seriousness of engaging with film, possibly converging with a simultaneous desire to do just that, . . . if only we could tame those images!! Another fine fellow in the same workshop, "W. R. Robinson focused on an essential difference between moving images and words"—great! Here,

Robinson articulates a version of Erskine's fear even as he hints at a compellingly moving desire as he insists that, "film imposes different kinds of relationships with the world and with ourselves. Because images are 'MORE CANTANKEROUS than words and won't be still, a new form is necessary with which to write about film" (*CCCC Workshop Report*, 1973, p. 311). Funny, the report indicates that *no one considered film as this new form*. Regrettably, the session ends with a consensus that had little to do with advancing uses of film over and above continued efforts at teaching—at a seemingly primitive level—print literacy: "Professor Robinson's statement that students have to learn to read before they can learn to see films met little resistance or reaction" (*CCCC Workshop Report*, 1973, p. 311). Even those who hoped to argue for increasing film's presence in composition classrooms wrote from a position of fear. Dale Adams and Robert Kline frame up their 1975 *CCC* article entitled "The Use of Film in English Composition" with a list of things that film can *not* do for students in composition classrooms. Their appeal to teachers hoping to include film is "humbly prefaced" by the following list:

1. It [film] will not guarantee that all students will write correctly or even interestingly.
2. It will not guarantee that all students will write with a new enthusiasm.
3. It will not guarantee that all students will write with insight and aplomb. ["aplomb"!]
4. It will not be the great elixir that will render easy the teaching or learning of writing skills. (1975, p. 258)

Damn. I want that elixir. Adams and Kline seem to describe it (though they do not offer this as a definition of "elixir") in the body of their article, which works with and against various fears that warrant their claims. Take number 7, "Lack of confidence in one's ability to use the film in a teaching situation," for example. Perhaps lacking confidence themselves, they explain that, "[T]his is a barrier that cannot be brushed aside lightly," (1975, p. 259) because audience (?). Why do they assume the gravity of this inability to move what is essentially an obstacle involving rethinking a pedagogical approach? Clearly, some "brave souls" (Dye, 1964) swiped left anyhow, apparently quite confident in rejecting this fear: "Too often the assumption has been made that all one has to do to use a film is to show it in class and let the film do the rest" (p. 259). Adams and Kline clearly intended this latter comment as a critique regarding an assumption ostensibly undertaken by earlier "brave souls," but from today's perspective, we easily see the validity of the option. Given today's affordances and the kinds of nearly spontaneous remix culture in which we live, write, compose, think, and play, we can see how showing up to "hit play" might be all one need do in order to initiate, shape, and sustain rhetorical sensitivities and to enact productive critical and rhetorical pedagogies. But again, like many early film-compositionists, hoping and fearing, working from a position of feeling overwhelmingly bound to the concerns for written discourse and "the primacy of the word over all other forms of communication," Adams and Kline refused the call. What they do concede is that "film does offer something which can improve student writing, this something does not lie, as some would have it, in the simple equation of frame to word, shot to phrase, and sequence to sentence" (1975, p. 260). (Are these Erskine's "cinema-writing equations"?) Another concession involves student's ease with film: "Students are generally not cowed by films" (Adams & Kline, 1975, p. 260). Yet, the "do not" list obtains as the frame. Adams and Kline feared the call.

Today, we know better—or, we operationalize a more capacious version of serious play as pedagogical approach, and we recognize that students can read films, and video games, and digital texts of many forms, "a multiplicity of discourses" (New London Group, 1996, p. 61). We also know that immersive study and play can be motivational, in the form of what many digital game scholars refer to as "serious play." Because digital game theory and practice seems to participate via the affordances of digital media and toward the goal of critical pleasure, I turn to game theory as a zone of optimism that works along with film-composition to resist and reject many of the overdetermined fears that have evolved alongside turf wars, power struggles, and disputes over the nature of identity and identification.

Game theorist and player Jan Rune Holmevik (2012) explains that we use "serious play in order to invent a new image of ludic ethics" (p. 149), and he appears to reject discourses of fear in the context of an emergent ludic ethics. Like one of Dye's "brave souls," Holmevik is up for new intellectual terrain. He resists the normative compulsion to view affectively inspiring multimodal texts as unworthy. Reclaiming the teaching of ethics from fearful voices who have conventionally seen playful multimodal texts, such as films, as "another bit of ephemera like yesterday's newspaper or the political cartoon" (Huss & Silverstein, 1966, p. 566), Holmevik insists,

> [W]e are inventing a new ethics through the act of ethics, through playing, where experiencing outcomes and consequences is the key element. . . . As an experience engine, the game makes possible the move beyond epideictic rhetoric and the topoi of praise and blame toward a new understanding of ethics in an electrate time. Through play we can experience the consequences of the ethical choices we make. (2012, p. 150)

This "brave" rhetoric rejects worry-filled discourses over the identities students perform in response to film spectation and even college study. Embracing

Holmevik's ludic ethics and serious play as pedagogical disposition, the fear that teaching film might corrupt is rendered quaint. From today's vantage, especially as contemporary pedagogy values invention, collaboration, improvisation, and play, we move beyond fear.

Seemingly presaging this critical zone of optimistic play, in 1966, Huss and Silverstein feared that a lecture-driven academic treatment of film might do more harm than good. To their credit, they feared a diminishing value for the integrity of the film, itself:

> When classicists, historians, philosophers, professors of art and music, and the like, praise films, they also do not want them taught, fearing the destruction, through pedanticism, of naivety and spontaneity that will be likely if films are subjected to the discipline of college courses. Put a movie in a syllabus, make it an assignment, allow the professor to dissect it, and its spontaneity is gone. (1966, p. 566)

A playful, improvisational pedagogy of play—inclusive of the production of the course content (a world within a game, designed by students; a film, produced by students)—is today's response to the fears Huss and Silverstein articulated. This is not to say that such pedagogies will not occasionally be(come) tainted by professorial oversight that defers to a lecture-driven, analytical venue, where "Bad analytical criticism destroys the movie organism" (Huss & Silverstein, 1966, p. 566). But even in such scenarios, there is room to move beyond the fear of destroying a film's integrity, especially if such moments are balanced with immersive making. Here, critical rhetorical knowledge is gained in production, and what is of critical value—rhetorical and ethical insights beyond the overdetermined readings—is illuminated more profoundly as it is experienced individually and collectively in the body and in the mind. The roomy affordances I am describing here and associating with film-composition shine brightly as a zone of optimism and is best understood as a form of techné.

Techné is historically associated with Aristotelean ethics as not so much art (product) but craft (process and product). Immersive pedagogies seem poised to revitalize our attentiveness to techné as a portal for valuing craft as a form of ethics. This is perhaps the sort of teaching that earlier scholars who spent time and pages worrying film both desired and believed possible, but it appeared to seem an area of pedagogical possibility exclusively through the lens of literary hermeneutics. Today, we know techné through a variety of academic practices and daily life—through our practical indwelling within digitally mediated cultures.

Defining techné "as a way of knowing by which something is brought into being not only with regard to how it functions, but also with regard to values such as beauty and goodness" (2016, p. 28), Belliger and Krieger explore the nature and ethics of body tracking and the information flows that emerge from digital self-monitoring practices that might have been seen as Orwellian doom in an earlier time:

> The informational self is neither the product of technologies of power (Foucault), but of an "ethical" technology of the self. The self becomes a hub and an agent in the digital network society. Body tracking transforms the opaque and passive body of the pre-digital age into the informational self. Networking is the way in which order—personal, social, and ontological—is constructed in the digital age. (2016, p. 25)

Body tracking practices hack conventional approaches to self-care, and though dystopian fears abide, the value of seeing networking as a practice for knowing a self seems aligned with our notions of an always already openness, one to another, or rhetoricity. Thus, I see hacking the self through self-monitoring as a zone of optimism (though I prefer selfies or Pokémon Go to conventional fitness trackers). Similarly, pedagogies that demystify cinematic texts not by analysis alone but in the making of films seem vitally able to teach rhetorical knowledge and skill even as we are immersed within networks of symbolic action[31] many associate with digital filmmaking.

Despite lingering fears, today's maker-driven pedagogies amplify the optimistic strategy; we are making new "studio systems" (galleries, journals, e-publication houses, courses, programs) for producing rhetorically moving texts, installations, memes, trends, interventions, and critical and creative communities. Informed by more than two decades of emphatic "student-centeredness" and "active pedagogy," today's "engaged" student is expected to be able to work with digital tools toward the crafting of sophisticated multimodal texts. Pedagogies devoted to this more expansive version of "writing" define the field today to the extent that discussion of conventional academic essays are often whispered rather than gavel-banged. Whereas hope seems to upstage fear, the range of fears articulated in the context of film-composition's emergence is powerfully tied to our historical constraints regarding the limits of our expertise and access to sophisticated tools. Some fears are rooted in a concern for rhetorical ethics in the form of a concern for piracy, remix work, and impoverished views on the capacious affordances of Fair Use policies (for works "protected"[32] by copyright), and they are also bound up in fears regard-

---

31   See Halbritter, B. (2012).

32   The rhetoric of "protection" demonstrates how fear is inscribed within the very discourses designed to alleviate fear. And who, really, is afraid? And how far down must this fear go in the pedagogical machine? This rhetoric is primarily and ultimately about ownership, which

ing the crusty old figure of The Master. Many worry their own levels of teacherly proficiency, especially up against their students' skills.[33] Our fears began, however, in a broader, more clearly demarcated concern for morality, and its worried grandpa, turf.

Rhetorics of fear largely defined the blossoming scholarship about film in composition classrooms. The momentum for such discourses gathered strength in the mid-to-late 1960s, interestingly aligning with the emergence of both the French New Wave, and the (then) New Hollywood (American New Wave). Both movements are associated with anti-establishment dispositions and desires for increased creative freedom from convention, often attended by radical DIY methods (Luzi, 2010). This generalized shift in film culture was marked by an obviously growing desire for films that boldly portrayed subversive forms of the good life, claiming new zones of optimism for desires that did not easily vibe with normative culture and convention regarding identity, privilege, and power. Happening within the emergence of the postmodern turn, filmic portrayals of shifting identities and identifications offered audiences alternative visions of success. In many ways, film culture articulated postmodern zones of optimism in the form of "new configurations of individuality" (Poster, 1995, pp. 24). to which many critical pedagogies turned for non-normative thinking and promising new forms of narrative and rhetorical expression. The story goes that these new figures offered lenses through which to see more clearly the limitations of normative culture, and this tracked with pedagogical efforts to enhance our critical vision.

Our fears had, however, often rendered as fear of the new that manifest in rhetorics of crisis regarding the diminishing old. Vibing with rhetorics of crisis that have long marked composition scholarship (Green, 2009; Spellmeyer, 1996), William D. Baker wrote in 1964 of film's capacity to function as a "sharpener of perception." Clearly emphasizing hermeneutics, Baker wrote of the nature and scope of film in composition classrooms, and this meant reading comprehension, an ability to see, a capacity for enjoying films not simply for affective pleasures but also as tools for the massive project—considered to be the appropriate moral range of writing classes—of "discovering what life and language have to offer" (1964, p. 44). Baker proposed that we halt our efforts to "nibble away at other rhetorical precepts," such as specificity and focus, and instead that we have a "primary need" to "look

is to say that it is about earnings potential. How can we shift our pedagogical concerns so that they are more critically and creatively attentive to the critical production of moving texts rather than the constraining, fear-inducing, creativity-destroying legalese?

33 See Prensky, M. (2001), and his concept of "digital natives" (students), and "digital immigrants" (teachers).

for something to help students learn to look at and record the details that make meaning" (1964, p. 44). In many ways, Baker saw rhetorical concerns as overly general, yet at the same time, he clearly wanted to use film as a tool to enhance perception of rhetoric, of strategic choices. This paradox appears often, as scholars attempt to argue for the use of film but appear constrained by their sense of allegiance to a disciplinary tradition. Perhaps it is a more straightforward matter of ethos. The upshot of this tentative framing—absent a direct rhetorical frame—is fearful discourse. Often, the fear doesn't take the form of a direct articulation of a threat, but it occurs more subtly, as when Baker frames up a concept by which to articulate his sense of the rhetorical value of film analysis for writers. The first task appeared to have been a need to claim that film is art. Baker begins with this project, making quick work of it and then moving on to coin a phrase he used to highlight film's rhetoricity:

> Film enters the realm of art in its form and its use of symbols. We may start with the assumption that the poet and the film director are both deliberate artists. That is, they don't let a word or scene just "happen-in" by itself. (1964, p. 44)

Baker wanted to assure teachers that their work might consist of helping students see how rhetorical choices have been made in a film, that, "We should assume that nothing 'happens-in'" (1964, p. 44), summarizing film's rhetorical nature by explaining that, "The point is to begin with the technique, not the message, of the film" (Baker, 1964, p. 44). Despite his emphasis on a valuable hermeneutic use of film in the composition classroom, Baker wanted to highlight how hermeneutics had been so prominently, albeit perhaps unsuccessfully taught; he proposed that students' engagement with the text might aid the project of teaching critical faculties. He defaulted to discuss poetry analysis as an exemplar, but his rhetorical emphasis is clear:

> No student, from kindergarten to college, enters the study of film with a clean, blank slate of non-experience. Would that he would. He has seen film, has been brought up on it, and resists an analysis of it because he has trained himself to concentrate on the message. Hence, he must learn to disregard the message temporarily, just as a good stenographer disregards the message when she transcribes her shorthand. Afterwards, she checks for sense and message. (1964, p. 44)

Baker describes several pedagogical moves he used to teach with film, including screenings followed by plot outlines and shooting directions, group work involving critique of such, and challenges to certain claims regarding shot angles and meaning. More tellingly for my claim regarding Baker's sense of film's rhetoricity and the pedagogical affordances of filmmaking for rhetorical study (and toward practice) is his assertion that, "Experience shows that students do not immediately see the relationship between film analysis and rhetorical principles" (1964, p. 44). Despite Baker's seeming assertion that there exists a "relationship between film analysis and rhetorical principles," (1964, p. 44) his approach nonetheless suggests uncertainty regarding trust in student immersion in cinematic culture as sufficient for university-level rhetorical study and learning. That is, Baker seems to imagine that (surely) if "he has been brought up on it [film]," he/she does bring a great deal of knowledge, and so working from that point would be (is) how we would approach rhetorical pedagogies involving film today—working from students' inherent knowledge of rhetoric, narrative, and cinematic content on the basis of our awareness of their immersion in screen cultures. Baker, though, was working in a fearful new ecology, hopeful and on the cusp of claiming emergent qualities, but fearful, just the same. Baker worked with/in institutional constraints that were less forgiving of border crossings or interdisciplinary foraging. This status is perhaps responsible for what feels like an old-man-on-the-lawn level worry: "You must teach them the relationship, as carefully as some teachers (fie on them) teach sentence diagramming, slowly, thoroughly, item by item" (Baker, 1964, p. 45). *Sigh.* Inasmuch as "The words have been in rhetoric texts for centuries, and film analysis is but a new twist to the old tried-and-true principles" (1964, p. 45), Baker could not move too far from a sense of systematic, disciplinary propriety. Thus, his pedagogy reads as particularly constrained and conventional—hopeful, yet afraid. Even within Baker's fear-tinged rhetoric, however, zones of optimism suggest potential momentum.[34] Note his awareness of situatedness in cultural scenes featuring film love as near-but-not-quite qualifying students to take on serious film work as rhetorical study. While missing the fuller immersion argument (rhetoricity) that positions us all within screen cultures indebted to filmic rhetorics and the pedagogical affordances of this rich, multimodal ecology, earlier scholarship, exemplified by works like Baker's, begins to foretell today's more rigorous rhetorical work in film-composition.

Like many who write from affective intensity, an adversarial dialectic often shapes the work, as scholars seek new syntheses that actualize new, transcendent, and otherwise non-normative potential. I am not an expert in affect, nor in Hegelian philosophy, but I have worked as a teacher-scholar in Com-

---

34   I can't help imagining an "underworld" of film-composition, where Composition teachers were doing radically progressive work but perhaps not publishing in conventional modes or routine academic venues. Researching this potential will be an ongoing venture that film-composition anticipates.

position long enough to appreciate the rhetorical registers of affective dialectic and to sense how these articulations vicariously radiate the wavering internal motivations of the rhetor. Reading Baker, I sense that he was working toward hope. Baker was not overt about fear. Perhaps he worked unaware of the extent to which disciplinary pride and tacit border policing constrained a clear view of the nascent desire to treat films rhetorically (even toward production). And so, perhaps Baker sensed the value of staging his argument as a potential zone of optimism for film work as rhetorical study (and practice). Others were more forthcoming with their fears. Announcing their fears at the outset, Roy Huss and Norman Silverstein introduced their 1966 *College English* article, "Film Study: Shot Orientation For the Literary Minded" by mansplaining that "[t]he serious filmgoer who would elevate cinema-study to the realm in which art, music, and literature are taught in American colleges is open to the charge of frivolity" (p. 566). In fact, the serious filmmaker who would do so is open to the charge of frivolity. I wish I could say otherwise. If I could see it as a valid descriptive move, this book might not be titled, *Cruel Auteurism*. Despite zones of optimism, one is right to fear. Or, less dramatically, one is wise to anticipate reactions that are less-than-ideal (this is just good process, if we can assume the filmmaker is primarily concerned with content rather than uptake in the form of rewards). I maintain that the challenge is worthwhile, for myself in terms of creative digital scholarship, and for my students, who so love multimodal composing and so clearly demonstrate rhetorical knowledge and skill in ways that are not nearly as movingly evident in their print work, alone. However, even when she is prepared with rhetorical training, narrative awareness, technical skill gained through auteurist practices, collaboration, and immersion in film communities, she is likely to receive responses to her work that register in only a few different configurations, 1.) Bemusement-erupting-into-anger, 2.) Pedagogy-grabbing inquiries about Fair Use, and 3.) Related, pedagogy-grabbing inquiries about technical skill (as in, "How can I do that?").

Her greatest fear—the primary auteurist worry—is that no one will appreciate the work for its ambient hopes. The ambient is critical, here, for a sense of today's auteur, for today's film-compositionist, working within multiple ecologies toward participation in a particular network of like-minded agents. Jeong and Szaniawski (2016) explain the shifting meanings of "auteur," and in doing so, they hint at the ambient rhetorics shaping our sense of (academic) filmmaking today, and an emergent film-composition. They explain the intention of their edited collection, *The Global Auteur: The Politics of Authorship in 21st Century Cinema*, beginning in an introduction cleverly entitled, "The auteur, then . . .":

> if auteurism has validity in this global age, it may express itself in the way film directors, old and new, capture the zeitgeist in a a multi-layered and faceted world, overtly or covertly. We see here a twenty-first version of la politique des auteurs—not a certain policy or politics of auteurs anymore so much as "the political" immanent to cinematic authorship. (2016, p. 1)

Jeong and Szaniawski recall the origin story of auteur theory, recognizing that in the earliest (1950s) writings of the *Les Cahiers du Cinéma*, auteurs were positioned in terms of their artistic "authenticity" so that they were "equivalent to artists in other media" (2016, p. 2). In this formulation, the auteur produced works that captured an ambient moment, a cultural scene, and thereby implicated a range of political potentials:

> When successful, this experiment established an original outcomes of theme-form chemistry [ambience] whose governing principle is nested in narrative structure as in mise-en-scene. (2016, p. 2)

So early auteurs were rhetorically attuned to ambience in ways that enabled them to render their works so as to capture the vibe rather than to mechanically stage an adaptation of reality. Jeong and Szaniawski complicate the "next phase of auteurism, 'auteur-structuralism'" by turning to Bazin, who had foreseen the potential to overplay incongruities inherent in considering the body of work that distinguished an auteur, "but subsequently begged the question of its contextual parameters," which would mean a rejection of "the quasi-mythical figure of the auteur" (2016, p. 2). They note that,

> Bazin had already defended "impure cinema" as naturally hosting hybrids, which required technological, sociological, and historical approaches and captured "the genius of the system". (2016, p. 3)

In other words, "Bazin's *politique des auteurs* was also a *critique des auteurs*," recognized by discerning film historians as "a wise man's warning against the fetishistic 'cult of personality'" (Jeong & Szaniawski, 2016, p. 3) that has marked the notion of the auteur throughout rhetorical renderings of cinematic history. Later, post-Barthes (1977), the spectator became implicated in a reading of a film's ambient potential, so that the auteur was further diminished, so that

> a film would work as an enunciative, performative écriture through which the auteur would then perform its "postmortem" agency by increasing spectatorship in a shifting discur-

sive configuration, at the crossroads of historically accumulated films and the ways in which they are received. In short,
the death of the auteur signaled the birth of the spectator, with
the next phase of auteurism emerging on the side of the audience. (2016, p. 4)

For Jeong and Szaniawski, the "spectatorial turn" begins to move toward a
sense of auteurism today. For while "auteurism has lost it semi-religious myth
of independent creativity," this fact "does not attest to its real death," which
they note as "rhetorical" in nature. Instead, "the auteur is now a critical concept indispensable for distribution and marketing purposes," and it has been
uptaken across a spectrum of writers and thinkers, making the concept available to "scholars who weave auteurs into a systematic web of critical ideas"
(Jeong & Szaniawski, 2016, p. 4). Witness my own playful effort to use Berlant's "optimism" for "auteurism," it's aural and ideational resonance hoping
to bypass fears of failure, fears of disciplinary over-reach, and fears regarding
critical and rhetorical validity. My brief turn back, to(ward) a justification
for the term "auteur" is similarly about overcoming fear via affect. It feels
right to play on "optimism," to project optimism altered just so to accommodate my DIY filmmaker's reality through the rich history of auteurism.
However, simply feeling that I've found the right beat for my intention isn't
enough. The auteur works with a desired message, toward the production of
agentially motivated rhetorical content. A sensational Orson Welles, a darling
(albeit "decidedly masculine") Francois Truffault, a daring "female director"
of the French New Wave, Agnès Varda, "has been called both the movement's
mother and its grandmother" (*Criterion*, 2016, para. 2). Oh yeah, being female
somehow amplifies the signifying strategy; of *Varda*, the *Criterion Collection*
site notices the compulsion to call it out:

> The fact that some have felt the need to assign her a specif-
> ically feminine role, and the confusion over how to charac-
> terize that role, speak to just how unique her place in this
> hallowed cinematic movement—defined by such decidedly
> masculine artists as Jean-Luc Godard and François Truf-
> faut—is. (*Criterion*, 2016, para 2)

I dare say that many female auteurists, and most filmmakers—because of or
perhaps regardless of gender or sex—work to generate effective films without
much consideration of their place in any particular "movement." Speaking
for myself, to worry how I am received over and above how my work is considered seems a waste of intellectual and affective energy. As an academic
filmmaker striving to discover increasingly roomy working conditions so

as to support my work (think jobs, promotion, grants), I *must* be thinking about how I am considered. And, as a rhetorician working toward a particular vibe and meaning, of course I worry reception. Nevertheless, to enable fears regarding the articulated perception of one's auteurist status is—while in academia nearly an autonomic cultural practice—to diminish the rhetorical force and attendant affective intensities the filmmaker labors to experience and render in the process of filmmaking. These fears require strategic compartmentalization and sensitivity, and this dynamic balance requires a great deal of attention. This balancing act seems to activate new forms of rhetorical sensitivity that are increasingly multivalenced and complex, well-suited to the range of audience needs to which we attend as filmmakers working in the interstices. These heightened rhetorical sensitivities may help in the process of generating more effective filmic texts, and they certainly re-animate long-held rhetorical knowledge regarding audience, knowledge that is amplified and rendered perhaps more forcefully via the multi-sensory affordances of digital filmmaking.

Of course, I would love to claim that I work fearlessly, but what I am getting at is that working without fear in service to a film is hard work. This has been a driving motivation for me in my work, to more fearlessly and forcefully use the affordances of cinematic rhetorics to radiate my particular purposes through my films, absent consideration of a certain range of certain kinds of audience reception, rejection, or other less-than-ideal response. In hindsight, gender may have even amped up my fears (and perhaps Varda's, as well), but I like to think that I work, like Varda, with a confidence in the potential and thus the potentially powerful rhetorical effects of my filmic work. As well, considering that the audience participates in the production of meanings and receptions, I trust that I alone will not be diminished should a work fall short of its desired effects. To be sure, I have not worried that my gender discredits me more than might a history of fears associated with doing rhetorical work in the academy in ways that move more forcefully beyond words, beyond print. For me and for many film-compositionists, the multimodal making in which we have engaged has been about a deeply felt drive to engage digital technologies toward the goal of generating especially effective filmic texts. This passionate motivation drives many multimodal makers and filmmakers. I have heard many filmmakers at the Sundance Film Festival say, "I simply had to make this film," as if some force of nature, some deep internal accumulation of desire simply could not be denied. The intensely felt drive to create cinematically testifies to the power of affect as exigence and as sustaining force for film-composition. Fear, too, motivates as an oppositional affect that nearly always attends deep passion and conviction. Fear obtains in shaping film-composition, but we "brave souls" (Dye, 1964) carry on, revising our fears into action, just as did may film-compositionists before us.

As a filmmaker, I identify productively with the rebellious auteurist filmmakers, many of whom worked with a conviction regarding their initial creative vision, undaunted by external efforts to alter their works. As noted, Jean-Luc Godard famously struggled against convention only to become a leading figure in a new cinematic movement, a new rhetorical genre in the French New Wave. Similarly, auteurist romantic Wim Wenders resisted studio control (an agent of convention) in his breathtaking cinematic works. He has argued that by working "through his conviction [affect, felt sense, purpose] . . . each film should reflect its own place within a certain tradition of filmmaking" (Cook, 1991, p. 34), intimating that good films find their place. In other words, focusing on the film and its rhetorical integrity may overtake concern for its reception, which is not to say that audience concerns are irrelevant (because, again, the contemporary, post-Barthesean auteur/spectator hybrid). Instead, according to Roger Cook, in "Angels, Fiction, and History of Berlin: Wim Wenders' *Wings of Desire*," Wenders

> became less concerned with critical self-reflexivity and more intent on making films that through the strength of story [rhetorical purpose] and narrative form [delivery] work against the grain of contemporary cinema. (1991, p. 34)

Is Cook suggesting that Wenders' films were so purposeful and narratively effective as to create a new form? If so, he hints at the iterative nature of textual production as it occurs on a timeline—drawing from what has worked, testing, and revising and working through hope to discover another/better way of achieving a desired purpose. So Wenders worked to move story along to/through new forms. Although Cook seems to say that Wenders wasn't evaluative of his work ("less concerned with critical self-reflexivity"), this does not mean that Wenders was unavailable for critique. He was perhaps more concerned that his creative vision was at stake when considered through the machinations of convention. Cook explains that during the making of Wenders' *Hammett*, the project received a great deal of what I will call "input" from Orion Studios and Frances Ford Coppola, who was hired to alter the original script "so that it better conformed to the conventional Hollywood detective genre" (1991, p. 34). As teachers, we worry that should we avoid teaching convention in favor of "creative vision," we miss out on pedagogical opportunities (not to mention disciplinary shoring up). Perhaps our fears need not render as a primary frame. Cook reveals that while Wenders felt reined in by the forces of convention, he was nonetheless able to take on valuable rhetorical lessons. Cook frames up these lessons to reveal Wenders' ability to maintain his creative and critical vision and to work within the given constraints, noting that Wenders learned that

> the conviction that the original concept for the film should remain open so that during the filmmaking the director can discover and incorporate into the film new images and ways of seeing. (1991, p. 34)

What I am highlighting here is how both creativity and fear inhabit the filmmaking process (and what we hope for in the convergence of teaching and learning). A director fears that he or she may not be able to enact his or her vision within the constraints of the particular process; this fear seems bound up in matters of trust. How can an auteur (or any composer, writer, rhetor, teacher, student) hope for her vision in light of institutional, generic, and other constraints? It seems to me that by thinking through the struggles of auteurist practices, we see a shared non-normative desire to work beyond constraints, perhaps as one path available for enacting the closest version of one's story or argument. By considering our own personal and professional histories, we may recognize a trend to iterate, moving with and against convention toward productive effect. Perhaps by trusting both fear and resistance in the context of teaching convention we may find room to improvise effectively. Perhaps as we learn to recognize the value of fear and resistance in our pedagogical and scholarly practices, we will discover their value rather than waiving them off as irrelevant in light of our proud explications and instead advance our disciplinary dispositions accordingly, iterating toward more holistic compositional practices. Attuning to affect, in other words, may mean recognizing the occasionally counterproductive nature of disciplinary constraints. We have not always been so feelingly available to think about affect.

Recognizing the "danger" (Barnes, 1976, p. 32) of struggling against disciplinary constraints are many earlier scholarly works articulating their desires and fears, both ignited to work with and against limitations that might afford film a broader audience in the academy. In 1976, Verle Barnes unveiled a "to do" list that might foreclose struggle in favor of a more direct series of strategies. In "Eight Basic Considerations for the Teaching of Film," Barnes ultimately describes eight ways of preparing to teach film as an end in itself, which is fascinating and sensible, I dare say. Though he does not elucidate how his considerations will play out shiningly for teaching film in a writing class, per se, his fearful rhetoric appears in *College Composition and Communication*. Though this turn to film seems like a natural for a writing course in the mid-1970s, Barnes nevertheless begins with the somewhat hopeful, slightly cynical, and vaguely fearful assertion that

The study of film as an academic discipline has grown rapidly in the last several years and has invaded, or should I say been snapped up by, various academic departments in the mad rush for students and for the attractive courses which can draw large numbers of students. (1976, p. 32).

That film was at the time becoming a discipline unto itself seems promising, though it might have been a more hopeful introduction had Barnes taken up that promise instead of quickly turning to fearfully viral rhetorics of "invasion" and the pragmatic buzzkill of drawing more students to courses. While Barnes tentatively celebrates the new discipline, he also thinks about the "danger" the new discipline faced, imagining that "they must also be a little worried about what might happen to the discipline itself" (1976, p. 32). Barnes worried too that

the characteristics of the cinema present special problems for an academic discipline. The nature of the medium, as both a medium and as an art, is so different from traditional disciplines that great care must be taken in the planning and offering of film-study courses to students. (1976, p. 32)

His eight considerations were similarly full of worry. However, reading them through the lens of my experience and thinking through affect, I see his fears as characters that Barnes uses to articulate his own qualifications for teaching film. For example, regarding "1. Preparation," Barnes worries the forms of experience he sees as essential for someone to qualify to teach film, which in his list includes graduate course work, publications, film criticism, and (finally!) directorial work. *3 out of 4 scholars prefer production!* Barnes ultimately asserts that these matters "should be confronted in order to assure meaningful, quality instruction" (1976, p. 32).

Fear is not great at mobilizing effective rhetoric. To support his claims regarding the need for teacher preparation, Barnes shares anecdotally that his Chaplin course was, in retrospect, flawed not so much because of the teachers but because of the students:

I naively registered for the course, believing I would be involved in a small seminar of serious students, but what I got was an auditorium full of, largely, undergraduates looking for a snap course. (1976, p. 33)

It's hard to take Barnes seriously when he argues out of a concern for bad pedagogy when what he does here is hold himself apart from other students he clearly sees as lacking. He carries on in this way, assuming a variety of things he can't reasonably assume, most of it emerging less from fear for quality and more from desire to teach these courses (!). Framing it not as a critique of the class but "merely as an example of what might happen in a given situation," Barnes goes on to further extol his intellectual skills while demeaning other students:

> I believe I can safely say that the experience as an academic experience was not meaningful for the majority of the students in the class. I have the utmost respect for Mr. Chaplin, and I believe more students should see his films, but his films should not be studied by relatively unsophisticated students until they have been given some basic instruction in the art of films. (1976, p. 33)

Reading Barnes' fear of underprepared teachers' unsophisticated students through the lens of affect, I imagine that Barnes is driven by his passionate affection for good films in ways that occlude his vision. He is, after all, writing about film courses for a journal concerned with composition pedagogy. He writes little about film and writing, nothing at all about film as writing. Continuing his list, he worries, "2. Independence." That is, Barnes makes clear that he is one of those possessed of the visual acuity to see film as "capable of carrying its own weight," finally arguing that "care must be taken to insure that film gets scholarly and critical treatment as film, and not merely as an adjunct to literature" (1976, p. 33). Here, Barnes misses the chance to advance the seemingly obvious notion that when we treat film as rhetoric, the "critical treatment" is afforded both the study and production of film. Film-composition is about this more contemporary and less competitively fearful treatment. Film-Composition recognizes that the fears of its rhetorical structuration as "adjunct to literature" (a common refrain in Composition scholarship) are no longer essential to a productive conversation on the nature of its emergent status in the academy. In his third consideration, Barnes moves toward something that begins to feel less fearful and more like a hopeful map of film-composition, with film's "3. Quality" discussed in terms of aspects of film that contribute to a whole—"critical-aesthetic aspects, . . . as artistic end product, . . . inherent 'messages,' [and] the structural and 'craft' aspects of the film which combined to communicate these messages to the audience" (1976, p. 34). Disappointingly, Barnes says nothing here of production, perhaps fearing that an initially strategic and administrative map must be established for film courses in composition. Even more regrettably because rhetoric, because complexity, in his next point, "4. Relevance," Barnes misses an opportunity to write of film's rhetorical affordances, but defaults to the logistical fear which forecasts that, "no film course might be relevant to a highly structured technical program in electronics which has given its students a timetable for completion" (1976, p. 34). Wow. How does a writing and rhetoric scholar swipe left so hard on "relevance"? Turning more specifically to affect, Barnes lingers on "5. Enjoyment." Oh, Barnes. Here, he vacillates between the more obviously hopeful proclamations about film courses and fearful "tssking" over, again, "3. Quality." Barnes recognizes that pleasure attends learning and cites *Sesame Street* as a pedagogical opportunity. While he might have chosen any number of more age-appropriate examples, he seems to get that, "planned learning does not have to be drudgery, that it can, in fact, be fun and still be effective" (1976, p. 34). Perhaps revealing his own attachment and maybe also his desire to teach film and to be recognized as an authority on its teaching, Barnes asserts,

> Film is one area that, by its very nature, is entertaining. Entertainment and enjoyment combine to form one of the major attributes of film study, as an academic discipline, one of the "attractions" [attachments] of the discipline itself and probably one of the major reasons why so many students enroll in film courses. (1976, p. 34)

Great! So . . . where's the fear? Barnes has got you covered:

> While it is possible to remove the "entertainment" from many film courses, there is no reason to do so. Since entertainment and enjoyment are positive attributes of film study, they should be maintained as much as possible in any film course. (1976, p. 34)

Right. Who said we need to take the fun out of film? Where is this coming from? Could it be from an entrenched set of conventions? Could it be from a more established field? Barnes offers

> The primary caution which should be taken in studying films that entertain and that bring enjoyment is one which has existed in the study of literature since the birth of literary study itself. That caution is simple: maintain the quality of study by differentiating between quality films and non-quality films. (p. 34)

Is Barnes confused? What is "non-quality"? He might have classified a group of films as "poor" but instead suggests zero quality, which is odd. Perhaps hoping to clarify, he argues that we must watch out for "non-quality films":

> When the purpose of the course is historical and the content
> is, for instance, "B Pictures of the 1950s," students should be
> made aware that some of the films they will be viewing may
> be second- or third-rate. (1976, p. 34)

Another rhetorical opportunity missed! Can you just see the remix project potential, here? *Of course you can. You are immersed in screen cultures that have emerged from cinematic histories that have intertextually prepared you to consume and produce in clever and rhetorically strategic ways! You are attuned to what works, what has worked, what worked in a given situation and how that working might be repurposed in the present moment for a variety of different and new purposes.* If only Barnes could have liberated himself from the fears of appearing to conform to academic convention and instead embraced film's pleasurable qualities, he might have articulated a more productive and rewarding vision for film study *and* production as rhetorical work; he might have begun to testify to the emergence of film-composition. Barnes concludes, "6. Time," by insinuating that this is the "easiest" consideration, which seems odd given that he goes on to list scheduling limitations and the need for extra time for screenings, discussion, and speakers as the main concerns regarding time and the teaching of film. From the perspective of film production, time becomes intensely important and perhaps higher up on the list of worries. From the perspective of film-composition, *time is the elemental space for writing a film.* The timeline is the essential conceptual tool, and so "easy" seems far too flippant. Barnes moves between attempting to argue for his serious consideration as a qualified film teacher (scholar?) and working to list the administrative concerns of offering film courses. He concludes with, "7. Assignments and Outside Activities," and "8. Budget" in ways that further reduce his fears and tend instead to amplify his sense of confidence as a verifiable judge of quality, meaning, and scope. He argues that another "danger" of teaching film is the potential to overplay extra activities, to "kill the films" with too much critical work such as "too much 'forced' discussion, too much 'significance searching,' [and] too much 'meaning'" (1976, p. 35). Perhaps Barnes is lingering with that notion of pleasure, here, hoping that there will be less need to explore a film's rhetorical structure and meaning, to say nothing of production, but it is one of the delights of reading early Composition scholarship, to find this sort of quiet dismissal of the mainstays of conventional classrooms in favor of keeping a film alive, so to speak. It is almost as though Barnes dismisses fear in favor of trust in attunement, trust in a shared knowing that might simply vibe out instead of suffering (dying!) at our pedagogical hands. Financially speaking, ("8. Budget"), Barnes writes of "cutting corners" by showing films on televisions, noting that, "the advantages far outweighs the drawbacks" (1976, p. 35). He also suggests showing "Good foreign films" as they "might cost much less than well-known American movies," (1976, p. 35) and, again, writes nothing at all about production. Of course, to fault these tentative gestures toward film-composition for not thinking about making films as a rhetorical and pedagogical approach toward learning how to write, how to compose, . . . well, it's too easy, and it may seem mean-spirited, but I do marvel at how ancient practices in imitation seem to have evaded these teacher-scholars. It seems that only imitation of print modes would do.

Hinting at potential approaches to take in and utilize the affordances of film for English courses, Stanley J. Solomon (1974) played it safe while arguing for "Film Study and Genre Courses." As you might guess, Solomon advocated using film without fear of disciplinary punishment by developing genre courses, with films as the central texts. While Solomon seems quite confident within the contours of his schema, he nevertheless betrays a fear that underlies his desire to work with film as an English professional. In part, the fear was about intra-and interdisciplinary disputes regarding course content, and how to proceed. Interestingly, Solomon seems to easily evade fears regarding the propriety of teaching film in English, and this is because he recasts film within the familiar context of genre, and sees film as simply given that "what an English teacher often considered his [sic] primary pedagogical responsibility" was "to guide a class through a close textual examination of a work of art" (1974, p. 283). By suggesting quite boldly that the way to use film in English would be to design genre courses that mimicked existing genre approaches routinely used by Literature, Solomon seems less than confident in the rhetorical skills of those English professors who would be teaching film. It seems such an obvious line of reasoning to follow in support of his desired ends, yet he does not address the kinds of rhetorical knowledge these genre courses might yield but instead uses the genre approach, well, generically as a way of bypassing worries over turf and to ensure that English departments would gain access to the growing student demand for film courses. I want to retroactively say to (belt out at) Solomon, "Don't fear the rhetor!" Interestingly, Solomon begins to unravel one of the more vexing concerns facing teachers and scholars working in visual rhetoric, multimodality, and film-composition today when he asserts that, "What is really essential for pedagogical dialogue in film studies . . . is constant practice in verbalizing the visual experience" (1974, p. 282). Solomon teases us with a hint of "ekphrastic hope," 1 of 3 modes of ekphrasis articulated by visual rhetorician, W. J. T. Mitchell. For Mitchell (2004), the hope that we might articulate verbally (via print) the nature of our reception of an imagistic entity is complexly related to our fears that should we do so we destroy the distinction between the objects' affective allure and our necessarily reductive articulation of its value and meaning. Solomon argued that we must take up exercises in ekphrasis, guided by a sense of disciplinary value and the conventional forms of evaluation that make a discipline's discursive practices valid as intellectual work. Solomon's view of the struggle inherent in this work of "verbalizing the visual experience," what I see as a type of ekphrastic practice, involves his overdetermined sense of the nature of academic work in English Studies. Considering the nature of ekphrastic rhetorical practices, Solomon says that

> [t]eachers will often have more trouble doing this than their students, for there is no textual passage to point to, once the film is completed, to support a generalization, no palpable line reference in hand for all to gaze at during a tour de force of explication. (1974, p. 282)

So, it seems that for Solomon, teachers are routinized toward explicating via guides and in a manner that calls for laudatory consideration of their performances. This seems about right for the time. Not "right" as in the better choice, but "right" in terms of how the professoriate functioned and conceptualized its own values in the mid-1970s. Moving to consider students' roles in processes of ekphrasis, Solomon defaults to a narrow view of student capacities even as he hints at their rhetorical attunement, which may be viewed from today's vantage (see Rickert) as a form of functional rhetorical knowledge. He argues that,

> [s]tudents may lack the words to spell out exactly what they have observed, but they sometimes can remember it better, being more attuned to the "literal level," more passive, and thereby less analytical than their professors. (1974, p. 282).

Exactly. But whereas Solomon feared that student reception of filmic texts may be too literal, that they were too ready to accept a film's narrative, its vibe, and its affects, it may be safe to say that at this point in (postmodern) time, Davis' "rhetoricity" and Rickert's "attunement" sufficiently theorize what Solomon saw as damaging. Instead of seeing the eager acceptance of a film's various affective and rhetorical shimmers as productive, Solomon (bless him) saw students' "literal" reception of cinematic experience as weak, inadequate, and in need of teacherly guidance. Solomon feared the reader where he might instead have begun to see the critical, pedagogical, and rhetorical affordances of film. This is not new. Regrettably, these fears of this kind continue to darken hopes, but film-compositionists, now as ever, persist in light of their fears.

Chapter 3: Desire (I)

... my desires have invented new desires . . (Helene Cixous, 1976, "The Laugh of the Medusa")

Like a moving film the flow of thought seems to be continuous while actually the thoughts flow stop change and flow again. At the point where one flow stops there is a split second hiatus [a cut]. The new way of thinking grows in this hiatus between thoughts. (William Burroughs, 1969, *The Job*)

Though my desire to make films had been embraced in certain venues by a handful of respected scholars, I continued to worry the matter. The worry was not unproductive. I was emboldened by my reading in the archives and in film histories, both of which illuminated challenges overcome by many fine artist-composers, and I have been nothing if not aspirational. At the same time and in spite of my fears regarding career identity and what began to feel like living in the academic interstices to an even greater extent than ever before, I continued making films. It felt essential. *Malkovich*. I'd found a portal to a sacred space for me to be in, to dwell in, to make in, a space where I could test out and refine a voice that might be heard in the midst of the vast range of academic voices that wanted to do what they wanted to do (help students, clear the way for new forms of writing, support existing forms, mark and remark/make identities—all attempts to move audiences).

I continued proposing conference presentations, as live performance seemed the optimal scenario for sharing my work. The responses articulated what I had been sensing in the archives, that many of us working in the field of Composition wanted more film. As had been the case with *i'm like . . . professional*, my 2007 CCCC presentation became an invited submission, this time not to a renowned digital publication, but to the esteemed and inviting print journal, *Composition Studies*.

The performance took place in the biggest conference ballroom situation I'd ever encountered, and I was presenting with two of my/our inspirational superheroes, Geoffrey Sirc, and Anne Frances Wysocki. As if that weren't enough to compel my intense gratitude, I recall a stillness in the hotel room, shortly before slipping silently down to the Grand Ballroom. I stood in the center of the room, the hum of the minifridge an ambient buzz profoundly silenced by the goth-symphonic vibe of my quiet joy. I said out loud and to no one in particular, "I am in New York City, presenting a cinematic tribute to Jean-Luc Godard."

The ground shifted beneath me. . . . I had hacked the sound system with the help of my filmmaking co-conspirator, Todd Taylor. We had earlier bypassed the AV team and cabled up so that the room would fill with the audio track that scored the film—The Art of Noise's "James Bond Theme." *Ready.*

The presentation offered both a tribute to Jean-Luc Godard and a historical consideration of the revolutionary status of 1963 Composition. I would reproduce it for you, here, as a point on the timeline of our disciplinary desire. You might loop the video I looped at the NYC presentation, if only I'd saved the micro-cassettes upon which the short film had been saved (alas, my moves to digital have meant some regrettable decisions to toss certain materials). Standing in is the text from that presentation, which was eventually published in *Composition Studies* as an invited submission. The piece intends to both articulate my/our desire to work in film—toward film-composition and it aligns that desire with early desires that shaped our field. This is, "'Totally, Tenderly, Tragically': Godard's *Contempt* and the Composition Qu'il y Aurait (That Might Have Been)."

A retiring adolescent, I started watching black and white movies on Saturday afternoon TV. I got hooked fast—the sharp contrasts, the slightly unreal look of black and white film, the busy and contemplative smoking. Nothing was exactly clear . . . but in that confusion I sensed something I could hold on to . . . I felt a part of something capital-M[35] Meaningful. A powerful sense of pleasure and belonging emerged from what felt like my shadowy find. Perhaps it's not surprising that these films, this art, should have taken hold of me, given my clinical outsiderism and attending vulnerability. I consider my desire to participate in film as fully as possible as a desire for belonging, for communion with something just slightly unknowable and possibly dangerous. This desire makes sense to me as I think through the lens of Walter Benjamin's (1936) contention that "artistic production begins with ceremonial objects destined to serve in a cult" (p. 224).

Benjamin's focus on "artistic production" gives way organically to contemplation on consumption; are film people cult members? There's something right-feeling about this notion, especially as I think about the cultural and intellectual importance of the films of Jean-Luc Godard, considered the most "intellectual" of filmmakers comprising the French New Wave of the late 1950s and early 1960s. Of course, this "cult" conceptualization of the films and filmmakers of the French New Wave is problematic, given what we understand of cults. But what I want to get at is the seductive nature of participating in a "movement" even as I experience a vibrant but hopeful internal melee that pits my awareness of the collaborative nature of text making with my

---

35   I intend here to hint at the masterful film noir work of Fritz Lang in his captivating film, *M*.

infatuation for the auteur (who would resist the cult but perhaps unwittingly participate in the production and consumption of its sacred artifacts).

I am trying to articulate a desire. I am thinking through my desire to produce "magic" objects that secure my belonging to a community, but at the same time, aware of this desire, I resist, mindful of the creative limitations of group membership. Take, for example, the ways in which working in Composition is so often about generic conventions and text-bound assignments. Writing on changes in English curricula (of which Composition continues to remain a part, if not a humble but evolvingly rebellious servant), Gunther Kress worries that generic thinking about curriculum is unlikely to assist learners as we experience literacies shifting and as we are increasingly learning to move among and between differing literacy contexts, arguing succinctly that, "[a] curriculum based upon theories of semiosis of convention and use cannot hope to produce human dispositions deeply at ease with change, difference, and constantly transformative action (1999, p. 67). Thinking with roomy wisdom about the coming convergences and the attendant rhetorical demands and affordances, Kress explained that

> There is . . . a coming together of developments—economic, technological, social, political—which requires a rethinking of the processes and the means for representing ourselves and our values and meanings, broadly . . . "literacy." (1999, p. 67)

Since the early 1990s, Kress had been encouraging us to think about literacy beyond our limited academic range, in many ways consonant with the converges of design and rhetoric initiated by scholars like Wysocki. For Kress, "the possibilities offered by electronic technologies of communication raise this question of the constant metaphoric extension of the term literacy sharply" (1999, p. 68). By now, this claim seems obvious, but I want to emphasize the dynamic and ongoing nature of this desire to move beyond constrained convention toward the increasingly rhetorical vastness of meanings inherent in digital media making. As Sirc (1999) had it, "Composition remains entrenched" ("After Duchamp," p. 190).[36] So too did Kress attempt to activate new curricular thinking; Composition had/has work to do:

> [c]urriculum now needs to be focused on the future; its task is to provide young people [students] with dispositions, knowledges, and skills which they will need in their future social lives . . . [and] 'conventionality' does not provide a means of understanding or using . . . new media. (1999, pp. 66–67)

---

36   Anis Bawarshi argues effectively for Composition as genre in his book *Genre and the Invention of the Writer*.

In increasingly new media-saturated literacy scenes, it seems obvious, now, that we have taken Kress' claims seriously in order to consider the ways in which our servitude to clear written discourse has sometimes, if not often, shaped and constrained Composition's identity. We miss a range of pedagogical and cultural opportunities when we—as individual teachers or as collective programs, as a discipline—are unwilling to stray from these conventions and postures, especially because it is now rhetorically purposeful, possible, appropriate and timely to do so. It is my hope that works like this, which hope to generate reflection by recursing in ways that move us, gesture toward fuller investment in the thrilling range of creative energies that manifest within the context of work in new media and film-composition.

As I attempt to honor early Composition by tracing my interdisciplinary investment in new media work (especially production), I hope you'll indulge me as I explore my particular filmic disposition. Explored through the lens of the year 1963, an iconic year for Composition, I look at the work of an iconic filmmaker—Jean-Luc Godard—whose work first found widespread critical acclaim in the early 1960s, and especially in 1963. I hope to generate associations that aid you in discovering criticisms that may manifest absent my overt articulation. Call it an experiment. Or subversive. Or self-indulgent. It seems to me a matter of form and content. A compositionist who now fancies herself a filmmaker has some serious investment in "self," and this seems appropriate, for by all accounts, Godard was an egomaniac. As well, early Composition struggled with self-assured nobility and conviction against Terrific Academic Odds.

More to the point, considering the variety of informed yet inventive pedagogical moves of early Composition[37] alongside my predilection for ambiguity and moves that gesture toward "the new," I am drawn to the work of French New Wave filmmakers because of their (past) attempts to generate the new even as they clearly paid homage to the classic, in this case, to classic film, to the established and beloved works that shaped their discourse community and redefined how they, and we, think about (film) texts. Jean-Luc Godard, Francois Truffaut, Eric Rohmer, and other filmmakers of the French New Wave worked together for years as writers for *Les Cahiers du Cinéma* (Cinema Notebooks, or Notebooks on the Cinema), *the* cinema journal of the day, so it seems inevitable that their work derives much from their longtime collaborations as they reflected together on the nature of film.[38] Yet many of these

---

37 See Stephen M. North's *The Making of Knowledge in Composition* for a neatly compartmentalized review.

38 Similarly, the teacher-scholars of early Composition had worked for years to teach writing without the benefit of a rich historical sense of itself, without a range of theories from which to draw. In part, my point is that this unknowing disposition compelled creative indi-

visionary filmmakers worked within the romantic milieu of the auteur-driven by a "unique" vision. I want to participate in this romantic sense of my work, within the interstitial work that emerges from a knowable place along with desires to move beyond; I seek always to maintain this indeterminate posture, despite the vast disciplinary odds, and practices of expressivism.[39] (Composition has been there—romanticism via expressionism—and few want to claim a desire for Return, despite laudable contemporary moves to retrieve the value, meaning.) To explain/apologize: I like to think that I invest myself in work that must be done, however seemingly unstable in its wandering, work that is compelled by both internal and external forces (personal desire and memory; identification with people, places, and cultural particularities; worry over "the state of the world"; longing to create "art"). Perhaps speaking to my various desires to participate in the "cult-y" French New Wave (via spectation, reflection, imitation, and, more hopefully, invention-in-production), Phillip Williams, in "The French New Wave Revisited," explains that

> What the [French] New Wave moviemakers improvised was a much more spontaneous, independent cinema, a cinema that lived in their world and spoke to their generation. It was often rough and unpolished, but seldom uncommitted. There was usually a strong voice behind the camera; a voice that spoke to aspiring artists around the world. (Williams, 2002, para. 13)

Based upon these identifications, it should be obvious that I value a Composition that is interested in more than clear, expository prose; I want (however idealistic) a Composition invested in composing (as) art, and this must surely mean that I am romantically seeking to work beyond the bounds of our discursive conventions. It has always been true. My first report home from first grade was a note informing my parents that I was doing "fine" but that I refused to color within the lines; this disposition continues to obtain in my work today, so that whereas I want to make art, I want to make it on my own terms, however culturally shaped and re-imagined, however resistant and unruly (and even if it means making "mistakes"). Here, my identification with Geoffrey Sirc's similar desire—articulated so beautifully in his book *English Composition as a Happening*—is clear. But it's not enough to cite Geoff and hope that you get my meaning. That is, I suppose that readers may be wondering exactly what I'm after. Essentially, I want to share my take on various scenes within both film and

---

viduals to discover the available means of getting the job done-humanely, creatively, compassionately, and in ways that privileged personal freedom from constraint.

39   See Sherrie Gradin's *Romancing Rhetorics* or Bruce McComisky's *Teaching Writing as a Social Process.*

Composition because there is value in this reflection. I will focus particularly on Jean-Luc Godard because I find value in seeing the ways in which early Godard operated—with little funding, with found moments, with something close to an egomaniacal bravado and certainty in his novice moves. This sort of novice confidence seems key to recalling early Composition and its motives and, most importantly, for the motivational value it offered/offers young writers.

In his *Senses of Cinema* essay on Godard, Craig Keller explains that Godard has been fairly vilified because of his bravado. Yet it seems reasonable to agree with Keller as he intimates (via reference to artists considered "masters") that it is necessary for an artist to maintain such bold confidence, especially in the creation of some outstanding new thing: "Godard is an artist of tremendous agency and authority within his medium, and through the uncompromised expression of his aesthetic and, therefore, moral convictions, demonstrates as little concern for the satiety of the 'audience that might have been' as Beethoven, Joyce, or Renoir before him" (Keller, 2007). Joining, then, in the esoteric stance (any self-respecting auteur is drawn to the esoteric), I want my writing to serve as a kind of image (the notion of text-as-image,[40] by now more than passé), one that comes into focus over time. Similarly, Keller says of Godard's longing for a more fully engaged cinema, "'qu'il y aurait' ['what might have been'] is a conception couched primarily in the language of 'hindsight' (projecting backwards into a memory of cinema/art/world to underscore and poeticize the associations between the films), and we might do best to make that leap into the future" (Keller, 2007, para. 6).

Reflection and becoming. Of course, I realize that I romanticize this very work by considering it as a kind of becoming that you should indulge. I find even greater clarification for my method in a W J. T. Mitchell (1995) interview with Homi Bhabha (1995). I want to identify with Bhabha's response to Mitchell's question regarding the "difficulty" of his prose. Bhabha explains:

> I feel that the more difficult bits of my work are in many cases the places where I am trying to think hardest, and in a futuristic kind of way-not always, I'm afraid, there may be many examples of simple stylistic failure, but generally I find that the passages pointed out to me as difficult are places where I am trying to fight a battle with myself. That moment of obscurity contains, in some enigmatic way, the limit of what I have thought, the horizon that has not as yet been reached, yet it brings with it an emergent move in the development of a concept that must be marked, even if it can't be elegantly or adequately realized. (as quoted in Mitchell, 1995, p. 91–92)

---

40 See W. J. T. Mitchell, *Picture Theory: Essays on Verbal and Visual Representation.*

Apparently, in Godard's writings on film, he worked in a similarly "rebellious" (or, from my perspective, "organic") manner. Craig Keller explains that, "Godard's method of writing about films involves elliptical, round about argument, the concatenation of seemingly unrelated disparities, and frequently coming down on the side of films deemed by critical establishmentarians as too vulgar or unpolished" (Keller). Godard's writings were considered the most deeply theoretical of those published within the pages of *Les Cahiers du Cinéma* (*the* cinema journal, you must keep in mind). Keller insists that "the cinema as put forth by Godard was therefore a 'cinema that might have been,' a canon (or anti-canon) that existed only as an ideal . . ." (Keller, 2007, para. 5). Sounds good to me, but I recognize its sentimental disposition as one that may make my comments unavailable for serious consideration in today's Composition programs, which are beholden to assessments both internal and external (and this means clarity, uniformity, not complexity or idealism). Nevertheless, what I'm after in this, my apologia, is an account of my desire, my longing to think about film and Composition as a scene, complex and overfull, idealistic and unavailable for easy analysis. In other words, this writing wants "to put our relation to the work into question, to make the relationality of the image and the beholder the field of investigation" (Mitchell, 2005, p. 49). For my purposes, "the work" is about both film (spectation, appreciation, and, importantly, production) and Composition, and I hope to think through the "relationality" I experience as both a filmmaker and a compositionist—a composer. The French New Wave represents the scene of my early and more recent identifications, associations that seem useful for thinking about film as rhetoric, filmwriting as appropriate work for Composition, as (a) composition.

So I will proceed. No more apologies for indulging my francocinephilicism and the clichés that attend imitating "The French" as I admit that while drafting this paper, I wanted to do Serious Academic Work by seeking a more theoretically deep and confounding lens through which to make my arguments. I have been contemplating Mitchell's consideration, *What Do Pictures Want?*, his concern for what images seem to desire as a way of thinking about images, a concern reflected in Godard's approaches to filmmaking, particularly in his trademark jump cutting techniques, which display motion-in-time but only imperfectly, as though the image wants to avoid capture and maintain a sort of freedom or integrity.

Again, desire. Godard's jump cutting moves as revolutionary rhetorical gestures that sought to destabilize conventional filmmaking. The jump cut. Craig Phillips defines a jump cut as "a non-naturalistic edit, usually a section of a continuous shot that is removed unexpectedly, illogically . . ." (2007, para. 7) and sort of re-imaged to create a version of the real that reflects our imperfect perception (think of how a blink intervenes to create a nano-temporal lapse in the fluid, linear progression of image-narrative). Working against the theory that regards Godard's decision to employ jump cuts in his films as rhetorically brilliant filmmaking (which I want to insist that it is), Keller explains the use of jump cuts as a convention that is

> commonplace today, but back in the late 1950s and early 1960s, this was all very groundbreaking. Jump cuts were used as much to cover mistakes as they were an artistic convention. Jean-Luc Godard certainly appreciated the dislocating feel a jump cut conveyed, but let's remember—here was a film critic-turned-first-time director who was also using inexperienced actors and crew, and shooting, at least at first, on a shoestring budget. (Keller, 2007)

Keller argues that Godard's jump cuts were, in essence, the product of novice skill and working conditions-more simply, mistakes. Phillips adds, "Today when jump cuts are used they even feel more like a pretentious artifice" (2007, para. 7) I am not sure that I can agree with Keller because of the over generalization he creates. But more to the point, his identification of Godard's (then) revolutionary move as a mistake, while not implausible, seems to emerge from ignorance about the nature of writing, the nature of filmmaking, the nature of reflection, and the nature of textual convergences that generate "ideas" about an expression-event (text, film, art work, etc.).[41] Filmmaker Tom Twyker (*Lola Rennt* or *Run Lola Run*; *Paris, J'Taime*) agrees as he describes the influence of the French New Wave filmmakers and their methods: "they looked for the moment," he argues, extending that visual inquiry to imagine the value of the jump cut along with Godard. Twyker recalls, "If you look at what Godard has said about his films—the jump cutting, for example—it was often there because they didn't have another take, so they cut inside a take just to move the shit forward. It's less conceptual, but it's still artistic" (as quoted in Williams, 2002, para. 16). Keller, as critic, wants to point out Godard's methods as mistake, whereas Twyker, as filmmaker, sees the jump cut/mistake as method that is nevertheless "conceptual" and "artistic" (as quoted in Williams, 2002, para. 16). From the perspective of the rhetorician and compositionist, pointing merely to Godard's inexperience and limited working conditions seems far beside the point; Godard invented an available means of persuasion in his given situation, and it worked, magically, ambiguously so (and in this way, perhaps we find the trace back from

41 I borrow the term "expression-event" from Brian Massumi, who describes our existing and emergent affective relationships to expression or external stimuli, be it image, image and words, text, *etc.*

the French New Wave to Italian Neorealism, a desire to create something that did not so much resemble a "film" in terms of Hollywood spectacle but more in terms of a story about "real" life, full of real human beings who remember only in pieces and imperfectly jump cut-rather than as fluid movement through clear, linear space-time).

Jaime N. Christley writes about another filmmaker who works in a similar rhetorical mood, Chris Marker, who famously wonders about "the nature of truth, how it is perceived, understood, and most importantly, how it is created, for ourselves as individuals and as members of this or that community" (Christley, 2007, para. 1). Marker's most famous work, *La Jetee*, which is comprised of a continuous series of discontinuous jump cuts,

> Clock[s] in at 28 minutes, [and] is one of the strangest movies ever conceived, and also one of the most beautiful and sad. It's made up almost entirely of black and white still photographs, depicting the events of the narrative. (There is one single, haunting exception-the woman, in repose, fluttering her eyelids open.) These stills are governed by a third party narration—the only voice we hear—as well as music, and sound effects. (Christley, 2007, para. 6)

In her *Senses of Cinema* entry on Marker, Christley explains that, "[t]aking an image, a simple image, . . . and 'scrubbing' it—closely examining its nature, its context, its subject, or any other aspect, in order to develop a relevant discourse—is what Marker does best. Scrubbing the image is Marker's bread and butter" (Christley, 2007, para. 8). For Composition, we find here an easy analogy to an emphasis on creativity and invention that leads to new methods, but perhaps more clearly, we see revision practices in writing processes (writing as "scrubbing" via revision). But we might/must also consider that while Composition has devoted itself more recently to studies of the image that aid in the teaching of elemental rhetorical knowledge and skill-rendering Marker's "scrubbing" valuable for our current theory and practice—I have to think about present-day Composition beyond the elemental/textual in order to conceive of it as more expansive and hopeful cultural work. Here, however, I think ambivalently with Soviet filmmaker Andrei Tarkovsky, who bluntly explains his take on what such critical work can accomplish as cultural work:

> It is obvious that art cannot teach anyone anything, since in four thousand years humanity has learnt nothing at all. We should long ago have become angels had we been capable of paying attention to the experience of art, and allowing ourselves to be changed in accordance with the ideals

it expresses. Art only has the capacity, through shock and catharsis, to make the human soul receptive to good. It's ridiculous to imagine that people can be taught to be good ... Art can only give food—a jolt—the occasion—for psychical experience. (Tarkovsky, 1989, p. 50)

It seems that we both comprehend and insist upon working against this ambivalence, and so, again, desire. Resisting Tarkovsky's seemingly self-evident claims regarding the failure of art to elevate us to the realms of the angels, it seems crucially important that we "become angels . . . capable of paying attention to the experience of art" (Tarkovsky, 1989, p. 50). Naïvely idealistic, the desire for it is essential; it is Composition's desire for reflection, our mobilization of reflection as the compulsion to effectively communicate desire and resistance, expression and argument, ambivalence and meaning. In the context of reflection on film and image texts, it is this desire that I imagine informing Deleuzian speculation on the "plane of immanence" where we find interplay between the virtual and the actual so that they "thus become interchangeable," where "[a]ccording to Deleuze, the actual is defined by the present that passes, the virtual by the past that is preserved" (Pisters, 2003, p. 4). Conversely, speaking primarily of representation via words-in-print-texts, and perhaps articulating the sense of permanence and status sought by Albert Kitzhaber in and around 1963, by 1965, in a report sponsored by the College Entrance Examination Board, we read that "we must distinguish between the passing and the permanent" (as quoted in Harris, 1996, p. 7). The reality and experience of immanent change had been associated with ostensibly harmful "progressive attempts to turn the [English] classroom into a 'catch-all' space for discussing what ever happened to be on the minds of teachers or students" (Harris, 1996, p. 5) . . . and this wouldn't do. But if we find value in Deleuze's take— "the actual is defined by the present that passes, the virtual by the past that is preserved" (Pisters, 2003, p. 4), in becoming rather than in establishing What Has Been, then we will want to explore Godard's jump cutting, montage, and other added effects in order to appropriately consider, along with Michael Temple and James Williams,

autobiography and memory in film; age and melancholia; twentieth-century history and historiography; the fate of European art and culture; the relation between aesthetics and identity; ethics and philosophy; the nature and status of authorship and literature; the evolution of the visual image from painting to film and video; speed and technology; and videographic montage as a new poetics. (2004, p. 9)

It is true that here I want to "discuss what happen[s] to be on my mind," and I will do so by paying homage to Godard's "new poetics." Thinking alongside my concern for a kairotic, responsive, and responsible Composition, I want to applaud Godard's efforts to both capture and liberate an image at the same time.

Less idealistically, as "a film person" (and as someone who is not actually French), it's humbling for me to return to Benjamin's comments upon the apparent charlatanism of the film spectator; he argues that "[i]t is inherent in the technique of film . . . that everybody who witnesses its accomplishments is something of an expert" (1936, p. 231). Humbling today, but back then, as a cranky teen with my Saturday afternoon movies, it seems plausible that I enjoyed certain films—even with my limited understanding— because of how they made me feel, like *one of us*. Rhetorical engagement as social process. Simple. Still, recognizing the weight of my tone and the nature of current Composition, it seems necessary to read against my somewhat dreamy and nostalgic sentiment and make clear that I find the "anything goes" disposition to composing and Composition somewhat problematic. But I will resist explicating this awareness as a form of Burkean identification with and in the spirit of Godard, who, speaking in terms of production on his work as critic, writer, and filmmaker, identifies "a clear continuity between all forms of expression" arguing, "[i]t's all one. The important thing is to approach it from the side which suits you best" (as quoted in Milne & Narboni, 1972, p. 171). So I will follow my sentiment as I shape my approach-identifying with Godard who has divulged that "[i]f I analyse [sic] myself today, I see that I have always wanted, basically, to do research in the form of a spectacle" (1972, p. 181).[42]

I realize that by identifying so closely with Godard's self-assured performative disposition, I may simply be exposing my narcissism. Possibly confirming this diagnosis is *New York Times* film critic Manohla Dargis' review of a film recently screened at the Berlin Film Festival, a film scrumptiously entitled *Exterminating Angels*. Setting up her review, Dargis (2007) writes, "Film criticism . . . is the rationalization of taste into theory. No matter how involved the argument, writing about the movies almost always comes down to a question of personal taste, [to] that web of influence through which we filter each new film" (Dargis, 2007, B3). I love the candor with which Dargis explains her take on film criticism. Aspiring to a similar effect and gesturing toward a kind of nostalgia that may be productively (re)motivational for contemporary Composition, I call upon my personal taste and experience,

---

42   This approach was multimodal as this paper was originally presented at the 2007 CCCC conference. During the presentation, I read the paper as I screened a short film, an homage to Godard that wanted to articulate my desire visually and aurally, in cinematic rather than in pure "conference-paper mode."

along with various historical accounts, in order to project a sense of "crisis" in 1963 film culture and argue that a similar disposition attempted to move 1963 Composition.

So, Godard (1963): in his "first and last" big budget, studio-financed film, *Le Mepris* or *Contempt*, made a move to "go big" in ways that diminished many of his most inventive and effective filmmaking moves. But in "going big," Godard failed to create a very good film. A few complaints: a shift from black and white into lurid color; loss of subtle montage and other added effects for linear narrative; big name Hollywood stars; hit-you-over-the-head references to Greek Literature—when, we get it. Contemporary analogues to the shift I'm lamenting can be found in films (famously, all iterations of latter-day Star Wars) that evidence the CGI effect, films that, because they can, create digitally crafted armies of millions—locusts, clones, aliens, what have you—but that lack a certain small scale intimacy and suffer the loss of the ambiguous charm, delight, curiosity, and terror that comes from not seeing, from not overwhelming the sensorium—absence is presence, or, as Baudrillard famously comments, "to dissimulate is to feign not to have what one has," (1983, p. 5) which is a pretty magical formula for the artifice of (film) composing. This is relevant to Godard and his early methods—hand held cameras, little financial and technical support, and a revolutionarily independent spirit. I'm inspired by Godard's charming ambiguity—how his work is both pleasurable and intellectually engaging without clubbing me with its studio-supported, effects-driven force (its obvious-to-the-point-of condescension rhetorical effects). I want to think about Composition through the lens of film culture and its various crises of aspiration. Specifically, as I contemplate early, present-day, and future Composition performances, I want to imagine with Jean-Luc Godard a "cinema that might have been" (Keller, 2007, para. 5). That is to say, I want to think with Godard about a phenomenon that often amounts to "the disconnect between audience spectatorship (ecstasy before the projected spectacle) and the ex post facto indifference and callousness of that same audience/world that once watched" (Keller, 2007, para. 7). In other words, I want us to think with Godard as he laments the rhetorical and affective intensity that occurs at the moment of spectation/experience but fades once the lights come up. Godard seemed to be after both affective intensity as well as rhetorical and cultural engagement. As Keller interprets Godard's desire, "The cinema, which disengages us from worldly considerations while engaging us in its world, that is, our world, ontologically resides in a zone of paradox. Between action (engagement) and inaction (disengagement), Godard was to set out on the path of the former" (2007, para. 8).

It seems, then, that Godard shares a sentiment famously articulated by Brian Massumi in "The Autonomy of Affect," which caught the attention of scholars in Composition. Wondering about affect is not a new practice within our field; Ann Berthoff and Sondra Perl famously explored affect in Composition's early days. More recently, Composition scholars Kristie Fleckenstein, Jenny Edbauer Rice, Lynn Worsham, and others have been exploring the affective as a way of theorizing writing and the teaching of writing. While not speaking within the context of Composition but nevertheless exploring issues of pressing concern for many teachers of writing, as Massumi theorizes responses to film and televisual texts (including print text-as-image), he seems to share Godard's concern for audience-experience as desire that engages a "free-flowing affect."[43] This phantom but, as I see it, necessarily desirable affect circulates, for Massumi, somehow beyond discourse, within and throughout what he calls "expression-event[s]" (2002, p. 27).

While Massumi's free-flowing affect provides us with a language for thinking through our seemingly non-conscious, visceral and heightened sensorial responses to certain expression-events, such as a film, the concept is clearly problematic for those compositionists who have gener(ic)ally accepted Foucault's various articulations of the ways in which nothing exists outside of or beyond discourse. My experience as a filmmaker who screens her films at academic conventions has shown me that some, if not many, compositionists believe that teaching, using, or producing film-as-rhetoric is problematic to impossible; film as composing (filmwriting, film-composition) moves us beyond convention and genre and traditional notions of "engagement" via affect, gesturing toward an "anything goes," extra-discursive play that may be counterproductive, even dangerous. Eager to argue for a more beautiful use of digital play in her 2007 plenary, "Fitting Beauties of Transducing Bodies," at the Penn State Conference on Rhetoric & Composition, Anne Frances Wysocki argued that some visceral forms of engagement may unwittingly contribute to a culture of violence that seems easily to tolerate violent representational texts and encourages audiences to participate with/in them (in the form of violent video games, new digital artforms that foreground the body's response to its status as "art object," and, we might imagine, film).[44] In my eagerness to embrace or simply to be after Massumi's "free-flowing affect" as I participate in film work as a spectator and film-compositionist, I initially resisted Wysocki's reading; however, working more carefully through some of my initial reservations (which I tried eagerly to deny), I see now that there is something quite important about what she is worrying. Still, I want to bypass this concern, for now, especially because of the ways in which it occludes my immediate desire.

---

43 I am indebted to Dennis Lynch for the term "free-flowing affect," and am grateful to him for talking through his reading of Massumi with me in a post conference extension of a paper I presented at the Penn State University's Conference on Composition (2007).

44 See *Saturday, 2002* by Sabrina Raaf or *Osmose* by Char Davies.

Thinking about desire is to think in terms of affect. Filmmaking engages desire, invoking its creativity and imagining (the experience of) its fulfillment; writing or talking about a film I've made is a far less complicated rhetorical activity. That is, the writing that attends film work seems to come with comparative ease. Because, while there's more to it than this, essentially, in generating words, I work with one track, whereas in generating a film I work with several visual tracks and possibly one or more sound tracks, as well. I work to integrate them into an audio-visual whole that resonates something I want, something I want to project, something I want an audience to imagine as new, something that moves, something an audience reanimates and in that way sort of helps to complete. Though somewhat problematically received, Marc Prensky (2001) popularly intimated that our "digital native" students were all about this complex, integrative, pleasurable rhetorical work (p. 1), and his terms resonated in a variety of compelling ways. Nevertheless, film work in our classrooms often defaults to analytic and cultural studies oriented work regarding existing films (Bishop, 1999, p. vii), and this is fine for purposes related to the production of standard written English and for critical academic discourse, but literacies shift, and we seem stuck. So this analytical textual work about film is fine, except that it's not. In many ways, we are not so much producing but still looking at film texts as bound by conventions and thereby throwing back to earlier versions of Composition that privileged literary texts that primarily served to polish up students for work in literary studies (Connors, 1997); we had been limited in terms of invention potential, discovery, creativity . . . we had diminished rhetoric's expansive range. In our recent film work, we are similarly delimiting our potential by clutching at what is, at what has been, and especially at what has been commercially successful; what I'm after is the "naive object," a term Geoffrey Sirc (2007) recently shared with me in an email discussion of this project, explaining that

> by "naive," I mean the stuff students do, which may not be naive at all . . . naive = must be as underdetermined as possible, which in a sense obviates a certain kind of over-determined criticism. So the rhetorical apparatus you bring to a textual/filmic/whatever object must be a kind of fresh encounter. You can't bring the received discourse in as an analytic for new objects. (G. Sirc, personal communication)

Agreed. And I want to compel us to do more interesting and inventive things in our film work alone, but I realize that we are still largely about orderly academic written discourse. Even so, it seems to me that film work may productively move (student) writers to greater rhetorical efficacy. So, what of the writing that emerges from or attends film? Here again, desire, desire for affective intensity, desire for a vital (and pedagogically valuable) engagement.

Engagement. I remember reading about early Composition and its groovy moves—"the sounds, the candlelight, the students on the floor, the dark" (Sirc, 2001, p. 1)—an inviting disposition that privileged and inspired spontaneity and creativity and desires to teach and learn with far less support than we were then receiving (by comparison, Godard's 1963 film *Le Mepris* is in many ways all about the horrors of what happens to one's creativity and integrity once massive support is secured: the breakdown of communication, trust, and tenderness; the loss of frivolity and joy; the absence of wonder). Briefly summarizing the film,

> *Contempt* deal[s] with a conflict between a European direc-
> tor (Fritz Lang playing himself) and a crude American pro-
> ducer, Jerry Prokosch (performed with animal energy by
> [Jack] Palance) over a remake of Homer's *Odyssey*. Prokosch
> hires a French screenwriter, Paul (Michel Piccoli), to rewrite
> Lang's script [in other words, seeking commercial gain over
> art, he hires a lesser-known writer to revise the work of an
> established "master"]. Paul takes the job partly to buy an
> apartment for his wife, the lovely Camille ([Brigitte] Bardot);
> but in selling his talents, he loses stature in her eyes [in early
> discussions of this paper, Geoff Sirc imagines Brigitte Bardot
> as Composition student, and this makes sense to me, espe-
> cially as . . . through] a series of partial misunderstandings,
> Camille also thinks her husband is allowing the powerful,
> predatory Prokosch to flirt with her—or at least has not suf-
> ficiently shielded her from that danger. (Lopate, 2007, p. 1)

Maybe I was drawn to Composition in the same way that Camille fell in love with Paul. In the film, lamenting the changes she experiences ever since Paul (the hack writer) pockets the check from Prokosch (the producer), she comments upon their earlier days, their carefree courtship, their spontaneity, the joy they knew despite their unknown status and modest financial circumstances. Maybe I was drawn to Composition because of its hopeful yet undecided nature. But I can't spend too much time on a literal comparison; casting myself is one thing, but it's too presumptuous to imagine our entire discipline as characters in a French film (although it is deliciously tempting).

We have been talking about film in Composition since at least 1939, when, as noted earlier, Hooper J. Wise noted the use of film as a tool that aids in the teaching of listening (*silenzio!*) skills as he discusses common practices in the University of Florida's First Year Writing classroom. Ever since then, we find references to film use in Composition's scholarly record. Apparently, we put film to the following uses: to engage students, discuss content, practice analytical skills, explore narrative conventions, discover and analyze cultural trends, and much more. More recently (obviously), we find ourselves thinking about film composition not merely as an artifact for consumption and analysis but also as end-text, as something to be produced in a Composition classroom (in fact, to avoid engaging with similarly popular "new" forms, Sirc has recently commented, seems "cranky and wrongheaded" ["Writing"]). Lacking production possibilities, we have in the past passed on film and other multimodal text-work. Or, the more likely cause of our inability to see film production as worthy (rhetorical) activity involves the continued privileging of the (correctly) printed word, (clear) written discourse as the primary vehicle of rhetorical power. We know that film, especially "intellectual," "foreign," or "independent" film can be provocative and engaging and rhetorically effective, but we seem to be conflicted about how and why we should be working with it. (As for the massive *Rambos* and *Pretty Women*, "no problem," we've been saying, for quite some time).

And "reading" these films is far too easy. Working in film production is vastly more interesting, challenging, and capable of engaging existing and shaping emerging rhetorical knowledge and skill. The ambiguity inherent in film work enables a kind of fluid possibility, a charming sense that what one says or does regarding film (as Benjamin earlier predicted and as Dargis intimates) can be said and/or done (e.g., YouTube, Slamdance, or the Free Form and Cell Phone Film Festivals). In other words, the current moment asks us to think about the ways in which the ambiguous and potential-laden multimodal disposition one must possess or develop in film work may productively reactivate and reimagine the "fearful" postmodern promise, "anything goes" (the sort of promise upon which early Composition perhaps relied, the promise we were persuaded to no longer trust post 1963). For "anything goes" is a threat to discursive power, a threat to the dominance of certain discourses that delimit what can be said and done in the context of thinking about and performing Composition—this issue of *Composition Studies* is, after all, devoted to thinking about shifts in culture that resonate within and throughout the emergence of our field. Film's inherent "anything goes" posture seemed/ seems likely to jeopardize traditional acts of composing by suggesting that it is free (not without consequence but that it is unconstrained by generic conventions). But somehow, desire for this posture seems necessary in the present moment, as forces-internal and external-continue to attempt to define the nature of our rhetorico-compositional work and the nature of what constitutes an appropriate "composition." It is this desire that turns me back to Godard.

For Godard, anything could and did "go." He is known for totally controlling his unorthodox methods of production. He worked fast, cheap, and, for the most part, without studio intervention. The parallels to early Composition are striking, it seems to me. And, just as early Composition pedagogy was in many ways born of—but could not break from—Literary tradition, in a parallel universe Godard has famously said of film work and its intertextual relationship to nearly 10 years of film theory (in the form of the *Les Cahiers du Cinéma*, for which Godard had been a chief writer) "we're born in the museum, it's our homeland after all" (as quoted in Howe, 2005, p. vii).

In addition to his thrift and cleverness, Godard likely appeals to the contemplative compositionist; introducing *Cinema: The Archaeology of Film and the Memory of a Century*, John Howe notes Godard's "explicit references to the physical process of filmmaking, [and] a reflective and reflexive element that has become central to his work" (2005, pp. ix–x). Leaving the measure of analogy (to Composition) to the reader, I will simply point out that when I consider the ways in which this reflexivity is in part responsible for Godard's early success, I have to laugh reading an anecdote from Philip Lopate's 2007 review essay of *Le Mepris* for the *Criterion Collection's* DVD release. Lopate, a cinephile who has himself borrowed dialogue from Godard's film for his own book on film entitled *Totally, Tenderly, Tragically* recalls that in "1963, film buffs were drooling over the improbable news that Godard—renowned for his hit-and-run, art house bricolages such as *Breathless* and *My Life to Live*— was shooting a big CinemaScope color movie with Brigitte Bardot and Jack Palance" (2007); so, even the counterhegemonic, revolution-minded arthouse regulars were excited to see what might happen if Godard were funded and loaded up with stars. It gets better: Angry over Godard's refusal to trade on Bardot's sexuality, the studios forced a compromise. The film opens on a scene of a nude Brigitte Bardot unwittingly offering a critique of the ways in which women are victims of the gaze as she asks her lover if he enjoys—one by one— each of her "parts" ("Do you like my feet? . . . Do you like my knees? . . ."). Following this "compromise," which one might be tempted to view as successful given the reflexive critique it actualizes even as it self-referentially exploits Bardot's appeal, Godard famously wondered, perhaps even then considering the horror of having sold out, "Hadn't they ever bothered to see a Godard film?" (as quoted in Lopate, 2007).

In many ways, I am thinking about selling out, selling out to correctness and clarity at the expense of engagement, creativity, and a counterhegemonic spirit enacted through early pedagogies. I'm nostalgically thinking about how, just as early 1960s Composition wanted to move away from the strange and stultifying posturing of Compositions A and B, we find, according to Youssef Ishaghpour, "Godard's . . . insistence on a sort of legal equality between image and text" (as quoted in Howe, 2005, p. xii). I'm seeing here an early form of Composition-as-Cultural Studies that had begun to deconstruct traditional distinctions within the arts. Godard wanted to see film-as-rhetoric-as-art-as action, not through the narrow lens of disciplinary or mercantile divisions that often diminish creative potential; to do so, he could not work effectively or with real satisfaction within traditional studio engines. Famously comment ing upon the "unpleasant difficulties" he encountered with his producers on *Le Mepris*, Godard commented that "the imaginary has completely flowed over into life" (as quoted in Brown, 1972, p. 37) which is to say that, like Paul in the film, Godard had found that selling out isn't worth it. It's a somewhat obvious critique, but it materializes my concern for Composition's continuing identification with what has been. My nostalgic turn both asks that I remember and compels me to imagine "the Composition that might have been."

Chapter 4: Desire (II)

> Desire is appetite with consciousness thereof. . . . in no case do we strive for, wish for, long for, or desire anything, because we deem it to be good, but on the other hand we deem a thing to be good, because we strive for it, wish for it, long for it, or desire it. (Baruch Benedict de Spinoza, 1677, *Ethics, Part III*)

> The term "desire" is understood here in a rather special way. It does not refer to the pursuit and possession of a love object . . . but to the visual figures of the text that elaborate a structure of opposition which expresses not so much the desire for an object as the psychic process of desire itself. (Linda Williams, 1987, *Figures of Desire*, p. xvii)

> I would still encourage somebody, if they wanted to make a movie, to just go take a movie camera. That's clearly been shown to work. (Nicole Holofcener, 2010, "Interview," *The A.V. Club*)

Desire radiates longingly, persistently, and in all directions. To support this claim, consider Spinoza's *Ethics, Part III*, in which he asserts that striving (desire) is a universal property shared by all beings and things. Cinematic desire, too, is ongoing; seeing a film from inception to production to projection to spectation/consumption, and possibly to critique (and *etc.*, *etc.*) requires intensely persistent desire, especially for the academic auteur who is working in affectively intense scenes of uncertain desire and without a clear sense of direction. Cinematic desire is polymorphous, disorientatingly open—consider the affordances of multimodal making and the activation of multiple senses. Yet cinematic desire is also constrained, rhetorically attuned to the structures of feeling attributed to a film through its screenplay, direction, acting, lighting, music, ambient sound, and all of the many attributes that comprise a film's ambient force and meaning. Speaking as a filmmaker, I can say that the will to sustain the force of (a) desire in the process of making a film is daunting, presenting one of the fiercest challenges a filmmaker faces. As an *academic* filmmaker, somewhat obstructed by my own awareness of my audience's expectations regarding how I will handle rhetorical conventions, I can say that the will to sustain desire is simultaneously met with a normative will to tame it. At times, this will to tame desire in filmmaking functions as a powerfully deflating, discouraging force, and at other times this admonishing angel lifts me up so that I am able to see the better choice(s). I will be arguing for the value of both impulses as intensely affect-laden experiences through which we reanimate existing rhetorical knowledge and revitalize hopes for the emergence of new ways of enacting our creative and rhetorical vision. To briefly describe this validating and vital desire for its rhetorical affordances and learning potential, a brief scene.

INT SAN FRANCISCO HOTEL ROOM (THE DRAKE)—3: A.M.

BONNIE is in the bathroom of the small but stylish room while MIKE sleeps in the bedroom. She is seated on the large, black tiles of the bathroom floor. They have a sheen, and they are cold. We see her Macbook Pro on the floor in front of her. She sits, legs splayed to either side, focusing on the screen's display of her edit and playback frames, eyes flickering between them as she types, considers, deletes, types, considers, and sends a status update to Facebook; she wants her friends and colleagues to know of her struggle. She writes to sustain her desire for scaling back from conventions toward shiny new potentials. She writes to identify this activity as furious 3:00 a.m. desire. She writes to pillow fight with her decision to forego title cards that she, in her fear regarding coherence, now, at 3:00 a.m. has "text-edited" in. The cards mark the three "acts" within her film, which will screen in the morning. She writes to say that she knows. She knows that this old convention will shiny up toward greater coherence for a film that had wanted to be about one quasi famous "stranime-ator" but turned out a case study of three because life, constraints, and etc. . . . She keeps the cards, re-renders, and . . .

> BONNIE
>
> (light sigh of something like resignation)
>
> (a beat)
>
> okay.
>
> . . . closes the case. BONNIE goes back to bed for an unsteady but somewhat more relatively possibly better sleep.
>
> END SCENE.

What seems essential in this scene, and going forward, is that film-composition honors creative and critical vision as advanced by the messy, nondiscursive, fully embodied, affectively responsive, cognitively and rhetorically capable film composer, the film-compositionist. In this chapter, I want to argue that we have good reason to do so. In fact, as I write, I am lit by the glow of Casey Boyle's (2016) "Writing and Rhetoric and/as Posthuman Practice."

Here, Boyle rethinks the nature of our work by moving beyond recent, officially articulated "frameworks" that seek to capture just what it is that we do and teach. Boyle, a digital scholar, pedagogue, and long-time editor of the digital journal *Enculturation: A Journal of Rhetoric, Writing, and Culture*, sustains a disposition to networked, ecological, and posthuman rhetorics, pedagogy, and praxis. Boyle's posthuman practice finds clarity in being and becoming, in emergence, immanence, and in moving beyond retrogressive notions of authors/auteurs, many of which have been complexified within the brief history of the term "auteur" that I sketched earlier, in chapter 2. Without directly referencing affect, Boyle here articulates a version of rhetoric that is attuned to affect, nevertheless:

> [R]hetoric, by attending more closely to practice and its nonconscious and nonreflective activity, reframes itself by considering its operations as exercises within a more expansive body of relations than can be reduced to any individual human. (2016, p. 552)

Boyle is careful to attend to networked being and/as rhetorical practice, but appreciation of this state of affairs need not diminish our attentiveness to particular nodes within our discursive assemblages. So whereas a "body of relations" defines our praxis in ways that are irreducible to "any individual human," (Boyle, 2016, p. 552), we are nonetheless affectively charged agents, and our attunements shape the nature of our various relations in ways that invoke care, study, and critique. Bound, as we are, within convention, we nevertheless follow our affective intensities toward our better articulations. This work that is aided by digital tools that enable us to capture, improvise, script, arrange, consider, critique, revise, and perform our sense of these orchestrations—and, importantly, how they (do or may) shape selves, communities, cultures, and other assemblages, other bodies of relations. Digitally mediated film-composition lights up a vast range of desires (from deeply conventional to radically non-normative) as radically and ongoingly productive. For though our composing efforts are met with a seeming counterforce—a will to tame desire, a force against which a good deal of progressive theory, scholarship, pedagogy, and praxis is in opposition—this force is both a challenging sort of obstacle and an illuminating, contour-defining light of shiny rhetorical wisdom. It seems likely that whatever the outcome, this will is at work in our lives as composers, as our choices are determined through processes of invention that call upon us to move with and against our desire, visions, and discovered purposes. Thus, while cruel auteurism meets desire with what may feel like outrageous demands and stifling constraints, these same desires may also, in the final cut, reveal themselves as Berlantian zones of optimism for desiring compositional choices that have made possible the effective cinematic object, the winning screening, the longed-for publication and perhaps at least some of the material and certainly the affective rewards that attend it.

The will to tame desire in this chapter is powerfully met with resistance, yet I make the curatorial effort. I want to talk about auteurist (and other forms of) desire and how DIY digital filmmaking moves rhetors to higher (including extra-normative, extra-conventional) enactments of their rhetorical practice. This means that I will write quite a bit about aesthetics and hint at the pleasures we seek through aesthetically curated compositional activity as activity bound up in the very perception of a pleasing aesthetics, and of being itself (see Spinoza, *Ethics III*). Additionally, I will think about student desires, pedagogical desires, and disciplinary desires, as these desires are both bound up in and are themselves binders of certain forms of rhetoric-aesthetic pleasure. That's a lot of binding. More simply, film-composition wants all the pleasures. As *Cruel Auteurism's* initial chapters make clear, the emergence of our desires for film in composition extends to the early twentieth century and the birth of film as an aesthetic, artistic, creative, and intellectual cultural practice. That is to say, filtered intimations of film as public rhetoric were initiated long before they gathered the kind of momentum we value today in film-composition. However, it was later on the timeline that film gathered overt force as rhetorical agent toward digital scholarship, cultural change, and academic pedagogy. This chapter explores our amplified desires, our sense of potential for,and enactments of vital, digitally mediated rhetorical choices.

Rhetorical Velocity and the Dialectical Automaton

It is difficult to know where to begin, but since we are incepting[45] and because this book is rendered in words, I want to begin with a clever phrase—"rhetorical velocity" (DeVoss & Ridolfo, 2009). "Rhetorical velocity" neatly articulates momentum both as a practice and as a way of characterizing a moment in time. Conceptually capturing the nature of our choices in the present, Danielle Nicole DeVoss and Jim Rodolfo articulate what I read as a sense of Deleuzian "movement-image," a way of coalescing images (in the case of their *Kairos* publication, screen grabs following a digitally mediated news story evolving over a three-day period) into a kind of metaphorical meaning, a sense of wholeness about an unfolding narrative. Their important *Kairos* webtext, "Composing for Recomposition: Rhetorical Velocity and Delivery"

---

45   See Christopher Nolan; see the timeline that moves in both redirections.

reveals that our choices play out in time contingent compositional practices; in other words, rhetorical velocity happens on something very much like a filmic timeline. DeVoss and Ridolfo consider the digitally mediated, revamped rhetorical canon of Delivery through the term "rhetorical velocity," a term that wants to articulate how we write for and enact desired rhetorical effects. They explain rhetorical velocity as

> a strategic approach to composing for rhetorical delivery. It is both a way of considering delivery as a rhetorical mode, aligned with an understanding of how texts work as a component of a strategy. In the inventive thinking of composing, rhetorical velocity is the strategic theorizing for how a text might be recomposed (and why it might be recomposed) by third parties, and how this recomposing may be useful or not to the short or long-term rhetorical objectives of the rhetorician. (DeVoss & Ridolfo, 2009, para. 1)

By thinking "ahead," toward how others might receive and remake a work, rhetors working for rhetorical velocity are attentive to the reception of a work, which is to "think ahead" on a timeline of rhetorical movement and open potential (think composing for counterargument—same as it ever was). We must appreciate the clever choice of incorporating a term denoting the movement of time into their effort to articulate a compositional trend and recognize the rhetorically interventionist nature of film-composition as capable of generating cultural change. Similarly, consider how Deleuze (1985) recalled how Eisenstein's view of chronologically determined emergence—movement-toward-meaning, meaning inclusive of how "the character experiences himself" as well as how "the way in which the author and the viewer judge him," which is convergence—"integrates thought into the image" (as cited in Deleuze, 1985, p. 161). This capacious rhetorical sensibility, this capacity to discern beyond agential rhetoric exclusively and toward a dynamic network of able actants was so impressive as to invoke Eisenstein's discernment of a "new sphere of filmic rhetoric, the possibility of bearing an abstract social judgment," (Deleuze, 1985, p. 161) a kind of cinematic public sphere, the very sort within which DeVoss and Ridolfo find "rhetorical velocity" vibrantly thrumming into being due to the affordances of digital media and the speed with which we share information. Regarding Eisenstein's "filmic rhetoric," and consistently articulating a mechanically correct concept regarding the velocity of key convergences, Deleuze theorized "[a] circuit which includes simultaneously the author, the film, and the viewer" (1985, p. 161), within which a dynamic range of affects and cognitive actions happen, glow, disturb, settle, brighten, flicker longingly, and despite all sorts of seeming chaos emerges as functionally meaningful. For Deleuze,

> The complete circuit includes the sensory shock [velocity's affects/effects?] which raises us from the images to conscious thought, then the thinking in figures which takes us back to the images and gives us an affective shock again. Making the two coexist, joining the highest degree of consciousness to the deepest level of the unconscious: this is the dialectical automaton. The whole is constantly open [and] . . . forms a knowledge . . . which brings together the image and the concept as two movements each of which goes towards the other (1985, p. 161).

Eisenstein via Deleuze shows that the sorts of dynamic, networked thought regarding the value of dynamic text events such as film are not new to us in the present moment. That we return to the notion of the "dialectical automaton" who is capable of processing affect and meaning dynamically and potentially absent the constraints of clear and certain purpose seems promising for both digital scholarship and pedagogy. Obviously, DeVoss and Ridolfo found kairotic value in meticulously reanimating that desiring zombie. With a zombie reference, I am applauding the propriety of resurrecting a knowledge that seems both self-evident and in need of critique. However we move with our understanding, though, "velocity" is movement. It is being with and being for (Nancy, as cited in Davis, 2010, pp. 4–10). I am essentially applauding the clever capture of this metaphorical happening. Though "rhetorical velocity" provides a rhetorically sophisticated term for analyzing and generating media texts and events, its rhetorical emplotment also functions ekphrastically to illuminate the emergence of film-composition. In other words, DeVoss and Ridolfo use language to articulate their sense that our multimodal choices might vibe with time contingent compositional practices, such as composing on a filmic timeline. This is the confident contemporary view, and it's been some time in the making, driven by our desires to demonstrate how film matters as intellectual, cultural, rhetorical work. Clearly, DeVoss and Ridolfo work toward rhetorical velocity quite optimistically, recognizing a zone of compositional potential rendered visible by seeing, over time, the unfolding rhetorical capture of a narrative event. This view might not have been possible in earlier, more fearful and less forcefully desiring theories that saw image and film as acritically devoted to little more than sales, or to power. With rhetorical velocity, we can read and produce effective texts on any range of affectively engaging and moving matters, and we may do so with a confidence that derives from the work of Composition scholars who study and circulate the complex nature of media events and their rhetorics in the present. We have not always been so confident in our skills or in our desires.

A History of Promises

A tentative disposition toward film in classrooms began to shift radically in the 1960s and 1970s. Breathtakingly outlining new zones of optimism in Composition, we find during this time in history a progressive movement that valued "the potentials of providing students with increased representational options" (Shipka, 2011, p. 4). Generously offering her uniquely loving take on the potential within Composition today, Jody Shipka (2011) details the emergence of this more vibrant range of compositional options in *Toward A Composition Made Whole*. She lauds this shift even as she worries that the term contemporarily used to denote it—"multimodality"—constrains abilities to imagine a vital range of compositional options that happen beyond digital technologies. Shipka privileges "the fundamentally multimodal aspects of all communicative practice" (2011, p. 13), and her work masterfully articulates the emergence of "multimodality" even as she is careful to extricate her particular concern for moving beyond screens in articulation of the term's fuller meaning and potential. *Cruel Auteurism* has been projecting a sense of multimodality that is primarily (but not exclusively) possible within the context of the screen. However, by theorizing affective intensities that occur in the processes of composing films as aids to teaching and learning, I share Shipka's concern for increasingly "whole" forms of compositional activity and rhetorical work. Shipka's work is thus crucially important to current theories and practices on "making," "makerspaces," new materialisms, installation work, and film-composition.[46] Shipka's work is profoundly important for contemporary theories and practices in film-composition. Her articulation of desire for theories and practices that value "other representational systems and technologies" (2011, p. 11) resonates with the ongoing desires of early film-compositionists, many of whom worked against limitations regarding moving off the page (and toward the screen). Written during a viscerally progressive era that seems to forecast emergent film-composition (and Shipka's "composition made whole"), Peter Dart (1968) wrote in *English Journal* that

> Teachers are encouraged to use films in their classes. Films, they are told, should be used to provide vicarious experiences, to provide focal points for discussion, and to provide comparisons of media and communication. But the

---

46 "Matter and meaning . . . are not separate elements" (Barad, 2003).

> film's most effective and profitable use is probably its most
> neglected function: students need to produce their own
> films. (p. 96)

Very hopeful proclamations radiated a desire to participate more fully in
the complexity, narrative vitality, and rhetorical potential of film. Referenced
earlier and due to its powerful presence throughout many efforts to map film
in Composition, Richard Williamson (1971) offered a rich and vibrant proclamation when he argued not simply for the inclusion of film for its potential to
teach analysis and enliven classrooms with engaging content. Instead, he advocated "The Uses of Filmmaking in English Composition," moving straight to a
consideration of production, articulating what had likely been circulating as a
kind of shared desire. Yet, perhaps haunted by earlier doubts and sensing that
English was still English and that disciplinary identity trumped interdisciplinary potential, the arguments were still somewhat brief and under-developed.

Later, as Cultural Studies inflected theories and practices in Composition,
we began to recognize that engaging content served a variety of ideological functions that rendered a host of popular texts available for critical inquiry. From
Raymond Williams' (1954, 1961, 1977) "structure of feeling," we began to think
more overtly about affective desire as it circulates through networks of rhetorical action, both oppressive and subversive, in the lived experiences of daily
life. For Cultural Studies scholar Lawrence Grossberg (1997), desiring or not,
perhaps resistant, "the political intellectual ha[d] no choice but to enter into the
struggle over affect in order to articulate new ways of caring" (p. 23). He recalls
Richard Hoggart's attempt to define cultural studies as a move to explore "what
it feels like to be alive" (as quoted in Gregg & Seigworth, 2010, p. 309). Tracking
with my own desiring motivations, some of the most exciting scholarship today hopes to think with "what it feels like to be alive" in the digitally mediated
present, with all of the affordances for consumption and production that we enjoy, worry, and utilize as tools for generating responsive, critical, and otherwise
intense forms of affectively charged rhetorical action. Digital tools enable us to
gesture at articulation of affect in the context of this rhetorically strategic work
so that we may render possible the critical desire of film-composition: contemplation of these affects as rhetorical and ideological work.

That a good deal of affect theory worries the Deleuzian "plane of immanence" (2001, p. 27) appoints it nicely as a tool for analyzing and composing
films and multimodal texts. Reviewing some of our most intense engagements
with Deleuzean thinking, Grossberg explains in an interview with Gregg and
Seigworth that it is especially in his studies of Deleuze that he finds a conceptual approach to thinking about emergence that gets at the affective intensities
we associate with experience and everyday life. At the same time, he finds that

some scholarship drawing upon Deleuze proceeds with too carefree an approach regarding the actual and the virtual. It seems that worries such as these, while vital to intellectual life and integrity, may also have shaped the earlier sense of futility towards the desire to work with film in English classrooms. Perhaps ironically, it is through Deleuzian desire, and, increasingly, through digital text production, lived experience, multimodality, and film-composition that many discover a timeline for actualizing their projects. Attentiveness to our critical projects is essential, yet it seems clear that uptake may vortex differently depending upon the nature of the desire, which is seemingly but not necessarily contradictory—past and present, being and emergence, ontological and empirical all at the same time. In this space of discontinuity or ambiguity, film-composition shivers with desire. But this sparklingly hopeful desire may, some argue, blind us to a potentially vaporous fog in which little actually happens. In particular, Grossberg worries that affect theory as intellectual tool "simply covers too much ground," and he asserts that this simplicity is problematic, especially because "[t]here are too many forms, too many effectivities, too many organizations, too many apparatuses" (1997, p. 314). For Grossberg, this diverse rhetorical terrain means, for affect theory and its studies that, "affect can let you off the hook," that affect "has come to serve, now, too often, as a 'magical' term. So, if something has effects that are, let's say, nonrepresentational then we can just describe it as 'affect'"(1997, p. 315). Grossberg is correct to worry the velocity of today's scholarship on textual dispositions and practices. However, it seems to me that simply by virtue of possessing a capacity to speak to experience in its various forms and through diverse types of rhetorical assemblage (especially those rendered possible due to the speed of digital processing), affect theory does indeed offer us useful frames for critical inquiry, invention, and composition. Reading through affect theory may begin to address Grossberg's worries over apparatuses, assemblages, and the nature of scholarship on affect even as it draws upon the indeterminacy of how affect theory is defined and uptaken. This point seems to drive Patricia T. Clough (2010) as she argues in "The Affective Turn: Political Economy, Biomedia, and Bodies" that a fog of indeterminacy need not be theorized as lacking critical potential but that instead: "Affect and emotion . . . point . . . to the subject's discontinuity with itself, a discontinuity of the subject's conscious experience with the non-intentionality of emotion and affect" (p. 206). More optimistically than others, Clough wants us to see how working through affect favorably addresses our longing to theorize bodily responsivity:

> The turn to affect did propose a substantive shift in that it
> returned critical theory and cultural criticism to bodily mat-
> ter, which had been treated in terms of various construc-

tionists under the influence of poststructuralism and deconstruction. The turn to affect points instead to a dynamism immanent in bodily matter and matter generally—matter's capacity for self-organization in being informational—[. . . as] the most provocative and enduring contribution of the affective turn. (2010, pp. 206–207)

The Biomediated Body

Clough brilliantly bypasses what she calls a troubling "circuit from affect to emotion, ending up with subjectively felt states of emotion." That is, Clough moves beyond "a return to the subject as the subject of emotion" (2010, p. 207). (This is a matter that worried Lynn Worsham, and rightly so, as it focused perhaps too narrowly on individuals in a critical moment within the Social Turn. As well, Boyle's contemporary turn to posthumanism as a productive frame for rhetorical practice seems implicated in Clough's shared concern). Working cleverly from within a constellation of scholarly works aimed at a form of rhetoricity, Clough instead develops the concept of "the biomediated body," and she is guided by scholars who have benefitted from the insights of Deleuze and Guattari, Spinoza, and Henri Bergson, scholars who see, rather as Hansen has argued regarding cognition and techno-rhetorical immersion, affect as a matter of radical inclusion. For Clough, we might take on a view of "affect as pre-individual bodily forces augmenting or diminishing a body's capacity to act," and thereby join these laudable affect and rhetoric scholars in the contemporary moment, those "who critically engage those technologies that are making it possible to grasp and to manipulate the imperceptible dynamism of affect" (2010, p. 207). Clough's major contribution here is that she is able to bypass a notion of affect as frivolously acritical and instead turns herself to the laudable task of arguing that

> focusing on affect—without following the circuit from affect to subjectively felt emotional states—makes clear how the turn to affect is a harbinger of and a discursive accompaniment to the forging of a new body . . . the biomediated body. (2010, p. 207)

With Clough, media theorist Chris Vitale (2011) speaks to the value of affect by looking to how it operates within the process of filmmaking. His claims resonate with my sense of film-composition as a productive space for enacting creative and critical vision in ways that both emerge from experientially derived rhetorical knowledge, and in terms of potential to move audiences (both particular and general), cultures, and worlds. Vitale frames his understanding of this potential as "film-art," but I see through my biomediated body a version of film-composition in the notion of a productive art, a rhetorical art. Vitale's film-art (our film-composition) conceptualizes the roomy affordances of filmmaking's rhetorical potential by considering our motivations to make films, suggesting that, "we make film-affects, and aim to make more powerful film-affects, so as to more powerfully sculpt our relations with our world, to harmonize with its greatest circuits"(2011).

Here, I take Vitale to mean that these "greatest circuits" with which we long to "harmonize" are extra-normative, fluid, dynamic, and in all the ways we might say it, "open." He sees the value in this openness in ways that resonate with Davis' "rhetoricity" as a state of being:

> [f]or the more a film harmonizes with the world, the more it furthers the project of a deep sync with what is. Such a notion of sync would be far beyond adaptation, for it would be a transvidual world-becoming. Film-art is a part of the world envisioning itself, in and through us. The more powerfully we create, the more our film has resonances beyond ourselves, resonances with the deep structure of what is. That is, the more a film resonates with the deep structure of the world, the more it is affected by the world through its creators, and therefore, the more it has the power to affect more than just the filmmaker, but also the world around it. And thus, the filmmakers must be able to be powerfully affected by the world, so as to powerfully affect it in turn. Filmmakers can become lenses themselves, part of the world's own perpetual re-envisioning. (2011)

Vitale's desiring work, "Towards a Cinema of Affects: A Manifesto, Part I—From Film-World to Film-Art" confidently lights up a path that many in Composition long to travel more and more routinely. Our attempts to engage with textuality in ways that move us, our audiences, and our students mark our sense of purpose. Often, we have turned to film in articulating that purpose, as our history of hopes, fears, and desires have hoped to make clear.

Hyperdrives

From today's vantage, particularly from the perspective of Composition scholarship that draws upon the thinking of Deleuze and through Deleuze scholarship, more generally, we are able to explore the affective intensities of film spectatorship, the potentials of embodied spectating and production, and convergent thinking regarding mind and body, the virtual and the actual, past and present, and a dizzying range of reconfigured binaries that want us to open out to creative and experiential potential. Extending this work in ways that elide the potential to think affect too narrowly, Daniel W. Smith (2007) explains Deleuzean desire by clarifying that this is no base desire; tending to the drives need not be(come) a static affair that reads exclusively through psychoanalytic lenses toward overdetermined meanings, actions, and potential. Instead, Smith argues that, "conscious will *and preconscious interest* are both subsequent to our unconscious drives, and it is at the level of the drives that we have to aim our ethical analysis" (Smith, 2007, p. 69; emphasis mine). In other words, Deleuze complexifies the drives in ways that attend to the non-discurive, the unassimilable, the unruly, the just-out-of-reach that both defines and encompasses desire as a matter of its existence. *Hyperdrives.* This existential desiring resonates with Composition's being, its purpose, and its history for affective and effective ethical and compositional activity. Deleuzean value for conceptualizing film-composition is a matter of rhetoricity, the *being with* and *being for* that attends consciousness and compositional capacities. As with much digital scholarship that has made room for film-composition, for Smith, Deleuze characterizes "modes of existence, with their powers and capacities," through a dynamic rather than static sense of what those modes might entail:

> Deleuze approaches modes of existence, ethically speaking,
> not in terms of their will, or their conscious decision making
> power (as in Kant), nor in terms of their interests (as in Marx,
> for example), but rather in terms of their drives. (2007, p. 69)

Optimistically attentive to drives—both known and unassimilable—in contemplation of ethics, we move more forcefully toward the value of affect theory for rhetorical ethics and film-composition. But how? There is a great deal of ephemeral feeling going on here, and as many may sense, not enough that is clearly articulable for ethics, pedagogy, or scholarship. If anything, though, Composition has a history of attending to visual metaphors and metaphors of complexity (kyburz, 2005) as a portal opening toward optimal conditions for intellectual work. In its capacious interdisciplinarity, our field has reached to find the more productive paths to better rhetorical practices. Film-composition is no different. As I see her complexifying Deleuzean value for thinking generative rhetorical work like filmmaking and multimodal composing, Media Studies scholar Amy Herzog (2000) explains why Deleuze matters for film theory in ways that get after the productive, the dynamic:

> The greatest achievement of the Cinema books is that they
> suggest a means of looking at film that explodes static views
> of the work that the work of art does. Rather than "repre-
> senting" something, film, for Deleuze, has the potential to

create its own fluid movements and temporalities. These movements, while related to formal elements of rhythm and duration within the film itself, cannot be reduced to specific techniques or concrete images. Similarly, the temporality that Deleuze locates within the cinema cannot be pinned to a specific type of shot, nor a particular moment in the shooting, editing, projection, or reception of a film. (2000)

Herzog adds her voice to a scholarly vortex that strives, desires, and longs for being in striving. The emphasis, here, is on movement. Striving as being and becoming, with options for rhetorical action evolving and clarifying and moving into and out of range according to the positionality of spectators, with their own fields of dynamic striving activated and inflecting the meaning-making process. Further highlighting the value of dynamic Deleuzean desire, Richard Rushton (2009) rejects the (retro)conventional approach to spectatorship as passive: "Rather than spectators passively deprived of their bodies and held in thrall to an ideological apparatus, Deleuze's writings gave rise to the possibility of spectators who engaged their bodies and senses" (p. 45). Through desire, we move beyond what Rushton calls Deleuze's "cinematic bodies," portals to "new cinematic territories beyond the ocularcentric, psychoanalytically focused discourses" (2009, p. 46) that had marked a notion of the passive spectator, a-critically receiving cinematic texts.[47] Instead, affect, through embodied Deleuzean desire, affords us a critical approach to film-composition. Speaking for myself and some of my students, I can testify to the validity of this claim, particularly as it hints at affectively derived intuition as motivational for key rhetorical choices (more on this in upcoming anecdotes and student commentary).

Our collective desire to look beyond constraining notions of spectatorship even as we began to proclaim more eagerly a desire to begin production work in film-composition marks a good deal of scholarship in this period. For example, witnessing the emergence of new forms of textual play, Sarah J. Arroyo (2013) examines a series of diachronically networked theories on the nature of compositional spaces and interfaces. She characterizes the productive inventional space of "chora" as "a threshold or conduit of pure exposure along which bodies, through relations of touching, experience the emergence of otherwise unknown capacities and the shaping of new assemblages" (2013, p. 68). This is the "agonizing" abyss, for Diane Davis, in which we confront our "unanswered desire to hit bottom so that one might start building one's way back up and out"

---

47 The older notion finding purchase in early film-composition scholarship, where professors worried student reception of filmic content, where they worried film's potential to shape morality over and above Literature's.

(2013, p. 76). Arroyo reads this abyss as a space of potential, referring to it via Deleuze and Guattari (1987) as a "fog," or "glare" (2013, pp. 262–263). For Arroyo, given her attentiveness to Ulmerian "electracy" as a frame for exploring contemporary video assemblages, this fog is a space of invention, of networked sociality and compositional being: "there is no way out, yet there is no trap." She explains that, "[t]he abyss is where we reside; it is not a place on which to stand or out of which to emerge, but the chora, the 'hole' that cannot be separated from life itself" (2013, p. 68). Concerned for the potential emergence of "multiple possibilities for invention and production" (2013, p. 69), Arroyo sees the fog, the abyss, and the glare as descriptive characterizations of chora, the interface that calls upon our highest rhetorical capacities even as it registers our fuller, often messier and less desirably projected characteristics. This reality is what Arroyo refers to as "electrate reasoning: the logic of the 'and'" (2013, p. 69), and it involves a great deal of theoretical contemplation within processes of invention, movement, and making. In other words, electorate reasoning, which guides a great deal of (digital) film-composition work, involves improvisational being within spaces of networked sociality, and in these spaces, film-composition insists along with decades of Composition theory, we can become even better makers, better rhetors and rhetoricians. Nevertheless, it feels important to further reveal some of the problematic notions associated with this better rhetor, newly emboldened through film-composition and the affordances of digital media, and re-animated by affective desire. It's no secret to Composition, even less surprising to film-composition, that affective desire is essential to rhetorical work that circulates toward any sort of moving signification. I want to suggest the rhetorically powerful nature of (making) affectively moving films (to note what may seem quite obvious, that they function as cultural politics). Because of film's powerful rhetorical potential, this work as scholarship and pedagogy has been viewed with fear, suspicion, and cautious reservation. Yet, desire persists. And, in the context of digital scholarship and thinking through the powerful notion of mattering, posthuman rhetorics, and rhetorical velocity, these fears may call for our attention but they are unlikely to diminish our desire. For, if we are persistently operating as dialectical automatons, radiating desires in ways that we tend to but cannot contain, what of our excess? What of our intensity?

In and Out of Formation

Worrying the "excess," Ben Anderson (2010) examines the value of thinking through affect as "an imperative that emerges from a nascent recognition that affect is modulated and transmitted in forms of power addressed to life" (Hardt & Negri, 2004; Thrift, 2005) (as quoted in Anderson, 2010, pp.

161, 162). Anderson cites Deleuzian (1992) efforts to map "the imbrication of different affects in power formations that modulate the circulation and distribution of affects" by disrupting "the prescriptive normalizations of forms of disciplinary power," and he lauds how this transformative notion of affect moves toward a glimmer of the agential:

> Here it is precisely the transmission of affect, its movements, disruptions, and resonances, that forms of vital or life power can come to harness. These forms of power do not prevent and prescribe but work in conjunction with the force of affect, intensifying, multiplying, and maturing the material-affective processes through which bodies come in and out of formation (Anderson, B., 2010, p. 162)

Anderson writes out of a concern for how affect has been taken up in cultural theory, and in many ways his concern seems to resonate with fearful discourses about the affective power of film in Composition—the worries of frivolity, ostensibly acritical rhetorics of play, and potential for exploitation of ways of being that slip between the normative and other. In short, Anderson worries hopeful claims that are made regarding affective "excess," and these are claims that seem central to a good deal of digital scholarship, particularly works that value imagistic rhetorical practice for its moving potential. Articulating these worries as a set of polar oppositions, Anderson explains that,

> claims to the unassimilable excess of affect over systems of signification or narrativization provide the ontological foundation for the promise of a new way to attend to the social or cultural in perpetual and unruly movement, whether codified in terms of the "autonomy" of affect (Massumi, 2002) or the "immeasurability" of affect (Hardt and Negri, 2004). (Anderson, B., 2010, p. 162)

The rhetorician will see the dilemma for film-composition. We glimpse a sense of potential, aporia for new ways of composing and being through our indeterminate efforts at making beyond normative signification, yet how are we to imagine ourselves beyond? How are we to imagine excess? These questions are troubled as Anderson explains the opposition to the notion of a promising affective excess:

> The transitive excess of affect is precisely what is targeted, intensified, and modulated in new forms of power—forms of power that themselves function through an excess of mechanisms that saturate and invest life, whether named as

"control societies" (Deleuze 1992), or "biopower" (Hardt and Negri, 2000). (Anderson, 2010, p. 162)

Anderson's troubling binary—claims for the excessive, autonomous, and immeasurable intensities of affect vs. affect as fertile ground for emergent forms of power—points in the direction of desires for filmmaking and of film-composition. Unable to clearly untrouble this binary, film-compositionists work from within it, ever driven by their desires to address a central question Anderson worries in his work, "[h]ow to attend to, welcome, and care for indeterminacy, for affect's virtuality?" (Anderson, B., 2010, p. 162). Speaking to a shared concern for the evolution of film-composition but more realistically claiming for myself a compositional desire, I find value in Anderson's effort to encourage us to wonder, to ask if we are capable of conceptualizing "the imbrication of affect in an excess of knowledges, procedures, and techniques without being enamored of a power that acts without limit or outside?" (Anderson, B., 2010, p. 162). I see here a desire that runs throughout the affects associated with discourses on film in Composition. We want to use and make films that move us and our audiences, potentially as a rhetorico-cultural politics of intervention. Yet at the same time, we recognize what is at stake in claiming affective excess as a tool for forecasting the value of such work as it exists in contradistinction to centuries of agential rhetoric that is formed in and delivered through words (or even through very obvious non-fictional rhetorical cinematic forms, like PSAs—Public Service Announcements, with their obvious rhetorical stakes and normative values, and documentaries). With Anderson, I want to claim that we must "care for affect's virtuality"; we must care for affective excess because "the ontological foundation for the promise of a new way to attend to the social or cultural in perpetual and unruly movement" is too rich to ignore (Anderson, B., 2010, p. 162). That is to say, despite the potentially troubling unruliness of affective excess, the history of its becoming includes

> intellectualist discourses about affect and its ability to escape, shatter, and seduce reason. It may also evoke a still too present equation between emotion and the gendered figure of the irrational woman or the classed figure of the angry crowd. Equating affect with excess is risky, even if it is far from new (albeit increasingly common) as a refrain across many contemporary affect theories. Hence, claims of excess have also been central to the disavowal of affect theory. Despite this troubled genealogy, addressing the equation between affect and excess is necessary because it opens up a question for a politics of affect: how to think the intricate imbrication of the

unassimilable excess of affect and modalities of power that invest affect through an excess of techniques? (Anderson, B, 2010, p. 163)

In many ways, film-composition wants to create a space for affective excess as a politics of affect, a politics of affect that werqs on a timeline rendered possible via the affordances of digital media, attunement to affective intensity, rhetorical knowledge and skill, and a Composition gracious enough to recognize the value of all of its embodied agents and the bodies of relations they inhabit, the assemblages they generate, and the communities they seek to move into and out of formation, always toward better versions of being with and being for. I am not alone in working with a sense of the value of the excess. I am certain of my own affective intensities and of their situatedness within an image-dense screen culture. Thus, I return to my compositional encounters with the notion of image pleasure as a way of advancing and promoting a vital motivational desire.

Desiring → Happiness

Toward this pleasant potential, Thomas Rickert kairotically offered his 2007 *Acts of Enjoyment*. Any discussion of this work seems to belong in the Pleasure chapter, but desire and pleasure are intimate, and we are approaching pleasure via desire that must be seen as its generous partner. Working to sustain both, Rickert worries aspects of a generalized suspicion regarding affective intensity and intellectual pleasure. Rickert rejects this resistance to a view of pleasurable affects as somehow acritical, explaining more broadly that "the negativity inherent in establishing critique as the ultimate sign of a student-citizen-rhetor remains problematic, if not actively detrimental" (2007, p. 202). Rickert encourages us to wonder why we might "give way" to our desire, rejecting a historical suspicion of pleasure (in the name of the postmodern subject and "The Turns"). He lights up a zone of optimism by thinking beyond this history to see that we may "navigate by a few rather nebulous although quite useful coordinates" as a way of introducing Žižek, on pleasure. Žižek is helpful in articulating the powerful nature of filmmaking as critical rhetorical work because of his emphasis on the "backwards glance" that fantasy demands. As Rickert explains

> Žižek argues that while we may never attain "it," the sublime object granting us full satisfaction (primordial jouissance), we are nevertheless structured via the "backwards glance" of fantasy that suggests it is still attainable. (2007, p. 203)

This retroactive, reflective fantasy glance seems to comport nicely with a view of the sorts of work filmmaking affords us. For documentary filmmaking, the point seems obvious; we have tons of footage, and in the reviewing, sorting, and editing process, we discover "it," the pleasures of critical making, critical and creative—rhetorical—vision. But even in the case of fictional narrative filmmaking, we are bound by time; we recognize that shooting on a set generates a range of powerful affects that may or may not be associated with what is revealed through editing. The range of sights, sounds, decisions, distractions, hungers, desires, and pleasures we find on film sets make the acquisition of this critical vision a matter of jouissance, an embodied pleasure associated with the replay(ing). As I've been arguing, critical play is important to film-composition. And for so much pleasure, we exert a great deal of energy glancing backwards to ensure the validity of and hope for our fantasies; it's a good thing that the stuff of our community ties exists in this scholarly activity. We want this. Our desire sustains, all the more so if it's enacted in the context of filmmaking and digital scholarship and pedagogy, where we find clusters of promises rangy enough to move us beyond the normative script and toward new forms of collective rhetorical action.

Happy Things

Sometimes, we see our way to a promise because of a thing. We develop desires and attachments, and we have often, in the academy, explored these attachments in terms of their deleterious affects. However, affect theorist Sara Ahmed articulates what I see as a zone of optimism by getting us to consider "Happy Objects" in her 2010 article of the same name. I see her argument as sharing vibratory space with many others in this book, works all attuned to one another via shared investments in rhetoricity (thus, all implicated as forms of rhetorical work that is dynamically and affectively about *being with* and *being for*). Through Ahmed, we might consider the "happy" nature of immersive experiences in filmmaking. Again, this might seem to belong to the Pleasure chapter, but Ahmed moves me to validate my desire in ways that keep her here, in Desire, moving toward happiness, flailing longingly toward pleasure.

Moving beyond any attempt to define affect as a particular thing that is or is not, may or may not compel us toward greater critical acuity, Ahmed instead sees affect as a valuable way to frame "the messiness of the experiential, the unfolding of bodies into worlds, and the drama of contingency, how we are touched by what we are near" (2010, p. 30). Ahmed's project is to identify and work toward happiness as a way of theorizing and working through contingency. She notes that happiness is historically defined in relation to a contingency that has far less to do with modern "faking 'til making." Ahmed works through the latter with Mihály Csikszentmihályi, who exemplifies this contemporary and widespread belief by proclaiming that

> happiness is not something that happens. It is not the result of good fortune or random choice; it is not something that money can buy or power command. It does not depend on outside events, but, rather, on how we interpret them. Happiness, in fact is a condition that must be prepared for, cultivated and defended privately by each person. (as quoted in Ahmed, 2010, pp. 30–31)

Like the kinds of hopeful self-help discourses widely ciruclating via authors like Deepka Chopra, Charlotte Kasl, and Anthony Robbins, Csikzsentmihalyi here suggests a preference for the agential. Happiness is not something you are but something you decide that you are. For Ahmed, however, this version of happiness "could be read as a defense against its contingency," which seems sensible in the context of thinking about creative making. I read Ahmed as articulating a valuing of rhetoricity and all that it entails—being, circumstance, desire, will, and happenings. That is, I see happiness via Ahmed as a happening, as a form of being. We render it happy, linguistically, as a "backwards glance," perhaps, but Ahmed insists that whatever the case, "[h]appiness remains about the contingency of what happens." She explains,

> It is useful to note that the etymology of "happiness" relates precisely to the question of contingency: it is from the Middle English "hap," suggesting chance. The original meaning of happiness preserves the potential of this "hap" to be good or bad. The hap of happiness then gets translated into something good. Happiness relates to the idea of being lucky, or favored by fortune, or being fortunate. (2010, p. 30).

Ahmed's valuing of happiness as relative to contingency forges a zone of optimism whereby we might see improvisation and/as invention as sources of compositional pleasure that we experience as filmmakers. It's not so much in what I force myself to think about what I have made, though Ahmed says that "to be affected by a thing is to evaluate that thing. Evaluations are expressed in how bodies turn toward things" (2010, p. 31). Okay, so while I may not be able to escape the evaluative gestures, it's about the being. I want to assert that happiness, pleasure in filmmaking is about how I/we experience the making—I want to assert the vital nature of this desire to see the event in the happening, and in this desire we may be both moved toward situations of enhanced pleasure *and perhaps we make better things.* As an emergent area within Composition already invested in a variety of compositional possibilities and increasingly interested in new materialities, I read with longing Ahmed's notion that "[h]appiness . . . puts us into intimate contact with things" (2010, p. 31). Here, I see a flickering desire for film-composition to evolve its ecology in tangible, material ways, in ways that align with the critical value of maker and hackerspaces, . . . toward the long-desired affordances of crews . . . studios (!). People and places, . . . actual networks emerging from and perhaps folding into and out of the virtual. Ahmed's attunement to attachments as potentially happy even in a state of contingency (the liminal norm, the interstitial) inspires me to continue in this desire. Film-composition exists in this state of happy longing. It's all so dreamy. More particularly, I'm thinking about the cognitive value of affectively pleasurable tactile experience; filmmaking affords a great deal of this sort of experience. Feminist filmmaker and early YouTube pedagogue, Alexandra Juhasz (2016), recently commenting on the importance of feminist filmmaking and attempting to encourage those who desire it, notes, "ideas about film change when your hand hits a camera and vice versa" (2016).

When Your Hand Hits a Camera

Back to One. To aesthetics. I return to Massumi. A brief scan of digital scholarship drawing upon Massumi's work, and in particular his attribution of "the primacy of the affective in image reception" (2002, p. 24) reveals that a great deal of digital and multimodal scholarship and pedagogy is inspired by this claim regarding both the attraction of images and how they render affective intensities in viewers and producers. The line of reasoning goes like this: If our audiences enjoy what they are seeing, if they are affectively moved, they are likely to want to engage in more intensely critical acts of speculation and production. This is the contemporary version of "write about what you know," but with the added BONUS TOY tag line, "write about what you like." I am not here to deride this strategy, and I hope I have sufficiently complexified the seemingly easy perfection of affect as relevant almost exclusively to subjective experience. That is, I hope that my work through Clough's "biomediated body," Davis' "rhetoricity," and other works attentive to seeing affect beyond individual subjective experience has been helpful in getting us to a notion of pleasure that is shared, immersive, encompassing, and constitutive of being for and being with. These works have helped situate my own desire to invest almost completely in a hedonistic experience of rhetoricity as a digital filmmaker, and this has meant that I have (I hope) become a better rhetor (analytics reveal that my digital scholarship is viewed by thousands more than those viewing my print scholarship). "Hedonisitc" is fun, but of course what I am hoping to attend to is *intensity*. I want to think about the ambient meanings circulating with Massumi's claim for affective intensity in image work, the notion that there exists some ephemeral, extra-rhetorical dimension of something like pre-cognitive experience, that it happens in and through the body, and that this affective intensity creates a space for potential inquiry and rhetorical power. I'm pretty much all about this, and I say it in full recognition of the kooky sound of it. In addition to the works that have hoped to clarify hedonism toward a more critical "appropriate" (scare quotes intentional) notion of pleasure, I will think with David Lynch, here, and simply reproduce his response to inquiries regarding the enigmatic boxed blue key featured in his film, *Mulholland Drive*. The key, so elusively meaning-full in the narrative, never quite materializes a clear attachment, and we are left to wonder. One might imagine that Lynch crafted with a central signifying impulse regarding the blue key. In his book *Catching the Big Fish: Meditation, Consciousness, and Creativity*, he says in a one-sentence chapter, entitled, "The Box and the Key," "I don't have a clue what those are" (2007, p. 115). Keenly true in unfamiliar rhetorical scenes is the shamanistic advice of the sort Lynch offers. We might learn a great deal about our rhetorical desires and our abilities to render them by avoiding efforts toward clarity of intention and control.

Vortexing with and against control is desire. Film-composition invests in broad rhetorical knowledge and skill while vibing insistently with what Kevin DeLuca and Joe Wilferth identify as the rhetorical nature of the "image-event." The image-event captures a sense of the dynamic nature of image work and film-composition. It encourages a vital capacity and a sensitivity to trust in the kinds of affect-laden rhetorical dispositions that compel—beyond convention and easy rationality—engaging forms of compositional activity. Film-composition supports and promotes desires to make films as even as it avoids a "will to tame images," a practice that "rarely captures rhetorical force" (Deluca & Wilferth, 2009, para 11).

In my auteurist efforts to capture rhetorical force, I have often turned to Massumi (2002) for his claims regarding "the primacy of the affective in image reception." However, aware of disputes regarding what many read as his intimation of a free-flowing affect that is somewhat outside signification, outside rhetoric, I have struggled because of the seductive notion of agency inherent in the concept of the unassimilable, the ephemeral corporeal infoldings of experience. I want to believe. Writing the book, I need to open it up. Open what up? The missing ½ second. It's been inspiring. It's been controversial. It's been used to discredit affect theory/studies as frivolous. So you know it, but to review, In "The Autonomy of Affect," Massumi cites a research project in which 9 year old children were shown three versions of a scene featuring a melting snowman—one without words, one with factual narration, and one with narration that articulated the plausible emotional tenor of the moment as the scene unfolded. The children were instructed to rate the films on a "happy–sad" and a "pleasant–unpleasant" scale. The children preferred the "sad" version; Massumi explains, "the sadder, the better" (2002, p. 24). In addition to the ratings, the children were also physiologically wired to monitor autonomic reactions at the level of heartrate, breathing, and, importantly, galvanic response monitors captured the rate of reaction at the level of the skin (2002, p. 24). It was the original, nonverbal snowman film that generated the strongest reaction from the children's skin. The researchers were confused by the children's "sad" rating as being most "pleasant," but Massumi saw in this that affectively intense image reception could be so intense as to be "overfull" to the point of evading clear articulation or "taming." The wordless version invited suspenseful anticipation that worked in opposition the factual version, because as Massumi explains, "The factual version of the snowman story was dampening. Matter-of-factness dampens intensity. . . . This interfered with the images' effect. The emotional version" caught up rather than interfered with the resonating level of intensity experienced by the viewers. Massumi summarizes: "An emotional qualification breaks narrative continuity for a moment to register a state—actually to re-register an already felt state, for the skin is faster than the word" (2002, p. 25). He goes on to cite another experiment involving skin and brain responses. Patients wearing corticol electrodes received pulses to the electrodes and also to the skin. As Massumi explains, "If the corticol electrode was fired a half second before the skin was stimulated, patients reported feeling the skin pulse first." Analyzing the researcher's findings, Massumi explains that

> Brain and skin form a resonating vessel. Stimulation turns inward, is folded into the body, except that there is no inside for it to be in, because the body is radically open, absorbing impulses quicker than they can be perceived, because the entire vibratory event is unconscious, out of mind. Its anomaly is smoothed over retrospectively to fit conscious requirements of continuity and linear causality. (2002, p. 20)

Massumi's claim of the missing half second as meaning-making activity beyond rhetoric, has been problematic. Yet, he does offer the productive theory of the ½ second not as empty, which being outside of rhetoric can only mean to language scholars, but "overfull," which works quite well for affect theorists. "Overfull" here means the ½ second of autonomic intense skin response is "in excess" . . . it is intense, whereas "will and consciousness are subtractive. They are limitative, derived functions that reduce a complexity too rich to be functionally expressed" (Massumi, 2002, p. 29).

Rhetoric scholars with whom I have explored the giddy potential of a ½ second of intensely felt, language free experience have proved skeptical. And they are not alone. Like a rhetorician's claim that nothing exists outside of rhetoric, Mark B. Hansen (2015) inquires of the missing ½ second by referencing a variety of media theorists devoted to network theories that grant agency only to the environmental, suggesting a nearly non-human theory of agency. But for Hansen's phenomenological approach, (studies on consciousness and the objects of experience), a

> radically environmental and ontologically neutral account of experience can enhance human experience precisely by throwing into question many of our received notions about the human—including the privilege of (agential) perception over (environmental) sensibility. (2015, p. 15)

So the very conflict over experience outside of rhetoric is at least worth pursuing and decidedly valuable for complicating notions of agency, meaning, and potential (all things that digital teachers and scholars worry toward the goal of creating intensely moving—thus engaging—pedagogies). For Hansen, to ask "what is at issue when an event is thought" is not to dismiss of the human as a kind of "theoretical revolution" but it is instead to study "a shift of emphasis" (2015, p. 29). Just as historical research predicts and reveals. Many early film-compositionists worked in the "language is subtractive" mode—toward the capturation, toward the simple will and ability to bring films into comp classrooms for exploration—through analysis, which often rendered through familiar literary terms and morality lessons. However, today's film-compositionists are confident about the project of revitalizing film in Composition through processes of immersion and nonlinear experimentation.

Aligned with the desires of contemporary film-composition, I am shooting for rhetorical force. *Cruel Auteurism* wants to materialize as a nonlinear cinematic timeline. Motivated by hope, tinged with fear, and shot through with desire, like so many early and contemporary film-compositionists, this may mean "less-than-ordinarily scripted." The timeline wants to move us, to evade a taming. Massumi: "Will and consciousness [aka language] is subtractive" (2002, p. 10). Hansen: We can't perceive free flowing affective intensity but from within technological apparatus designed to perceive it (2015, p. 232). I can't resolve the philosophical conflict over the missing ½ second between "effect and content," but I'm certain of the intensity. And because, as Hansen argues, I am only able to perceive that gap from within the technological machine, I've created a version of the infamous melting snowman film Massumi cited to support the popular claim attributed to him, "The primacy of the affective in image reception" (2002, p. 24). Those critical of the idea of affect as a rigorous frame for rhetorical agency and innovative ways of being and composing have had me doubting. Yet, from within these frames . . . I am vaguely at home . . . [watch the film[48] that screened with this presentation, a film[49] that was later screened at CCCC 2016]. My experiences in the classroom reveal that students enjoy this space of ambiguous compositional pleasure, as well.

Where I am not quite so comfy is in the conversation about desires for correctness and ethical clarity when it comes to open access images, video, and audio, and their uses in digital scholarship and pedagogical stagings. Here, too, Berlant's (2011) cruel optimism is operational. So too are zones of optimism. I have been the grateful recipient of a good deal of feedback during conference presentations on the matter of DIY digital filmmaking. Prior to any discussion of the content of any of my films, I am routinely asked about Fair Use, first, and "How can I do that?," second. Both questions may be read through the lens of cruel auteurism, and both shimmer brightly within critical, intellectual, and pedagogical zones of optimism.

At the 2014 Conference on College Composition and Communication, I gave a talk on Fair Use as a "bad object" that enables what I called "Open Aesthetics." "Open Aesthetics" sounds good, right? So why refer to its central support system as "bad"? Because some works emerging from liberal Fair Use(s) operate as disruptive, creative, rhetorical works that may or may not register with academic audiences in ways that render conventionally "good life" outcomes (tenure, promotion, etc.). Yet, I continue to rely fairly radically upon Fair Use to make the arguments I want and need to make, and I encourage colleagues, students, and friends to do the same. I believe that many of you are with me. But there is that pesky sense that maybe the constraints aren't clear (enough) and that perhaps we are (I am) "getting away with" something, some form of creativity that I'm compelled to pursue by a desire that seems to promise some other forms of "good life" that may be within my reach. This desire to constrain our work has in many ways created career-length projects, and so it is at work in the construction of some "good lives." I didn't want to go there. I have always wanted to make beautifully thoughtful films that emerge from my lived experience as a creative, observant, immersed, and critical rhetorician freely moving within two ecologies, academia, and film. Consonant with the notion of Edbauer's "mattering texts," I have tried to go there, to make these happen. In doing so, I rely upon reports from sources like the Center for Social Media, reports indicating that not only is Fair Use fair

48 Visit https://vimeo.com/285368334. Password = snowpeople
49 Visit https://vimeo.com/208253147. Password = onemoretime

and flexible but that we aren't pushing with nearly enough passion and force. We must move more boldly in the direction of our rhetorico-aesthetic moods, confident in our ability to articulate the nature of our "rewards" and the status of our work as "transformative." Yet, up against the forces of fear (regarding copyright and correctness), and power (market, industry, and disciplinary voices of "what's right"), our liberally fair uses may function as vibratorily promising forms of Berlant's "cruel optimism," which, as you'll recall, exist "when something you desire is actually an obstacle to your flourishing" (2011, p. 1). My sense of this potential meaning for Fair Use comes from my emic's perspective of academic rewards. In other words, if the work that gains "conventional" rewards (publication, jobs, grants, tenure, promotion) is the work that matters, and if that work is disproportionately about convention, correctness and surveillance, over and above disruptive critical attunements derived from creative indwelling, can we say that our optimistic attachments deny us fuller and more gratifying forms of transformative success? Yes, (a beat) and also, no. Berlant explains

> the magnetic attraction to cruel optimism [by noting that] Any object of optimism promises to guarantee the endurance of something, the survival of something, the flourishing of something, and above all, the protection of the desire that made this object or scene powerful enough to have magnetized an attachment to it. (2011, p. 48)

Here, I can't help thinking of the something we both seek and passionately want to protect as the good life of the conventional tenured academic, for whom a sense of certainty about the foundations of her academic identity is precious, its survival to be ensured. "The good life" means support, academic freedom, . . . it advances critical play, and in many ways it creates sites of inquiry and critique that afford us opportunities to engage with cultural texts in ways that may sustain these very freedoms. However, our ideas about Fair Use are bound up within theories on composing in ways that create confusion about just what we are constraining with our pedagogical inclination to "teach against plagiarism" or otherwise limit our own creative potential by imagining that we dare not use certain media files (or portions thereof)— these moves function as sustaining rhetorics of another kind of "good life," the life of the ethical rhetor who plays fair and by the rules. But these rules exist in many ways to create a kind of threshold ["aka learning"] experience. Shouldn't they be flexible? Speaking for myself, I have been frustrated in my digital filmmaking career by discourses of fear regarding Fair Use. But I use it, push it radically and informed in many ways by my lived experiences in the Sundance Film Festival community, where it's understood that certain rights are acquired in-process, as a filmmaker workshops a scene or the use of a certain audio track, video clip, or still. Unless there is much at stake in the way of financial gain, there is a great deal of freedom in the context of festival screenings, which I liken to sites like the classroom, and the university conference, where we work it out—the creative, critical, rhetorical affordances of the use our primary concern. In fact, I have become so enamored of these threshold experiences, of live performance, live screenings, sharing and receiving feedback on my creative and critical works that my book project on the matter has languished in the dressing room while my film productions shimmer in the making and the afterglow.

I am theorizing Fair Use in the context of multimodal text production in the modern but still fairly constrained university as a "bad object" sufficient to generate cruel optimism. But it's more . . . and it's the overspill here that's interesting. It's about the visceral experiences of digital filmmaking—especially when the work can play freely with a wide variety of licensed cultural texts that have both shaped the desire to use them *and* perhaps brought to consciousness the very critiques a rhetor's creative work hopes to project. Berlant's potentially soul-crushing theory offers room for optimism. On the "bad object" and the attachment to it, Berlant says

> the hope is that what misses the mark and disappoints won't
> much threaten anything in the ongoing reproduction of life,
> but will allow zones of optimism a kind of compromised
> endurance . . . that will allow the flirtation with some good-
> life sweetness to continue. (2011, p. 48)

Many of my colleagues are devoted to this sort of flirtation, especially as digital media enable us to enact our creative and transformative rhetorical work and to share it in a thrilling array of performance spaces. We are thus more able than ever "to pay attention to the built and affective infrastructure of the ordinary" (Berlant, 2011, p. 49) that shapes our ambient rhetorics in the Fair present.

In another way of thinking about this hopeful flirtation, I'm thinking about DIY digital filmmaking and the conflict of the auteur vs. the constructivist perspective and citation networking that makes our creative and rhetorical works matter (via publication and circulation). Does creative work that surrounds itself more with the cultural texts that generate affective intensities for the "auteur" and less with a series of citations limit itself in ways that invite a kind of contemporary "failure"? Does the production of filmic texts for rhetorical purposes and the affective intensities of composing and screening stand in the way of more static and conventional forms of academic success? If we continue to worry The Academic Essay or The Book as the compositional object that moves us into scenes of successful living, maybe. However, if we are talking about digital filmmaking that inquires into what Malcolm McCullough (2013) worries as the age of embodied information, maybe not so much. Many of the short films-as-scholarship I enjoy—Arroyo, Lestón, and Carter's (2011) "Chora of the Twin Towers," and Arroyo and Alaei's (2013) intensely moving remix work, starting with "The Dancing Floor" and including everything they make together, and Lestón's (2013) delightful, contemplative object-oriented piece "Table Without Organs," and even my own *screencube* (2013). For McCullough (2013), these sorts of works compel "inquiry into attention and an environmental history of information" that is "interest[ed] in apertures" and constructed spaces—rhetorics of The Screen over The Frame, because screens ". . . in the form of shutters or blinds can be quietly gratifying to configure on demand" (p. 154). Many of the creative and critical rhetorical films we're producing enact intense desires for interaction with networks and portals that demand critical attention. For McCullough, such "facades, [which both invite, and potentially transport] fill[s] a view, enduringly, often inescapably, in embodied space" (2013, p. 154). And any more, gallery, installation work, 3D projection, virtual and augmented realities further manifest this fullness. I'm hinting at interfaces. Borrowing from Alexander Galloway (2012):

> This book ~~talk~~ is about windows, screens, keyboards, kiosks, channels, sockets, and holes—or rather, about none of these things in particular and all of them simultaneously. For this is a book talk about thresholds, those mysterious zones of interaction that mediate between different realities.[50] (p. vii)

I've been living a threshold experience, seeing that film work wants more from me than this book. Film work wants more from us than the production of academic essays, and books-toward-success, and even webtexts. So despite feeling grateful for the ability to enact my vision in two distinct ecologies, I worry the cruel optimism of digital filmmaking as scholarship. However, I embrace the "good life sweetness" of what I'm calling "cruel auteurism."

In her own attempt to compress the heliotropic[51] dynamics of "cruel optimism," Berlant explains that this state of affairs is responsive and generative, that it is

---

50   For the purpose and mode of the presentation, this passage was delivered as follows: "This ~~book~~ talk is about windows, screens, keyboards, kiosks, channels, sockets, and holes—or rather, about none of these things in particular and all of them simultaneously. For this is a book talk about thresholds, those mysterious zones of interaction that mediate between different realities" (p. vii).

51   For more on heliotropic rhetorics, see Mucklebuer, John.

> about living within crisis, and about the destruction of
> our collective genres of what a "life" is; it is about dramas
> of adjustment to the pressures that wear people out in the
> everyday and the longue durée; it is about the blow of discov-
> ering that the world can no longer sustain one's organizing
> fantasies of the good life. (Published Interview, 2012)

In my own attempt to describe my life's work of the past 11 years, here I am,
currently in the process of working toward completion of my first single-
authored manuscript. Lamentable? Sure—I got my doctorate *way back in* 1998.
Life choices, challenges . . . obstacles amounted to a timeline of six full years
for publishing even one article based upon my dissertation, by which time, I
was done with its subject, (chaos theory) though chaos continues to provide
an appropriate metaphor for my life as a scholar, writer, teacher, composer,
and filmmaker. In my book, which my editor recently suggested I re-title "A
Beautiful Vision" <blush> but which I continue to refer to as, *Cruel Auteurism*
[a bunch stuff post-colon], I argue that writing, composing, filmmaking—it's
all rhetorical work that self-organizes as an affectively intense performative
venue for enhancing and reanimating our given rhetorical knowledge and
skill and moving us toward ever more dynamic relations with that range of
desirable work, with this desiring state of being, a state marked by identifications across a range of "fantasies of the good life" such that any talk of
"organizing" seems futile in light of self-organization's inarticulable vortices
of attempting, performing, revising, reflecting, bitching, hating, fearing, rev-
eling, embracing, fucking it all and generally giving in to the dynamics of
contemporary life. Berlant sees the value of this state of being, explaining that

> In all of these scenes of "the good life," the object that you
> thought would bring happiness becomes an object that dete-
> riorates the conditions for happiness. But its presence rep-
> resents the possibility of happiness as such. And so losing the
> bad object might be deemed worse than being destroyed by
> it. That's a relation of cruel optimism. (Published Interview,
> 2012)

So inasmuch as Fair Use, or DIY filmmaking may be the bad objects to
which I've attached myself, what seems optimistically available for additional
critique is the conventional path in academic life as yet another form of cruel
optimism. I'm thinking about the path to tenure at a research-oriented institution, where you are recognized as "worthy," intellectually, productive, clever.
Your workload is manageable, enviable, even. This scripted good life fantasy
obtains within the academy and without, truth notwithstanding. In the 2015

Sundance Film Festival Grand Jury Prize and Audience Award winning film, *Me and Earl and the Dying Girl*, actor/comedian Nick Offerman plays the father of the film's protagonist. He wears a kimono and is mostly featured at home, eating various boutique items such as pig's feet and fried cuttlefish, and it's established that this grand eccentricity may be attributed to his "good life" as a tenured professor (of Sociology). However, fiction rarely radiates the fuller complexity. And most of us know that tenure rarely means kimonos and unproblematic indulgence in foodporn. It seems to me that many of us who do favor working in jammies are doing so out of need and desire, flirting with new forms of the good-life in our present state of crisis over just what the good life "bracket" [may] mean, not because we are so lovingly supported and nurtured by our institutions.

I'm hitting play on a short film I made (in jammies), inspired by the Chicago based performance collective, "Manual Cinema." [If you have the desire, please prepare to hit "play" to accompany your reading. Play at "public presentation" speed. Start the film just as you finish reading this paragraph]. Their performance of *Mementos Mori* live-produced a 90-minute film noir experience, all enacted through shadow puppetry and the brilliant use of overheads, live actors and their silhouettes projected onto side screens that were then captured and projected onto a center screen. [hit play[52]].

I recall learning about the cuttlefish. Discovery Channel. I thought I'd been THE ONLY PERSON WATCHING, the identification so strong that I myself had discovered the cuttlefish's remarkable adaptation techniques, its trippy visuals, and how it could live successfully in a variety of scenes, so long as it psychotriggered its visual display systems to physiologically alter its appearance. I saw the special while I was in the process of generating my (2009) short film, *i'm like . . . professional*. With that film, I literally "followed in the wake of" DIY filmmakers M dot Strange, Andy Blubaugh, and Jonathan Cauoette, and its premiere screening was all vibratory pleasure. But prior to audience response are the rhetorical entanglements. Against identifiable notions of constructivism, obviously linking my work to the works of others in my field (publishing others, powerful others), I work(ed) alone. I used M's YouTube videos and audio tracks from published and at least one unpublished track by Beck, a file gifted to me by a former student who had been friends with the artist. Here, now, you hear a track from the brilliant Brian Eno. It is used in *Me and Earl and the Dying Girl* as the score to a film the lead character has made. An emotive, lovingly quirky avant-garde film he'd made for his girl. We finally get to see the film when he shows it to her in the hospital as they lie together in her standard unit hospital bed. It's all very

---

52   Visit https://vimeo.com/285638299. Password = shadows

constrained and institutionally valid, she is medicated and calm, he is there during visiting hours.

I was a DIY filmmaker as scholars were beginning to say "multimodality." Making films overshadowed The Book. Berlant:

> This is not a time for assurance but for experiment—to have patience with failure, with trying things out, to try new forms of life that also might not work—which doesn't make them worse than what's there now. It is a time for using the impasse that we're in to learn something about how to imagine better economies of intimacy and labor. (Published Interview, 2012)

In light of academic economies that want ever more in exchange for "the good life," Berlant imagines various "good lifes," as cruel optimism "tracks the rise of a precarious public sphere":

> the world as in an impasse and . . . situation[s] beyond the normative good life structures, where people have a hard time imagining a genre that makes sense of life while they're in the middle of it. I'm saying that intense personal emotions about the shape and fraying of life are also collective, and have to do with an economic crisis meeting up with a crisis in the reproduction of fantasy. (Published Interview, 2012)

I wonder about fantasies—the conventional good life associated with traditional publications and academic labor. I worry that my own desires to work within vital emerging hybrid ecologies may represent a cruelly optimistic version of the good life that will leave me fewer and fewer options for engaging what I have come to embrace as creative and critical practice. More than ALL THAT WORRY, I want to be optimistic from within these benevolent, productive, and sometimes lonely fantasies. It's only fear fair.

Chapter 5: Pleasure

A man [sic] is as much affected pleasurably or painfully by the image of a thing past or future as by the image of a thing present. . . . (Baruch Benedict de Spinoza, *Ethics III*)

The mind, as far as possible, endeavours to conceive those things which increase or help the body's power of activity (III. xii.); in other words (III. xii. note), those things which it loves. But conception is helped by those things which postulate the existence of a thing, and contrariwise is hindered by those which exclude the existence of a thing (II. xvii.); therefore the images of things, which postulate the existence of an object of love, help the mind's endeavour to conceive the object of love, in other words (III. xi. note), affect the mind pleasurably . . . (Baruch Benedict de Spinoza, *Ethics III*)

. . . impulses are extracted from the real modes of behavior current in a determinate milieu, from the passions, feelings, and emotions which real men [sic] experience in the milieu. And the fragments are torn from objects which have effectively been formed in the milieu. . . . Actions go beyond themselves toward primordial acts which are not their components, objects toward fragments which would not reconstitute them, people toward energies which do not "organise" them. (Gilles Deleuze, 1883, *The Movement-Image*, pp. 124–125)

Fantasy and jouissance . . . are neither arcane nor ephemeral. They are part of our everyday doings and are integral to communities and communication. (Thomas Rickert, 2007, *Acts of Enjoyment*, p. xvi)

. . . we cannot land, and we must keep moving. (Cynthia Haynes, 2003, "Writing Offshore," p. 670)

To compose a chapter on pleasure requires chocolate . . . toward energies which do not organize but most certainly sustain me. Obviously, I have some pleasurable (and, surely, painful) memories of past and projections of future chocolates. I could claim that the chocolates I ate at around 5:00 a.m. were productively amping up my compositional practice. Physiologically speaking, this is factually true. I took on an early breakfast (though I hate breakfast), and I have thus "increase[d] . . . the body's power of activity" (Spinoza, *Ethics III*). That I did so in a languid state of trance-like being might be read as slovenly or worrisome. I'm choosing "mysticism." In fact, my films often strive to exist as testaments to being, being just so in this moment, and often being "okay" with things as they are, however lovely, however troubling (though, to be honest, I am surely inclined to labor toward the lovely, perhaps a form of what Lev Manovich refers to as "Instagrammism" (2016b), showing my desire to conform with routinely hip, urbane stagings of aesthetic value). From this perspective, I have developed a pedagogical inclination to teach toward what I call "enchanting the mundane," and filmic work that is more invested in affective pleasure and contemplative *being with* rather than overt, storyboarded (up) meanings for easy viewing, analysis, and articulation as "rhetoric." You may by now sense that I have an experientially derived sense of what film-composition is, wants, and may be(come). Toward integrating film-composition within existing webs of discourse within the field, it may be most useful to begin this chapter by exploring the present vitality and "velocity" of film-composition.

The way I have seen and experienced it, film-composition has shimmered into existence via the desires and rhetorical enactments of many friends, colleagues, students, and teacher-scholars in Composition, all of whom responded to many of our discipline's most vital theories and practices, enacting them via the affordances of digital media and driven by inspiration and a compelling responsivity to rhetoricity's call. Notably, the nature of their response aligns with a vision of progressive critical work as happening in nonlinear fashion, relatively unconstrained by convention, and experimental in nature. Thus, film-composition is marked as a form of cruel auteurism as its theories and practices do not intend to serve limited compositional and pedagogical aims exclusively, but they are also quite expansively aspirational. They seek forms of pleasure associated with uniquely moving experiences of affective intensity that film-composition-ists associate with being and being with/in emergent cinematic rhetorics in contemporary screen culture, where "screen culture" refers to the ubiquity of screens for rhetorical enactments of seemingly infinite variety. Though I immediately conjure in my mental cinematic space *The Minority Report* for a cinematic definition of "screen culture," Patricia Pisters (2012) references *Michael Clayton*, ekphrastically recalling "the omnipotence of media screens" to project a sense of it:

> [t]hroughout the film, small and large screens appear everywhere: navigation displays, computer screens, cell phones, television sets, urban screens, and surveillance technology;

> they are the markers of both a typical twenty-first century
> media city and the practices of everyday media use. (p. 2)

Pisters lays out an argument for the value in studying screen culture in order to take on critical work in what she calls the "neuro-image," a project that aims to understand relationships between "schizoanalysis, digital screens, and brain circuits" (2012, p. 1). Referring to the "delirious and intelligent" Arthur Edens, a central character in *Michael Clayton*, Pisters describes the neuro-image as a depiction of contemporary immersion in screen culture. Because of emergent mental states that border on troubled, such immersion seems to demand "collective analytics" that might worry mental states as they exist and evolve within networks of power and resistance. I dare say that this is the work of rhetorical studies, and so perhaps the reassuring (I'M NOT ALONE IN THIS FEELING!) worries and pleasures of film study and production, as both enable us to discern our shared cultural dispositions to uncertainty, vertiginous experiences of daily being-projected-at, and our simultaneous desires to project our particular images, scenes, stories just so (the latter, being the project of art, resistance, and pleasure).

Film-composition is invested in rhetorical arts that enable a sense of making and being that also act as critique and invention for new forms and new stories. That is to say, our films are films, not exclusively instructional videos or process-pieces documenting a compositional strategy—though they may be in whole or in part composed with these purposes in mind. We make from within scenes of our own making, being, and becoming; aesthetics as rhetorical strategy, as compositional force, as matter(ing). Aesthetics and pleasure are powerful collaborators, and together they comprise moving arguments regarding being, self, identity, communication, culture, power, and more. The Deleuzean scholar and rhetorician Daniel W. Smith (1998) helps out on this point. Smith, in his introduction to Deleuze's *Essays Critical and Clinical* explains that we are, as academic makers, always invested in analytical work that makes sense of selves and cultures, together: "Authors and artists, like doctors and clinicians, can themselves be seen as profound symptomatologists" (1998, p. xvii). Smith recalls that, "It was Nietzsche who first put forward the idea that artists and philosophers are physiologists, 'physicians of culture' for whom phenomena are symptoms that reflect a certain state of forces" (1998, p. xvii). This brief detour wants to frame up our sense of film-composition as rhetorical and artistic practice that is capable of rendering affective truth from within screen culture, from within scenes of emergent intelligence and uncertainty. In the rendering, we share resources, hopefully toward the production of new scenes of vital life through rhetorical sensitivity and re-animated critical performances.

A Certain State of Forces

The pleasures of critical making are, in the present moment, enjoying themselves. That is to say, we are today talking more openly about pleasure and academic work and life. Some will grumbleslough this into a file along with the "neoliberal agenda" or the "commodification of higher education," and there is merit to this worry. However, a more critically rewarding view on critical and creative pleasure may derive from witnessing rhetorical change that happens in anticipation of, in-process, and as the result of our textual production. Digital media and analytics enable far more of this type of vision, and exploring the uptake of our circulating texts is engaging, instructive, and illuminating work. Take, for example, Lev Manovich's (2016) *Instagram and Contemporary Image*, which "combine[s] traditional qualitative approaches of humanities and computational analysis of 16 millions [*sic*] of Instagram photos in 17 global cities carried out in Manovich's lab (softwarestudies.com)." The determination to use big data as a way of seeing the nature of culture and its technologically mediated shifts and orientations makes the work of critical making seem rhetorically illustrative on a massive scale. But such work may also reveal the particularities of the local. Manovich explains,

> Our Instagram analysis suggests that the subjects and styles
> of photographs are strongly influenced by social, cultural,
> and aesthetic values of a given location or demographic. (2016)

Manovich's studies of large data sets seem to suggest the potential to generalize on a massive scale, but he is quick to insist that these studies also render small variations and various ways in which they create vital new forms. Many Composition scholars are using their work to similarly examine how images and other multimodal texts circulate and toward what sorts of ends. In chapter 4, I invoked "rhetorical velocity" as a way of marking variations in the speed of our contemporary compositional practices as potential signs of certain forms of affective intensity. In this chapter, I am thinking about "pleasure." Here, DeVoss and Ridolfo's highly lauded *Kairos* publication on "rhetorical velocity" raises questions about the speed with which texts may be composed, recomposed, delivered, remixed, and otherwise put into (re)circulation. Such questions are important for twenty-first century rhetoricians and echo importantly with questions about pleasure, questions attending to an alleged dearth of critical value in film-composition, especially as film-composition wants to do more than record our processes; it wants also to radiate cinematic value through its aesthetics toward affective pleasure as rhetorical practice (and yes, so much of this calls for book-length treatments in the post 2016 Election era!). For my purposes, I want to continue to work toward a "concluding" chapter with a broad agenda on pleasure. However, because of the activities of various right-wing makers in Election 2016, it seems important to consider how a pedagogy grounded in consideration of rhetorical velocity may open up more productively should it tend perhaps more powerfully to compositional pleasure as a part of its central project. The current emphasis on the somewhat less-than-ideally pleasurable project of attempting to think through to the uptake and circulation as a sort of primary compositional activity is laid out effectively and persuasively by David M. Sheridan, Jim Ridolfo, and Anthony J. Michel (2012). They explain that

> We're increasingly posting, publishing, and circulating our compositions in media conducive to composing for recomposition. While the printed word encouraged the illusion of a fixed security, the realities of digital publishing radically undermined any sense of fixity. In a digital context, compositions fluidly emerge from earlier compositions and are recomposed into subsequent compositions. (96)

Film-composition seems to approximate compositional fluidity in ways that structurally mimic the fluidity of emergent meanings. The dynamic, multisensory pleasures afforded via film-composition seem capable of amplifying a rhetor's awareness of this fluidity in ways that may render a pedagogy framed by teachings on rhetorical velocity increasingly effective. A pedagogy emphasizing pleasure may also provide access to critical literacy knowledge regarding how and why we have witnessed the emergence of rhetorical artifacts like "Pepe" (the racist frog image associated with the alt-right during Election 2016). As Sheridan, Ridolfo, and Michel argue, rhetors increasingly confront the affordances of digital texts" in ways that help them shape "a pedagogical framework for addressing issues pertaining to rhetorical velocity," they confront "the challenges associated with the way compositions travel when they are finished" (2012, pp. 96–97). Sure. Yes, we need this. Film composition wants to offer a suggestion and a structural framework that is both dynamically capable of enacting this pedagogy and affectively up to the task. That is, instead of devoting such focused energy on contemplating uptake and circulation (important stuff to be very sure), an emphasis on compositional pleasures affords contemplative space for, a.) invention pleasure, and b.) sensitivity to how Pepe and why Pepe, and maybe even c.) responsive strategies for hearing, comprehending, and countering Pepe.[53] In other words, I may still *feel* it's okay to punch a Nazi, but then, maybe I don't *think* or *believe* it's an effective rhetorical strategy for enacting the kinds of changes we

53 See Samantha Bee's *Full Frontal* talk with the founder of the anti-hate group outreach organization, Life After Hate, Christian Piccolini.

need. Perhaps if we could comprehend the giddy fervor of alt-right meme and remix artists, we might begin to imagine ways of ethically, responsibly, and responsively teaching digital rhetoric and writing via film-composition. I will continue to work toward advancing film-composition as a pedagogical and scholarly activity that aims first at compositional pleasure even as it worries, hopes, and delights in imagining audience reception, remixability, uptake and circulation, and suasive academic and cultural power.

Earlier scholars in digital rhetoric and writing have worked to create value for and of pleasurable compositional potential, and I dare say many film-compositionists have taken inspiration from their projects. Speaking to the matter of extra-conventional meanings and affective registers of the sort I am hoping to describe, Cheryl E. Ball (2011) has addressed the question through a well-reasoned and critical assertion regarding the value of pleasure in our scholarship. Echoing Massumi's (2002) concern for the "subtractive" nature of language that is flatly assertive rather than vibrating with pleasure as it articulates a kind of felt affect that may not enter easily into reasonable assertion, Ball insists that "If we rely on rigor as our scholarly touchstone, we miss the value that supposedly nonrigorous (e.g., nondiscursive, affective, imagistic) meaning-making strategies can have in our scholarship" (p. 76). This chapter hopes to advance that insistence on Ball's rigorous "nonrigorous," Massumi's "unassimilable," and Murray's "non-discursive" into the realm of the obvious by illuminating our increasing sensitivity to the rhetorical and pedagogical necessity of affective intensity in our scholarly and pedagogical projects. Screened through affect theories that explore pedagogy and the pleasures of affectively intense striving toward certain accumulative joys, the resonant notions of rhetorical velocity, and the problematized version of rigor which holds affective intensity as pedagogically important, we begin to see ever more clearly the kairotic, rhetorical propriety of film-composition and its pedagogical promises.

What I'm channeling is an effort to curate a sense of the value of pleasure as rhetorical work. Here, I am referring to pleasure in ways that exceed conventional academic notions of pleasure that are often associated with discerning a cultural trend, worrisome practice, or other critique-worthy thing. These things bring pleasure, "the pleasures of the mind," as it were. They are pleasurable insofar as they extend our being, our abilities to exist purposefully, notions on the essence of being articulated by Spinoza in his *Ethics* and troubled by various theoretical schemas both before and ever since. Thriving requires more than conventional critique and intellectual pleasures that are ordinarily scripted. For Spinoza, thriving requires both an effort along with cognition, along with awareness of the effort to thrive (*Ethics, Part III*). These attempts to thrive, this striving is embodied—happening intellectually and simultaneously in and through the body in ways that help us recognize pleasure and aesthetics as essentially interrelated. Compositionists have long theorized the value of affect, and indeed embodiment discourses run through most contemporary digital scholarship.[54] This notion may be important for film-compositionists working to generate films as scholarship and craft filmic projects for and with their students. In many ways, it's a simple re-minder. Our bodies matter. The affects matter. Intuition matters. As affective enactments of some ghostly knowledge, as intuition that flickers into view, intuitive compositional knowledge materializes as a hovering, the illumination happening through an ethereal scrim just beyond easy articulation. Intuitive affects are acquired through rhetoricity, immersion in literate cultures, their vibratory whisperings hinting toward critical consciousness. Hunches matter. They move us with and against aesthetic pleasures toward effective articulation.

Recuperative Affect

Megan Watkins (2010) affirms my clunky poetry with her "Desiring Recognition, Accumulation Affect." She works beyond a mis-characterization of affect based in its perception as "a preliminial, preconscious, phenomenon" (2010, p. 269). Arguing that the view of affect as "autonomous and ephemeral" has shadowed reception of affect theory as attentive to individual experience in ways that elide the social, Watkins draws upon Spinozan distinctions that help recover for us the value of affect for pedagogy. For my purposes, here, Watkins' recuperative work gets at affirming my bold claim regarding how affectively felt intuition (like Perl's "felt sense") rises up through the residue of what is perhaps unwittingly, immersively-received rhetorical knowledge. She outlines Spinoza's terms and how they make way for a sense of "residue," a space I am imagining in terms of accumulated rhetorical knowledge that we perhaps access through affective intensities guiding our compositional choices. *Vibrational pedagogy and scholarship. Ambient?* Watkins troubles the worrisome consequence of seeing affect exclusively in terms of the individual for

> the ways in which affect can arouse individuals or groups in some way but then seem to dissipate quickly leaving little effect. While this distinction is a productive one for dealing with particular types of affective experience, it doesn't account for the distinction Spinoza makes between affectus and affectio, the force of an affecting body and the impact it leaves on the one affected. Affectio may be fleeting but it

---

54   See Arola and Wysocki (2012) for their provocative collection, *Composing (Media) = Composing (Embodiment): Bodies, Technologies, Writing, The Teaching of Writing).*

> may also leave a residue, a lasting impression that produced particular kinds of bodily capacities. (2010, p. 269)

Watkins explains her interest in what is left as "residue" because of "this capacity of affect to be retained, to accumulate, to form dispositions" (p. 269). In many ways, Massumi's "½ second," Murray's "non-discursive rhetoric," Ball's "supposedly nonrigorous" rhetoric, Rickert's "ambient rhetoric," Davis' "rhetoricity" and Berlant's "zones of optimism" all get after a sense of potential, possibility, compositional hope, fear, desire, and pleasure, and I see each of these notions sharing in spaces of epistemic rhetorical potential sufficient to suggest lasting affects/effects or "residue" in the form of situated, experientially acquired rhetorical knowledge. What I am hoping to argue in this last chapter is that composing and revising in ways that give us access to that affectively ephemeral knowledge can be massively rewarding and extraordinarily pleasurable, and at the same time, this pleasurable compositional activity re-sensitizes us to many types of rhetorical knowledge and gives passage to new forms of creative and critical potential.

A Different Place to Begin

To attempt further comment on film-composition amped up on aesthetic pleasure, I want to think beyond the easy turn to the drives, and at the same time tend to the body. Such a move may happen more productively in an interdisciplinary mode, at a convergence that allows for such seeming contradiction. Here, I turn to Art History, where, as with the uncertainties that attend new disciplinary trends, theories, and practices, we find a great deal of academic investment in troubling "meaning." Art historian Susan Best writes of an emergent investment in a rhetorically capacious sensibility in "Visual Pleasure: Aesthetics and Affect." Best gets after the sort of pleasure I have always associated with film spectation, production, and rhetorical value—the delightfully felt sense of heavy import or airy joy. I purposefully invoke embodied metaphors that intentionally fluctuate just beyond sexual innuendo as a way of elaborating film-composition's pleasures in ways that are disinclined to silliness (though silly is pleasurable, as well—see memes, see animal videos, *etc.*). Best re-imagines visual pleasure and art appreciation beyond the realm of the libidinal drives that have often come to define the "meanings" of art works via critical analysis. Drawing upon American psychologist and affect theorist Silvan Tompkins' theories of affect, Best resituates pleasure so that it is not necessarily articulating a kind of sublimated libidinal desire but may instead resonate affectively, differently, in ways that open us to new meanings, new forms of pleasure and attachment/detachment. I needed to spend time with Tomkins, so I turned to affect theorists who had gone there before. For the purposes of articulating pleasure through affect theory and consistent with my desire to explore the pleasures of new forms of enacting rhetorical desires, I found Tomkins' value for non-normative theoretical dispositions that move us beyond convention. Eve Kosofsky Sedgwick and Adam Frank (1995) looked to Tomkins for non-normative readings of affect that might avoid, in particular "heterosexist teleology" (p. 7), and in their work they claim to have found in Tompkins a theorist who had found "a different place to begin" (p. 7). Different, that is, from sexual and other drives (but mostly sexual). Sedgwick and Frank seem to find this fresh origin story gratifying and also somewhat "terrifying" (1995, p. 3), despite its resistance to heterosexist frames dominating the sciences and seeking to understand human motivation. They see a refreshing way of theorizing affect through Tomkins, one that many working in film-composition will likely appreciate for its emphasis on *affective pleasure as a way to begin composing* (rather than from a linguistically overdetermined idea, carefully researched, written as an essay and *then* rendered cinematically or otherwise multimodally). Focusing upon affect itself, received in the body and experienced linguistically (emotionally), Tomkins emphasized the felt sense of the possible, the "may" that structured so much of his writing seeming to exist as a leap[55] or aporia for new meanings that evaded normative thought on meaning, value, and experience. Tomkin's evasive tactics (or perhaps they were not evasive; though it seems unlikely that he was wholly unaware of dominant theories of affect and heterosexist norms) worked not from an easy correlation between the affects and the drives, "(*e.g.*, to breathe, to eat)," but instead from an inspiringly non-evaluative position regarding our attachments, the relations that generate affective pleasure:

> It is enjoyable to enjoy. It is exciting to be excited. It is terrorizing to be terrorized and angering to be angered. Affect is self-validating with or without any further referent. (3:404)
> (as quoted in Sedgwick & Frank, 1995, p. 7)

For Sedgwick and Frank, and, I am arguing, for film-composition, "[i]t is these specifications that make affect theory such a useful site for resistance to teleological presumptions of the many sorts historically embedded in the disciplines of psychology" (1995, p. 9) and Composition, and composing. As a DIY digital filmmaker driven by hopeful inquiry, curiosity, desire, and pleasure, I am drawn to Tomkins' for his inclination to the "may," for his recurrently open circuit for potential, manifesting in, among other delightful findings,

---

55 See Rickert, T. (2006). *On the Leap: Reason, Faith, Legitimation.*

his theories of affect and their relevance for, of all things, cybernetics. Indeed, Sedgwick and Frank found in Tomkins an intellectual space of potential for the actual that was yet virtual. Important for film-composition, they sense in Tomkins a non-evaluative correlation between pleasure and meaning that feels refreshing and capable of supporting contemporary claims regarding film's propriety as rhetorical scholarship in digital mediascapes and in terms discernibly pleasurable and eager for student engagement with film as rhetorical work. Further implicating the value of Tomkins' work for film-composition, Sedgwick and Frank historicize the moment of Tomkins' highest intellectual output, this neither modern nor postmodern moment as the "'cybernetic fold,' roughly from the late 1940s to the mid-1960s" (1995, p. 12). Amplifying the interdisciplinary rhetorical potential of the "may," Sedgwick and Frank identify this as a "moment of systems theory . . . part of a rich moment, a rich intellectual ecology, a gestalt . . . that allowed it to mean more different and more interesting things than have survived its sleek trajectory into poststructuralism" (1995, p. 12). In other words, Sedgwick and Frank found in Tomkins a resistant theory of affect that did not obediently start with libidinal drives (and the overdetermined notions association therewith) and move headlong toward an oppositional politics. Instead, they laud the path Tomkins created for an "early cybernetic notion of the brain as a homogeneous, differentiated system [that] is a characteristic and very fruitful emblem of many of the so far unrealized possibilities of this intellectual moment" (1995, p. 12). Arriving at cybernetics via affect theory may seem tangential to work in Composition, but in digitally mediated literacy worlds we inhabit, this route may not seem quite so strange. As well, it may resonate with the desires and pleasures found in digital scholarship and film-composition, both of which find value in and through new potential that has less to do with overdetermined readings of self and other (and other such pairings that crunch meanings) and more to do with affect, attention, and motivation. Noting a "characteristic structure" (1995, p. 8) in Tomkins' writing, Sedgwick and Frank detail a portal to new potential for affect theory, and they do so with clear reference to the ideational fundamentals of cybernetics:

> What appears to be a diminution in the power assigned to the sexual drive nonetheless corresponds to a multiplication—a finite and concrete multiplication, it will emerge—of different possibilities for sexual relevance (residing in this case in the distinct negative affects shame, anxiety, boredom, rage). Sexuality is no longer an on/off matter whose two possibilities are labeled express or repress. Sexuality as a drive remains characterized here by a binary (potent/impotent)

model; yet its link to attention, to motivation, or indeed to
action occurs only through coassembly with an affect system
described as encompassing several more, and more qualita-
tively different, possibilities than on/off. (1995, p. 8)

In other words, by limiting attentiveness to the drives as first causes, we
open up new portals for new kinds of linkages, new potential assemblages
that are activated in an affective universe that offers more than "on/off" as
our range of affective realities. Going beyond the drives moved us far beyond
heteronormative binaries that imbricate in a variety of theories in psychology and affect. Because Tomkins worked energetically but in ways that did
not validate or even really much recognize Freud, his work has accordingly
been received in various states of discomfort. Sedgwick and Frank, driven to
read beyond the disputes, found valuable new ways of enjoying the pleasures
of theoretical work on human motivation and meaning through Tompkins'
affect theory. Echoing many in film-composition who delight in discovering
new forms of rhetorical action through affectively charged processes of filmmaking, they describe the nature of the aporia Tomkins provided and the
space of doubt from which it emerged:

> The moralistic hygiene by which any reader of today is
> unchallengeably entitled to condescend to the thought of
> any moment in the past (maybe especially the recent past)
> is globally available to anyone who masters the application
> of two or three discrediting questions. How provisional, by
> contrast, how difficult to reconstruct and how exorbitantly
> specialized of use, are the tools that in any given case would
> allow one to ask, What was it possible to think or do at a
> certain moment of the past, that it no longer is? And how are
> those possibilities to be found, unfolded, allowed to move
> and draw air and seek new voices and uses, in the very dif-
> ferent disciplinary ecology of even a few decades' distance?
> (1995, p. 23)

How are those possibilities to be found, unfolded, allowed to move and
draw air and seek new voices and uses, in the very different disciplinary ecology of even a few decades' distance? For Sedgwick and Frank, the beloved
labor of uncovering Tomkins' distinctly non-normative theory of affect was a
project about which they were somewhat uncertain. Like my own, like Composition's foray across the disciplines, and like my identification with enigmatic figures in film (Bazin, 1967) and affect (Berlant, 2011) theory, I identify
with their proclamation regarding the pleasures of such work, as they ask,

> What does it mean to fall in love with a writer? What does
> it mean, for that matter—or maybe we should ask, what
> else could it mean—to cathect in a similar way a theoretical
> moment not one's own? . . . Some of what we're up to is the
> ordinary literary-critical lover's discourse: we want to propa-
> gate among readers nodes of reception for what we take to be
> an unfamiliar and highly exciting set of moves and tonalities.
> As people who fall in love with someone wish at the same
> time to exhibit themselves to others as being loved, we've also
> longed to do something we haven't been able to do more than
> begin here: to show how perfectly Tomkins understands us;
> to unveil a text spangled with unpathologizing, and at the
> same time unteleologizing, reflections on "the depressive,"
> on claustrophilia, on the teacher's transference; on the rich
> life of everyday theories, and how expensively theories turn
> into Theory. (1995, p. 23)

So, for the cultural critic attentive to the changing tides of what counts as
theory-of-the-moment, Tomkins puzzles and pleases due to his resistance to
overdetermined origin stories for cultural theory. For the Art historian seeking
to consider affect and its value for contemplating aesthetic pleasure, Tomkins
more simply delights. For our purposes in articulating the pleasures of film-
composition via aesthetics, valuing of Tomkins' seems essential. Best (2007)
finds productive ways of viewing aesthetics and affect via Tomkins because

> he separates and yet entwines the drives, affects and cogni-
> tion. It is this model of the embodied, feeling, thinking sub-
> ject that promises to reach what most people seek or expect
> from the experience of art. (p. 506)

For Best, Tomkins' work seems to forge a synaptic capacity for understanding meaning beyond conventionally determined registers, such as those
that evolve into theories and then practices. This move resonates with other
extra-conventional approaches to theorizing affect and aesthetics, and Best
goes there in ways that might please film-compositionists and other teacher-
scholars seeks new portals for enacting affectively intense pedagogical and
scholarly projects.

Spontaneous Feeling

Best is also important for film-composition and pleasure as she works
across disciplines to characterize the nature of interdisciplinary theoretical

disputes. She productively cites Brian Massumi's call to tend to the "embarrassed silence" in literary and cultural theory about terms such as expression, beauty and aesthetics (Massumi, 1997, p. 745, as quoted in Best, 2007, p. 508). She notes two of his concerns that align with some of my own worries as a DIY digital filmmaker. The first of Massumi's critiques involves an overly Romantic tendency that privileges "the investigation of the nature of artistic production, and the role of the artist in that production, over the work and its reception" (2007, p. 508). Here, I refer to many screenings, and some comments on my published films that attended almost wholly to questions on technique, ability, and copyright. I have seen this painfully constrained set of worries attend others' screenings, as well. Very little time and effort was given over to the work and its affective reception, and this trend indicates the nature of many of the challenges of film-composition. If our works have rhetorical force, how might we reorient ourselves as audiences so that we are capable of receiving the work on its terms. Chocolates? Best turns next to the second of Massumi's worries over aesthetics, which involves "The second pole that Massumi (1997) identifies—the concern with judgments of taste, an approach most closely identified with Kantian aesthetics" (2007, p. 509). Best reminds that for Kant, taste was, "the ultimate arbiter of art, both the production and the reception of it," (2007, p. 509) which is also to say that taste—if is it to be judged, and it must be as a condition of its being—is a matter of agential rhetoric. Best notes the uptake of Kantian aesthetics in terms of a kind of affective sidestepping, a dampening. That is to say, for Best, the articulation of aesthetic value has often been about articulations and critical proclamations regarding "something like a cultural norm" (2007, p. 509). At the same time, Best worries that this characterization "ignores the fact that taste is not just a cultural imposition, it is also linked to spontaneous feeling" (2007, p. 509). Best, like myself and many film-compositionists who are compelled to work from and toward affective intensity, returns to Kant:

> Indeed for Kant the viewer's affective response is central to the conception of art. For Kant . . . , an aesthetic judgment is not, as we now think of it, primarily about the appearance of the object judged; instead it concerns the sensation that the subject experiences in relation to the representation of an object—the assumption being that others should share this same feeling of pleasure. Indeed, we act as if our response is universally shared, we presume others will feel as we do: share our taste in the beautiful and our standards in judging the sublime. (2007, p. 509)

Film-composition has a long way to go if our films-as-rhetorical work may register variously, movingly, and absent overdetermined rhetorical frames for valuing what we shoot/edit/curate, how, and why. This is to say, while films about writing, and films by students engaged in compositional practices and about composing may be illuminating and joyful and moving and instructive, they need not define film-composition's aesthetics in order to matter, to "count" (empirico-positivist metaphor intended). There must be room for the sublime that does not depend upon classrooms, pedagogy, and overdetermined notions informing certain kinds of cinematic value. *All are welcome!* Best, again, helps articulate concern for cinematic pleasure and aesthetics that do more than record what we are doing and have been doing in composition classrooms. Tending to aesthetics and affective pleasure as we theorize the rhetorical affordances of digital filmmaking is vital for film-composition. For Best,

> aesthetics is not simply an embarrassment for cultural theory; it contains some of the clues for rethinking the gaze, visual pleasure and affective engagement with art. As the part of traditional philosophy that originated in the attempt to confront what is not fully captured by reason, it offers important insights into the domain of "non-reason" that unfortunately art history and cultural theory have forgotten or disavowed in their rush to be interpretative disciplines dealing with clearly communicable knowledge. (2007, p. 509)

We are, many of us, driven by hopeful desires for a productive rhetorical practice and pedagogy. Image work and the visual turn gave us access to ways of rendering the affective in moving and rhetorically provocative ways. Existing as both optimistically available and at the same time cruelly distant from mainstream recognition, film-composition is pleased to extend this work. It joins many contemporary rhetorical practices that support and sustain us as composers even as these compositional choices help us see our ways clearer to effective pedagogies toward teaching—re-animating existing—rhetorical knowledge and skill. Maybe it's clear that I'm not an expert in Philosophy, but I hope that my interdisciplinary foray into conversations about various implications regarding aesthetics, compositional pleasure, and rhetoric help make the case for the indeterminate yet affectively pleasurable and discriminating curatorial work of film-composition. I am certain that more collective efforts will help to ameliorate concerns regarding Kantian aesthetics and the problems of a worrisomely isolated compositional vision and energy. Rethinking "rhetorical velocity" in ways that may more routinely embrace, study, and critique compositional pleasure may aid in these efforts toward a fuller and more culturally impactful film-composition. I hope this work begins to extend just such a conversation.

A Return Approach

Because the pleasures of film-composition exist in and through aesthetics and so much of the aesthetic value of filmic work is visual, I want to approach a conclusion by returning to an ongoing exploration regarding the pleasures of images as central to so much digital scholarship and pedagogy. In a way, this image focus is subtractive, and yet image theory affords a dynamism that resonates throughout discourses on image, film, multimodality, and film-composition. My own long history of image pleasure will exceed the pages of this chapter, this book, this lifetime. Thus, toward an articulation of one aspect of film-composition's motivational and rewarding pleasures, I will share here a revised version of a presentation I shared at the 2008 Conference on College Composition and Communication. The slides and script, together entitled, "image pleasure," wanted to encourage us to consider movement, not static images but how images move us (thus, are rhetorically powerful in addition ago being affectively evocative). I was moving toward this place, where we are now; I hoped to share experientially derived aesthetic pleasures that I associate with film-composition. I hope that this reproduction is also helpful for those of us who have found our way to film-composition by way of an investment in the pleasures of aesthetics found in what we have come to embrace as "visual rhetoric," or as I call it "image. pleasure." Thus, a detour, a moment frozen from a scrolling timeline but yet contained within it. Toward an emergent sensitivity, reanimated within Composition, elaborated by my brilliant scholarly colleagues, produced and (hopefully) consumed with glee, and illuminated with purpose.

Image Pleasure

It started with good design—my response to it—the pleasure experienced both taking and appreciating this image. The typeface, clean and nostalgic. The shadowing and erasure of line. The exotic "MILANO," and the approval of age ("1913"). The taxi. The passerby. Me and my camera and my bag of expensive chocolates. Something about elite product, the unattainable, and the thrill of "taking" PRADA, all vibing out ambivalently and pleasurably at the same time. Desire and melancholy, the best and worst of our compulsions to ownership and participation. It's all so desperate, so romantic, so noir. But more . . . in the perspective achieved by the framing of the various elements within this windowpane—to borrow a phrase from Erwin Panofsky (1927) in

Perspective as Symbolic Form, perspective emerges from a "refashioning of the world"[. . . so that it is . . .] unified but still fluctuating luminously"(2005, p. 49).

I sense in my digitally enhanced pleasure a desire and potential to share the complex range of affective intensities activated while viewing (and within) the scene. Panofsky (1924–1925) explains that "exact perspectival construction is a systematic abstraction from the structure of . . . psychophysiological space" (1927, p. 30), and that in our attempts to represent that space, we seek to capture and express a, "boundlessness foreign to the direct experience of that space" (1927, p. 31). Exactly. In viewing the scene, I experienced one form of pleasure; in framing it up so effortlessly with my cheap digital camera, quite another; it was all there, the images in relation to one another, saying something about desire and my experience of the moment. It was a joyful moment. My joy—"the passion one experiences in the transition to an increased power to strive"—Spinoza's definition of desire (Stanford Encyclopedia of Philosophy, 2001, 2.1, para. 10)—resonated pleasurably with desire, and I want to think about how resistance is bound up with desire. Regarding this image: We might read "power to strive" as a decision to conform to cultural conventions (in this case, desiring just so), but we may also read it as resistance, depending upon the nature of our experience of a scene, and both readings interest me.

Shortly after my NYC trip, I watched Jean-Pierre Melville's *Army of Shadows*, a film that deploys muted grays and greens, a palette of subdued colors that have always pleased me enormously; set walls were washed with a particular hue, so as to cast a grey-greenish demeanor on the actors' faces. The actors portray characters living passionately and fearfully as key participants in the French Resistance, and I'm all over dramatic, heroic, and resistant. It seems essential, vital to my creative process. And I'm certain that my pleasure was bound up in both the visual (the palette) and the ideational (resistance). I'm also certain that resistance is bound up in image pleasure, a term I'll use to gesture toward an indeterminate space for image production, appreciation, and pedagogy. As I see it, we've not been resistant.

We share little agreement about pedagogies of the visual, virtually no consensus about visual communication as "argument" vs. what a prominent colleague has called "mere stimulus." Nevertheless, many of us put into play an immense range of rhetorically sophisticated practices in the context of teaching (with) the visual. Yet, it's no secret that [First-Year] Composition remains devoted to teaching clear written discourse; but, anymore, to what extent? We have questions about shifting academic literacies, hope for student engagement, and Marc Prensky (2001) reminding us of our status as "digital immigrants" whereas our students are, he argues, "digital natives" (p. 1). Perhaps more appropriately, we have been/become digital occupiers, demarcating the lines of possibility, the range and scope of what "counts" and what is "off limits," rounding up the opposition for censure via evaluation, "punishing" those who would evade or deride our post-haste rules and conventions. To shift the metaphor from occupier to comrade, something has to change, and it's not as simple as "incorporating visuals," or a "few guiding principles."

Diana George (2002) famously covered our historical engagement with the visual in her *CCC* piece, "From Analysis to Design: Visual Communication in the Teaching of Writing." George explains that many visual pedagogies have "commonly used pictures . . . as prompts for student compositions, [adding that] the [general] aim . . . was to bring students to a more vivid or accurate use of written language" (2002, p. 21). Right. And even in more progressive scenarios, we frequently frontload the work, staging a pedagogy that involves explanation of a few design concepts, analysis of existing works, and exploration of an issue, image, or event that usually manifests as a representational or what Sol Worth and Larry Gross call a "symbolic sign" (as opposed to a "natural sign," say, a cow in a field as opposed to an orchestrated message such as a stop sign). From early analytical work, students are expected to say and/or write something of value about an image. And whereas George insists that "Literacy means more than words," which might seem to gesture toward image pleasure, perhaps it's more about image analysis and production of a certain variety; for George, "visual literacy means *more than play*,"(2002, p. 215; emphasis mine). I remember reading George's piece in 2002, prior to but with my eye on filmmaking. I recall delighting in her move toward production, but while she seems to desire increased opportunities for image production as literacy work, image production is, I have been arguing, also and especially bound up in image pleasure. Visual literacy may be more than play, but *it is playful*, and playful need not mean uncritical or irrelevant—in case that point has not been (ha!) sufficiently made. The challenge for image work, for film-composition is about holding visual play as literacy while avoiding a pedagogy that would foreclose unrestrained passion and image pleasure in deference to more conventional textual work.

In today's more progressive pedagogies, students not only analyze but also produce images and films. But pedagogies that privilege filmic production over analytical pedagogy that finds expression in written discourse seems to be quite rare. And where and when we find it, it's about: What will we expect our students to produce? This is fine and to be expected, but such questions tend to foreclose the value of pleasure as itself an inventional, compositional, rhetorical heuristic. To their credit, and working at a moment in Composition's history when the "potentials of providing students with increased representational options" (Shipka, 2011, p. 4) was just emerging as a growing sensibility within the field, both Doug Hesse, and Kathleen Blake Yancey argued in their respective CCCC address(es) that we needed to be thinking about these potentials, about the kinds of texts—especially in the digitally mediated present—we value as writing professionals tasked with "teaching writing." Easily, many will say, "argument"; thus, "visual rhetoric" surfaced to describe our work with the visual. But need we have narrowed the work so conveniently? As early as 1996, we had philosopher J. Anthony Blair arguing for the possibility of visual argument that manifests entirely through "non-verbal visual communication" (p. 26), and this casts a different sort of light on Composition's concern for rendering a visual argument-qua-argument in/through verbal or written language. Blair's visual communication-as-argument is promising and I dare say rather obvious, because if we read an argument that is not intended as argument (say, Worth & Gross' "natural sign," the cow in the field), doesn't it still argue? Is our definition of argument necessarily contingent upon an active agent creating a purposeful communication for an audience imagined just so? Given our highly evolved understanding of communicative events as immersive, is the active agent necessary for constituting a rhetoric, a rhetorical move, an argument? Contemporary theories like Actor-Network Theory suggest not. But even before ANT, to complicate the question of whether or not images argue absent contextualizing written or verbal discourse, say, an essay that explains their meaning, we had iconologist W. J. T. Mitchell. Creating distinctions between "pictures" and "images," Mitchell (2005) argued for the somewhat easy comprehension of the rhetoricity of pictures because of how they support or contain images (images relate most essentially, for Mitchell, to icons). With regard to pictures, we might discuss line, angle, lighting, proximity, and other design elements as a way of getting at what an agent is after in the framing of the image(s) within a picture. But, for Mitchell, images are far more dynamic, as they possess the potential to seduce us into consuming and reproducing them; they have the distinctive ability to "go on before us," (2005, p. 105) [sic] as if they possess some vital force that exceeds or at the very least is animated by and through rhetoricity. Mitchell moves us beyond "What can I teach?, and, what do I need to do to prepare myself to teach it?" to wonder about, "the question of images and value [that] cannot be settled by arriving at a set of values and then proceeding to the evaluation of images" [the latter, describing our frontloaded pedagogies of the visual] (2005, p. 105). Rather, Mitchell argues that, "[i]mages are active players in the game of establishing and changing values. They are capable of introducing new values into the world and thus of threatening old ones" (2005, p. 105). Images themselves seem to possess agency, for Mitchell, and to divorce that agency from the image by intervening with a verbal rendering of the image's meaning seems somehow wrong—recall DeLuca and Wilferth's "will to tame images" vs. the "image-event." We might be especially struck by the reductive expectation for an image's accompanying verbal or written discourse because, here and now, new media technologies enable us to produce not only "pictures" but, with artful or perhaps even chance juxtapositions and playful tensions, "images."

Image pleasure is, to be sure, disorienting and paradoxical. On the one hand, images are impotent because they lay beneath our pedagogical concern—why worry them at all? On the other hand, we recognize the widely resonating power of images—they are powerful because we place them beneath us, as though to do away with or desacralize them, perhaps fearing their power because of how they reveal our own lack. This paradoxical (im)potence underscores the nature of images' enigmatic power and makes image work important for rhetorical pedagogies. Mitchell explains that

> [f]or better or for worse, human beings establish their collective, historical identity by creating around them a second nature composed of images which do not merely reflect the values consciously intended by their makers, [as with the rhetoricity of pictures] but radiate new forms of value formed in the collective, political unconscious of their beholders. As

> objects of surplus value, of simultaneous over- and under-
> estimation, [. . . images] stand at the interface of the most
> fundamental social conflicts. (2005, p. 106)

In particular, Mitchell sees images in terms of their rhetorical agency:

> they are phantasmatic, immaterial entities that, when incar-
> nated into the world, seem to possess agency, aura, . . . which
> is a projection of a collective desire that is necessarily obscure
> to those who find themselves . . . celebrating around or inside
> an image. (2005, p. 105–106)

For many, the obscure nature of the mutual desire of images seems to be what pedagogies of the visual might be after. That is, images "radiate" cultural values and desires; we respond to the desire of the image as we discern a will to engage with and participate with and in images. "Celebrating around or inside an image" seems to suggest unwitting participation (as with the golden calf), and here we may find space to imagine image work as an endorsement of acritical dispositions (and thus, many have privileged writing about images rather than with them as the most appropriate pedagogy). However, taking images, creating pictures and films and image-events seems contingent upon at least an elemental consciousness and perhaps a far more sophisticated rhetorical awareness of iconology that forecloses a simplistic reading of image pleasure.

What was it that I experienced on that New York City street while "taking" PRADA and Vuitton? It was more than recognition of irony in the icon "con-tained" within a (reflective) frame within which decidedly UN-PRADA and UN-Vuitton people and objects shared the same space. It was more than a basic compositional concept or an awareness of my "false consciousness," my overdetermined desire for participation with status beyond my reach. Similarly, teaching the visual, it seems to me, must be more than elemental de-sign concepts and the teaching of or about false consciousness to students via analysis of visual images. Here, I think of my students, many of whom tell me (often) that I read too much into images. And while I often think that they read too little into images, might I be somehow wrong or delusional . . . in need of some critically jarring work that destabilizes my awareness of the received discourses on images and pictures and design and Composition and power?

I worry these questions because, regarding image work, I have wanted to avoid the will to pedagogy. I worry that should I come in with my apparatus all posse'd up, I may offend or infantilize my students by assuming all that they don't know. Because I believe that students know a lot about design, a lot about the visual, a lot about image. Our students' tacit design knowledge may more appropriately register as "unwitting awareness," and this may complicate our ideas about their image arguments as agent-directed and intentional; that is, it may encourage us to find value in Mitchell's distinction that would discover a vitalism in images that may exceed our abilities to fully comprehend them in ways that make them available to conventional pedagogy. Yet, I'm invested in this indeterminate space for pedagogy. I can't know what my students know. I'm often unsure of my own responses to image and image-making, so how much do I prepare, and how much do I leave to negotiation? If we do participate in what J. Anthony Blair characterizes as "a systematic tendency to indeterminacy about visual expression" (1996, p. 27), we may find valuable spaces for image pleasure as pedagogy, and perhaps we may then begin to discuss image pleasure as both play and visual literacy as more than play.

To be clear, Blair intends to critique this "indeterminacy about visual expression" as he gestures toward a more concise pedagogy of the visual that may wonder about how images argue, how we argue with and through images, and how we might begin to create images that do the rhetorical work that we find valuable. And this is fine, but I find myself happily inhabiting this indeterminate space differently, living within a Berlantian zone of optimism within which I might not be thinking so much about what images mean and how I can make them mean for my ends. Instead, in this indeterminate space, I find myself producing images and discovering ways in which composing—making, doing—is the place for pleasure and discovery, trusting the immanent glances, hunches, and seemingly spontaneous insights that are symptomatic of rhetoricity. And I'm back to "just" writing, as opposed to rules and formats. Back to discovering the available means of persuasion and inventing from a less rigidly constructed place of knowing. It's a desiring force that enables me to create and complicate and perpetuate desire. And if desire is about the ability to reproduce itself, then my digital image qualifies as a picture of desire. My image aligns with what William J. Mitchell (not W. J. T.) defines as an "algorithmic image," one that is

> to a large extent automatically constructed from some sort of data about [an] object and which therefore involves fewer or even no intentional acts, gives away much less about the artist but provides more trustworthy evidence of what was out there in front of the imaging system. (1994, p. 29)

Ambiguous intention and pleasure but nonetheless capable of arguing? Sign me up.

In my recent work over the past decade, and especially working with images in the classroom, I tend to email my students via our campus email system one week prior to the first day of class, asking them to take a picture—not something they'd downloaded or pulled from a previous collection or a magazine—

and bring it to class. I request an "original" composition," something you find engaging, problematic, and significant." The point is that I am trying to develop a pedagogy that begins with student compositions, with doing, with doing absent instruction (channeling Peter Elbow's 1973 masterpiece, *Writing Without Teachers*). My student film projects begin with a similar admonition, one recently echoed by Bump Halbritter (2015), who explained that when he and his colleague and collaborator Julie Lundquist assign film projects, they tell their students to "write about what you love" [sic] (2015, "Multimoral"). So too does Sarah J. Arroyo assign works formed in and through pleasure (personal communication, August 18, 2016), including one project that invited students to take me up on the invitation to use video rather than text alone as a mode for creating a playful status update. Often, students enter into embarrassed silence about their choices, offering their images and clips tentatively, or perhaps performing a kind of ambivalence about their choice: "I don't know why I chose this." I worry that we are embarrassed about pleasure, and I hope that film-composition helps us get over it. It seems likely that Halbritter, Lundquist, Arroyo, myself, and many other film-compositionists begin with pleasure. In a brief interview, I asked Arroyo to describe her relationship to pleasure as a filmmaker. She replied in a way that likely sums up the DIY in DIY digital filmmaking that largely defines film-composition, explaining that

> Pleasure for me in filmmaking is watching my movies come to life as I/we are assembling them. As I've said many times, I usually don't have a "plan," but rather I have some sort of fuzzy vision for how to perform an argument or concept by way of video/audio. The pleasure in finding that something that seems like pure coincidence works beautifully in a video composition simply can't be matched. (personal communication, August 18, 2016)

Arroyo's response resonates with my sense that we might trust ourselves and the student writers and film-compositionists with whom we teach and learn. This is not to say that all we need to do is "have fun!" Though this is a good place to start, film-composition pedagogies nuance variously, radiating from this originary affect toward the production of similarly moving affects through the rhetorical nature, vivre and force of their productions.

At a more elemental level, it wouldn't be too far off to imagine that we are designing pedagogies for ekphrasis, driven by a desire to help students attenuate themselves more fully to their circumstances[56]—to be where they are more attentively, and to see what emerges from the critical indwelling. For W. J. T.

56   see kyburz, b., Enchanting the mundane (https://www.slideshare.net/blkyburz/enchanting-the-mundane), assignment prompt for university level writing courses.

Mitchell, the poetic mode of ekphrasis gestures at explaining desire for image pleasure as pedagogy. Mitchell describes ekphrasis as "giving voice to a mute art object" (Hagstrum, as quoted in Mitchell, 2005, p. 153) or, "the aestheticizing of language into . . . the 'still moment'" (Kreiger, as quoted in Mitchell, 2005, p. 153); . . . where we shape "language into formal patterns that 'still' the movement of linguistic temporality into a spatial, formal array" [that accounts for] a kind of ". . . silent presence" (Mitchell, 2005, p. 154). This is "ekphrastic hope," a desire for the visual arts to "speak" (or perhaps, "argue"). Mitchell explains that ekphrastic hope quickly gives way to ekphrastic fear, "a moment of resistance or counterdesire that occurs when we sense that the difference between the verbal and visual representation might collapse and the figurative, imaginary desire of ekphrasis might be realized literally and actually" (2005, p. 154). In other words, the image has both activated and fulfilled our desire. Fulfillment, the death of desire . . . so we resist because "meaning" is achieved . . . participation (in a conventionally academic sense) is no longer required.

Considering ekphrasis through the rhetorician's lens, we fear that what we say about the image cannot be said, that it cannot be rendered effectively as argument via verbal or written discourse, the driving engines for rhetorical—especially agential—action. Perhaps, in unwitting efforts to secure the indeterminate experience of (taking and enjoying) the image, students say they don't know why they took the shot, that they just did—they just liked it. *There can't be nothing in this response.* And yet, we feel compelled to cajole; I have found myself prodding and offering up readings that sound "academic." At the same time, I want to honor the resistance. Maybe, the non-response or resistance or silence is a kind of "ekphrastic indifference." For Mitchell, "Ekphrastic indifference" is "the assumption that ekphrasis is, strictly speaking, impossible" because of "the network of ideological associations embedded in the semiotic, sensory, and metaphysical oppositions that ekphrasis is supposed to overcome" (2005, p. 156). If we assume that images may not speak, perhaps there is some pleasure in this; images—still and moving—may speak differently, may mean differently. The overspill. The irrepressible nature of image pleasure. The resistance to verbal or written expression or "meaning making" in light of image vitality. My storefront images—something about taking them "through" the glass of a reflective surface, a practice I now engage routinely . . . a transformative experience I'd rather not attempt to articulate.

Maybe I saw in this image a design element (the iconic PRADA) in relation to other objects, an image that deconstructs obvious logocentric notions of beauty . . . that's fancy (and maybe it's related to why this woman scowls at me; I challenge her PRADAbility) . . . and it feels relevant, but only as a fairly obvious insight, the kind of insight we might applaud in a student response to an analysis assignment . . . or maybe the kind of response we would urge upon their silent "I don't know why I took it." Maybe "I don't know" means, "I don't know." Or maybe it means, "I know, and I think I know what you want to hear, but what you want to hear is simply too obvious. There's more. . . ."

There is more, so much more beyond image pleasure and toward film-composition. On the not knowing yet successful capturations and remakings of desire. Beyond metacognition toward a posthuman perspective that explores the immersive experience and the desires for making and where that making may lead. Making and labs and studios. Collaboratories. Deconstruction and Reconfabulation. Friends and colleagues sharing in this work include those working with home movies, travel documentaries, aesthetically moving efforts to demonstrate the  value of a particular rhetorical theory and contemporary practice, immersive installations, and more. Because this book sees the emergent history of film-composition through affectively charged arguments (which is to say, through always already embodied experiences and their particular affordances), I have found myself sticking close to that script. However, I want to encourage you to experience the work of some top film-compositionists for yourself. I hope that you find pleasure in doing so. I could continue to write about, hope for, fear that I'm not getting at, and long for it, but I can best point you toward the pleasures of film-composition by encouraging you to spend time with the cinematic works of Dan Anderson, Jonathon Alexander, Sarah J. Arroyo, Sarah J. Arroyo and Bahareh Alaei, Jamie "Skye" Bianco, Anthony Collamati, Geoffrey V. Carter, Bump Halbritter, Bump Halbritter and Julie Lindquist, Alexandra Hidalgo.[57] bonnie lenore kyburz, Robert Lestón, Jacqueline Rhodes, Anthony Stagliano, Todd Taylor, and all of you who are making out there, in your own dreamscapes and from your own special delights and fevermares . . . or from whatever space of affective intensity and lived potential you call your scene.[58] I have been inspired, nurtured, challenged, and schooled by you. To all of the hopeful film-compositionists reading, I hope this book invites you to hop onto this shimmering timeline so we can play, together, toward that perfect beat, that well-lit scene, that most vital vibe. Hit it.

---

57   Alexandra Hidalgo's *Cámara Retórica: A Feminist Filmmaking Methodology for Rhetoric* and composition notably became the winner of the 2017 *Computers and Composition* Distinguished Book Award.

58   Search the film-compositionists' Vimeo, YouTube, and personal/professional websites.

References

Adams, D. & Kline, R. (1975). The use of film in English composition. *College Composition and Communication, 26*(3), 253–262.

Adams, D. (1987). "An historical perspective." In *Report on film study in Amercian schools* (pp. 3–7). Urbana, IL: NCTE.

Ahmed, S. (2010). "Happy objects." In M. Gregg & G. J. Seigworth (Eds.), *The affect theory reader* (pp. 29–51). Durham, NC: Duke University Press.

Alaei, B. & Arroyo, S. J. (2013). The dancing floor. *Kairos: A Journal of Rhetoric, Technology, and Pedagogy, 17*(2). Retrieved from http://kairos.technorhetoric.net /17.2/topoi/vitanza-kuhn/arroyo_alaei.html.

Alexander, J. & Rhodes, J. (2012). Queered in technoculture. *Queered. Technoculture,* 2. Retrieved from https://tcjournal.org/vol2/queered/.

Anderson, B. (2010). Modulating the excess of affect: Morale in a state of "total war." In M. Gregg & G. J. Seigworth (Eds.), *The Affect Theory Reader* (pp. 161–185), Durham, NC /London, UK: Duke University Press.

Anderson, D. (2010). I'm a map, I'm a green tree. *Kairos: A Journal of Rhetoric, Technology, and Pedagogy, 15*(1). Retrieved from http://kairos.technorhetoric.net/15.1 /topoi/anderson/index.html.

Aristotle. (1924). *Rhetoric* (W. R. Roberts, Trans.). Oxford, UK: Oxford University Press.

Arroyo, S. J. (2013). *Participatory composition: Video culture, writing, and electracy.* Carbondale, IL: Southern Illinois University Press.

Aufderheide, P. & Jaszi, P. (2011). *Reclaiming fair use: How to put balance back in copyright.* Chicago, IL: University of Chicago Press.

Baker, W. D. (1964). Film as sharpener of perception. *College Composition and Communication, 15*(1), 44–45.

Ball, C. E. (2011). Assessing scholarly multimedia: A rhetorical genre studies approach. *Technical Communication Quarterly, 21*(1), 61–77.

Barad, K. (2003). Posthumanist performativity: Toward an understanding of how matter comes to matter. *Signs: Journal of Women and Society, 28*(3), 801–831.

Barnes, V. (1976). Eight basic considerations for the teaching of film. *College Composition and Communication, 27*(1), 32–35.

Baudrillard, J. (1983). *Simulations.* (P. Foos, P. Patton & P. Beitchman, Trans.), New York, NY: Semiotext[e].

Bawarshi, A. (2003). *Genre and the invention of the writer.* Logan, UT: Utah State University Press.

Bazin, A. (1967). *What is cinema? Volume 1.* Los Angeles, CA: University of California Press.

Belliger, A. & Krieger, D. J. (2016). From quantified to qualified self. *Digital Culture & Society, 21*(1), 25–40.

Benjamin, W. (1969). The work of art in the age of mechanical reproduction. In H. Arendt (Ed.), *Illuminations* (pp. 217–251). New York, NY: Schocken.

Berlant, L. & Greenwald, J. (2012). Affect in the end times: A conversation with Lauren Berlant. *Qui Parle: Critical Humanities and Social Sciences, 20*(2), 71–89.

Berlant, L. (2011). *Cruel Optimism.* Durham, NC: Duke University Press.

Berlin, J. (1988). Rhetoric and ideology in the writing class. *College English, 50*(5), 477–494.

Berthoff, A. E. (1978). Tolstoy, Vygotsky, and the making of meaning. *College Composition and Communication, 29*(3), 249–255.

Berthoff, A. E. (1982). *Forming/thinking/writing: The composing imagination.* Upper Montclair, NJ: Boynton/Cook.

Best, S. (2007). *Theory & Psychology, 17*(4), 505–514.

Bianco, J. S. (2013). Dog walking in cemetery woods. *Enculturation: A Journal of Rhetoric, Writing, and Culture, 16.* Retrieved from http://enculturation.net /dogwalking.

Bishop, E. (Ed.) (1999). *Cinema-(to)-graphy: Film and writing in contemporary composition courses.* Portsmouth, NH: Boynton/Cook.

Blair, J. A. (1996). The possibility and actuality of visual arguments. *Argumentation & Advocacy, 33*(1), 23–39.

Bogost, I. (2012). *Alien phenomenology, or, what it's like to be a thing.* Minneapolis, MN: University of Minnesota Press.

Boyle, C. (2016). Writing and rhetoric and/as posthuman practice. *College English, 78*(6), 532–554.

Brand, A. (1980). *Therapy in writing: A psycho-educational enterprise.* Lexington, MA: Lexington.

Brand, A. (1985–1986). Hot cognition: Emotions and writing behavior. *Journal of Advanced Composition, 38*(4), 5–15.

Brand, A. (1987). The why of cognition: Emotion and the writing process. *College Composition and Communication, 38*(4), 436–443.

Brand, A. (1989). *The psychology of writing: The affective experience.* Westport, CT: Greenwood.

Brand, A. (1991). Social cognition, emotions, and the psychology of writing. *Journal of Advanced Composition, 11*(2), 395–407.

Brannon, L. (1985). Toward a theory of composition. In B. W. McLelland & T. R. Donovan (Eds.), *Perspective on research and scholarship in composition* (pp. 6–25). New York, NY: MLA.

Brody, R. (2008). *Everything is cinema: The working life of Jean-Luc Godard.* New York, NY: Henry Holt.

Brodkey, L. (1994). Writing on the bias. *College English, 36*(5), 524–547.

Brown, R. S. (Ed.). (1972). *Focus on Godard.* Englewood Cliffs: Prentice Hall.

Burke, K. (1950). *A rhetoric of motives.* Berkeley, CA: University of California Press.

Burke, K. (1968). *Counter-statement.* Berkeley, CA: University of California Press.

Burroughs, W. S. & Odier, D. (1989). *The job: Interviews with William S. Burroughs.* New York, NY: Grove Press.

Carter, G. V. (2008). From gallery to webtext. *Kairos: A Journal of Rhetoric, Technology, and Pedagogy, 12*(3). Retrieved from http://kairos.technorhetoric.net/12.3 /topoi/gallery/index.html.

Carter, G. V. (2016). The MLArcade: Ten multimedia projects on the rhetoric of pinball. *Itineration*. Retrieved from http://tundra.csd.sc.edu/itinteration/submission_pages/mlarcade/carter/index.html.

Chion, M. (1994). *Audio-vision: Sound on screen*. New York, NY: Columbia University Press.

Chopra, D. (1994). *The seven spiritual laws of success: A practical guide to the fulfillment of your dreams*. San Rafael, CA: New World Library.

Chopra, D. (2004). *Synchrodestiny: Harnessing the infinite power of coincidence to create miracles*. London, UK: Rider & Co.

Christley, J. N. (2001). Chris Marker. *Senses of Cinema, 21*. Retrieved from http://sensesofcinema.com/2002/great-directors/marker/.

Cixous, H. (1976). The laugh of the medusa. *Signs, 1*(4), 875–893.

Clough, P. (2010). The affective turn: Political economy, biomedia, and bodies. In M. Gregg & G. J. Seigworth (Eds.), *The affect theory reader* (pp. 206–225). Durham, NC: Duke University Press.

Coleman, L., and Goodman, L. (2003). Introduction. "Rhetoric/Composition: Intersections/Impasses/Differends." *Enculturation: A Journal of Rhetoric, Writing, and Culture, 5*(1). Retrieved from http://enculturation.gmu.edu/5_1/intro.html.

Connors, R. (1997). *Composition-rhetoric: Backgrounds, theory, and pedagogy*. Pittsburgh, PA: University of Pittsburgh Press.

Cook, R. (1991). Angels, fiction, and history of Berlin: Wim Wenders' *Wings of Desire*. *The Germanic Review: Literature, Culture, History, 66*(1), 34–47.

Cox, M. H. (Recorder). (1969). Workshop reports: *College Composition and Communication, 20*(3), 242–265.

Cushing, H., D'Cruz, J. & Gay-Rees, J. (Producers) & Banksy (Director). (2010). *Exit through the gift shop*. London, UK: Paranoid Pictures.

Cushman, E. (1996). Rhetorician as an agent of social change. *College Composition and Communication, 47*(1), 7–28.

Dargis, M. (2007, September 16). A film festival as a showcase for the wacky, the naughty and the oh-so-deep. *The New York Times*. Retrieved from https://www.nytimes.com/2007/02/14/movies/14comm.html.

Dart, P. (1968). Student film production and communication. *English Journal, 57*(1), 96–99.

Davies, C. (1995). *Osmose*. Retrieved from http://www.immersence.com/osmose/index.php.

Davis, D. D. (2010). *Inessential solidarity: Rhetoric and foreigner relations*. Pittsburgh, PA: University of Pittsburgh Press.

Deleuze, G. (1985). *The time-image* (H. Tomlinson & R. Galeta, Trans.). Minneapolis, MN: University of Minnesota Press.

Deleuze, G. (1983). *The movement-image* (H. Tomlinson & B. Habberjam, Trans.). London, UK: The Athlone Press.

DeLuca, K. M. & Wilferth, J. (2009). Foreword. *Enculturation: A Journal of Rhetoric, Writing, and Culture, 6*(2). Retrieved from http://www.enculturation.net/6.2/foreword.

Derrida, J. (1977). *Limited, inc.* Evanston, IL: Northwestern University Press.

Detweiler, E. (2015, March 17). What isn't rhetoricity? *Rhetoricity* (Podcast). Retrieved from http://rhetoricity.libsyn.com/what-isnt-rhetoricity.

DeVoss, D. N. & Ridolfo, J. (2009). Composing for recomposition: Rhetorical velocity and delivery. *Kairos: A Journal of Rhetoric, Technology, and Pedagogy, 13*(2). Retrieved from http://kairos.technorhetoric.net/13.2/topoi/ridolfo_devoss /velocity.html.

Dobrin, S. I. (2011). *Postcomposition.* Carbondale, IL: Southern Illinois University Press.

Drew, J. (1999). (Teaching) composition: Composition, cultural studies, production. *Journal of Advanced Composition, 19*(3), 411–429.

Dye, R. (1964). The film: Sacred and the profane. *College Composition and Communication, 15*(1), 41–43.

Dyer, W. (1997). *Manifest your destiny: The nine spiritual principles to getting everything you want.* New York, NY: Harper Collins.

Edbauer, J. (2004). Executive overspill: Affective bodies, intensity, and Bush-in-relation. *Postmodern Culture, 15*(1). Retrieved from http://pmc.iath.virginia.edu// text-only/issue.904/15.1edbauer.txt.

Elbow, P. (1998). *Writing without teachers* (2nd ed.). Oxford, UK: Oxford University Press.

Erskine, T. (1973). Film as art form and mode of communication. *CCC Workshop Reports, 37,* 311.

Fleckenstein, K. (1999). Writing bodies: Somatic mind in composition studies. *College English, 61*(3), 281–306.

Galloway, A. (2012) *The interface effect.* Cambridge, UK: Polity.

Godard, J. L. (1972). *Godard on Godard: Critical writings* (T. Milne, Trans.). New York, NY: Viking.

Godard, J. L. & Ishaghpour, Y. (2005). *Cinema: The archaeology of film and the memory of a century* (J. Howe, Trans.). New York, NY: Oxford.

Gonzaléz, R. M. (2008). *The drama of collaborative creativity: A rhetorical analysis of Hollywood film-making of documentaries* (Masters thesis). Retrieved from http:// scholarcommons.usf.edu/etd/266.

Gradin, S. (1995). *Romancing rhetorics: Social expressivist perspectives on the teaching of writing.* Portsmouth, NH: Boynton/Cook.

Gregg, M. & Seigworth, G. J. (2010). An inventory of shimmers. In M. Gregg & G. M. Seigworth (Eds.), *The affect theory reader* (pp. 1–25). Durham, NC: Duke University Press.

Gries, L. E. (2015). *Still life with rhetoric: A new materialist approach for visual rhetorics.* Logan, UT: Utah State University Press.

Grossberg, L. (1997). *Dancing in spite of myself: Essays in popular culture.* Durham, NC: Duke University Press.

Halbritter, B. (2012). *Mics, cameras, symbolic action: Audio-visual rhetoric for writing teachers.* Anderson, SC: Parlor Press.

Halbritter, B. (2015, May). *Multimoral video pedagogy: The role of emotion, empathy, and engagement in audio-visual writing.* Paper presented at the Computers and Writing Conference, Menomonie, WI.

Hansen, M.B. (2015). *Feed forward: On the future of twenty-first century media.* Chicago, IL: University of Chicago Press.

Hardin, J. M. (2001). *Opening spaces: Critical pedagogy and resistance theory in composition.* Albany, NY: State University of New York Press.

Hardt, M. & Negri, A. (2000). *Empire.* Cambridge, MA: Harvard University Press.

Hardt, M. & Negri, A. (2004). *Multitude: War and democracy in the age of empire.* London, UK: Penguin Books.

Harmon, G., Deer, I. & Deer, H. (1973). The popular arts and introductory courses in English. *College Composition and Communication, 24*(3), 311–312. https://doi .org/10.2307/356866.

Harris, J. D. (1997). *A teaching subject: Composition since 1966.* Upper Saddle River, NJ: Prentice Hall.

Hawk, B. (2007). *A counter-history of composition: Toward methodologies of complexity.* Pittsburgh, PA: University of Pittsburgh Press.

Hawk, B. (2007). Hyperrhetoric and the inventive spectator: Remotivating the *Fifth Element.* In D. Blakesley (Ed.), *The terministic screen: Rhetorical perspectives on film* (pp. 70–91). Carbondale, IL: Southern Illinois University Press.

Hayles, N. K. (1991). *Chaos and order: Complex dynamics in literature and science.* Chicago, IL: University of Chicago Press.

Haynes, C. (2003). Writing offshore: The disappearing coastline of composition theory. *Journal of Advanced Composition, 23*(4), 667–724.

Héroux, C., David, P. & Solnicki, V. (Producers) & Cronenberg, D. (Director). (1983).*Videodrome.* US: Universal Pictures.

Herzog, A. (2000). Images of thought and acts of creation: Deleuze, Bergson, and the question of cinema. *InVisible Culture: An Electronic Journal for Visual Studies, 3.* Retrieved from: https://www.rochester.edu/in_visible_culture/issue3/herzog.htm.

Hesse, D. (2005). Who owns writing? *College Composition and Communication, 57*(2), 335–357.

Hidalgo, A. (2017). *Cámara retórica: A feminist filmmaking methodology for rhetoric and composition.* Logan, UT: Computers & Composition Digital Press/Utah State University Press. Retrieved from http://ccdigitalpress.org/camara.

Holdstein, D. (1990). *Computers and writing: Theory, research, practice.* New York, NY: Modern Language Association.

Holmevik, J. R. (2012). *Inter/vention: Free play in the age of electracy.* Cambridge, MA: The Massachusetts Institute of Technology Press.

Howe, J. (2005). Foreword. In J. L. Godard & Y. Ishaghpour (Eds.), *Cinema: The archaeology of film and the memory of a century* (pp. vii–xv). (J. Howe, Trans.). New York, NY: Oxford.

Hull, G. & Rose, M. (1989). Rethinking remediation: Toward a social-cognitive understanding of problematic reading and writing. *Written Communication, 6*(2), 139–154.

Huss, R. & Silverstein, N. (1966). Film study: Shot orientation for the literary minded. *College English, 27*(7), 566–568.

Hustwit, G., Swiss Dots & Veer (Producers) & Hustwit, G. (Director). (2007). *Helvetica.* US: Plexifilm.

Hansen, B., King, J. & Simpson, M. (Producers) & Jennings, G. (Director). (2005). *Hell yes*. US: Interscope.

Hustwit, G., Swiss Dots & Veer (Producers) & Hustwit, G. (Director). (2009). *Objectified*. US: Plexifilm.

Ingram, B. (2013). Critical rhetoric in the age of neuroscience. (Doctoral dissertation). Retrieved from https://scholarworks.umass.edu/cgi/viewcontent.cgi?ref erer=https://www.google.com/&httpsredir=1&article=1696&context=open_ access_dissertations.

Jarratt, S. (2003). Rhetoric in crisis: The view from here. *Enculturation: A Journal of Rhetoric, Writing, and Culture, 5*(1). Retrieved from http://enculturation.net/5_1 /index51.html.

Jeong, S. & Szaniawski, J. (2016). Introduction: The auteur, then . . . . In S. Jeong & J. Szaniawski (Eds.), *The global auteur: The politics of authorship in 21st century cinema* (pp. 1–20). London, UK/New York, NY: Bloomsbury.

Juhasz, A. (2016). Feminist filmmakers Twitter roundtable. Hosted by Alexandra Hildalgo & Agnés Films. Retrieved from http://tinyurl.com/gphetlh.

Kasl, C. (2005). *If the Buddha got stuck: A handbook for change on a spiritual path.* New York, NY: Penguin.

Keller, C. (2007). Great directors: Jean-Luc Godard. *Senses of Cinema*. Retrieved from https://web.archive.org/web/20071211053031/http://www.sensesofcinema .com/contents/directors/03/godard.html/.

Kellner, D. (1994). *Media culture: Cultural studies, identity, and politics between the modern and the postmodern.* New York, NY: Routledge.

Kent, T. (1999). *Post-process theory: Beyond the writing-process paradigm.* Carbondale, IL: Southern Illinois University Press.

Klein, J. T. (1990). *Interdisciplinarity: History, theory, practice.* Detroit: Wayne State University Press.

Kress, G. (1999). English at the crossroads: Rethinking curricula of communication in the context of the turn to the visual. In G. E. Hawisher & C. L. Selfe (Eds.), *Passions, Pedagogies, and 21st Century Technologies* (pp. 66–88). Logan, UT: Utah State University Press.

Kress, G. (2010). *Multimodality: A social semiotic approach to contemporary communication.* New York, NY: Routledge.

Kuhn, V. (2008). Metonymy. In From gallery to webtext. *Kairos: A Journal of Rhetoric, Technology, and Pedagogy, 12*(3). Retrieved from http://kairos.technorhetoric .net/17.2/topoi/vitanza-kuhn/kuhn.html.

Kuhn, V. (2011). Filmic texts and the rise of the fifth estate. *International Journal of Learning and Media, 2*(2–3). Retrieved from http://scalar.usc.edu/anvc/kuhn/index.

kyburz, b. l. (2004). proposition 1984. Retrieved from https://vimeo.com/13354536.

kyburz, b. l. (2008). bones. In MoMLA: From panel to gallery. V. Kuhn & V. Vitanza (Eds.). *Kairos: A Journal of Rhetoric, Technology, and Pedagogy, 17*(2). Retrieved from http://kairos.technorhetoric.net/12.3/topoi/gallery/index.html.

kyburz, b. l. (2010a). *i'm like . . . professional*: Notes on the film. *Kairos: A Journal of Rhetoric, Technology, and Pedagogy, 14*(2). Retrieved from http://kairos.technor hetoric.net/14.2/topoi/kyburz/index.html.

kyburz, b. l. (2010b). Status update. *Enculturation: A Journal of Rhetoric, Writing, and Culture, 8.* Retrieved from http://enculturation.net/status-update.

kyburz, b. l., Sirc, G., Taylor, T. & Wysocki, A. F. (2007, March). *The origins of modern composition, part I.* Panel at the Conference on College Composition and Communication, New York.

Lestón, R. (2013). Anomalous horror: A horror in video. *Kairos: A Journal of Rhetoric, Technology, and Pedagogy, 17*(2). Retrieved from http://kairos.technorhetoric .net/17.2/topoi/vitanza-kuhn/leston.html.

Lestón, R. (2016, February). A table without organs. In G. V. Carter & R. Lestón (Eds.), The MLArcade: Ten multimedia projects on the rhetoric of pinball. *Itineration: Cross-disciplinary Studies in Rhetoric, Media, and Culture* (Multimedia). [Journal status uncertain, so access via Lestón's Vimeo page. Retrieved from https://vimeo.com/116427769].

Lindquist, J. (2004). Class affects, classroom affectations: Working through the paradoxes of strategic empathy. *College English, 67*(2), 187–209.

Lopate, P. (2002). *Contempt: The story of a marriage.* Retrieved from https://www .criterion.com/current/posts/240-contempt-the-story-of-a-marriage.

Luzi, E. (n.d.). The French new wave: A cinematic revolution. The Black and Blue: Tips for Camera Assistants [Web log post]. Retrieved from http://www.theblack andblue.com/2010/03/29/the-french-new-wave-a-cinematic-revolution/.

Lynch, D. (2007). *Catching the big fish: Meditation, consciousness, creativity.* New York, NY: Penguin.

Manovich, L. (2016a). Instagram and contemporary image. Retrieved from http:// manovich.net/index.php/projects/instagram-and-contemporary-image.

Manovich, L. (2016b). Instagrammism and contemporary cultural identity. Retrieved from http://manovich.net/index.php/projects/notes-on-instagrammism -and-mechanisms-of-contemporary-cultural-identity.

Massumi, B. (2002). *Parables for the virtual: Movement, affect, sensation.* Durham, NC: Duke University Press.

McComiskey, B. (2000). *Teaching composition as a social process.* Logan, UT: Utah State University Press.

McCullough, M. (2013). *Ambient commons: Attention in the age of embodied information.* Cambridge, MA: The MIT Press.

McLeod, S. (1996). *Notes on the heart: Affective issues in the writing classroom.* Carbondale, IL: Southern Illinois University Press.

Melville, J. P. (Director). (1969). *Army of shadows.* Les Films Corono.

Metzger, D. (2004). The call for rhetoric. *Enculturation: A Journal of Writing, Rhetoric, and Culture, 5*(2). Retrieved from http://enculturation.net/5_2/index52.html.

Micciche, L. (2005). Emotions, ethics, and rhetorical action. *Journal of Advanced Composition, 25*(1), 161–184.

Miller, S. (1991). *Textual carnivals: The politics of composition.* Carbondale, IL: Southern Illinois University Press

Milne, T. & Narboni, J. (Eds.). (1972). *Godard on Godard: Critical writings.* New York, NY: Viking.

Mitchell, W. J. T. (1994). *Picture theory: Essays on verbal and visual representation.* Chicago, IL: University of Chicago Press.

Mitchell, W. J. T. (1995). Translator translated: An interview with Homi Bhabha, *Artforum, 33*(7), 80–84. Retrieved from http://prelectur.stanford.edu/lecturers/bhabha/interview.html.

Mitchell, W. J. T. (2005). *What do pictures want? The lives and loves of images.* Chicago, IL: University of Chicago Press.

Murphy, J. (1963). *The power of your subconscious mind.* Upper Saddle River, N.J., Prentice Hall.

Murray, J. (2009). *Non-discursive rhetoric: Image and affect in multimodal composition.* Albany, NY: State University of New York Press.

Nebenzal, S. (Producer) & Lang, F. (Director). (1931). *M.* Germany: Nero-Film A-G.

The New London Group. (1996). A pedagogy of multiliteracies: Designing social futures. *Harvard Educational Review, 66*(1), 60–93.

North, S. M. (1987). *The making of knowledge in composition: Portrait of an emerging field.* Portsmouth, NH: Boynton/Cook.

Palmeri, J. (2012). *Remixing composition: A history of multimodal writing pedagogy.* Carbondale, IL: Southern Illinois University Press.

Panofsky, E. (1991/1927). *Perspective as symbolic form.* (C. S. Wood, Trans.). Brooklyn, NY: Zone Books.

Parr, A. (Ed.). (2005). *The Deleuze dictionary, revised edition.* Edinburgh: Edinburgh University Press.

Perl, S. (1980). Understanding composing. *College Composition and Communication, 31*(4), 363–369.

Phillips. C. (2011). French new wave. All about film. Retrieved from http://kimmikong.wordpress.com/2011/12/01/french-new-wave/.

Pisters, P. (2003). *The matrix of visual culture: Working with Deleuze in film theory.* Palo Alto, CA: Stanford University Press.

Pisters, P. (2012). *The neuro-image: A Deleuzian film-philosophy of digital screen culture.* Palo Alto: CA: Stanford University Press.

Poster, M. (1995). *The second media age.* Cambridge, UK: Polity Press.

Poulakos, J. (1983). Toward a sophistic definition of rhetoric. *Philosophy & Rhetoric, 16*(1), 35–48.

Prensky, M. (2001). Digital natives, digital immigrants. *On the Horizon, 9*(5), 1–6.

Raaf, S. (n.d.). Saturday, 2002. *Sabrian Raff :: New media artist.* http://raaf.org/projects.php?pcat=2&proj=10&sec=images#.

Rice, J. (2003). The 1963 hip-hop machine: Hip-hop pedagogy as composition. *College Composition and Communication, 54*(3), 453–471.

Rice, J. E. (2002). Big time sensuality: Affective literacies and texts that matter. *Composition Forum, 13*(1–2), 23–37.

Rickert, T. (2006, May). On the leap: Reason, faith, legitimation. Paper presented at Rhetoric Society of America Conference, Memphis, TN.

Rickert, T. (2007). *Acts of enjoyment: Rhetoric, Zizek, and the return of the subject.* Pittsburgh, PA: University of Pittsburgh Press.

Rickert, T. (2013). *Ambient rhetoric: The attunements of rhetorical being*. Pittsburgh, PA: University of Pittsburgh Press.

Rieder, D. M. (2015). Introduction. *Hyperrhiz 13*, kits, plans, schematics. Retrieved from http://hyperrhiz.io/hyperrhiz13/introduction/1-introduction.html.

Robbins, A. (2008). *Unlimited power: The new science of personal achievement*. New York, NY: Simon and Schuster.

Rushton, R. (2009). Deleuzian spectatorship. *Screen, 50*(1), 45–53. Retrieved from https://doi.org/10.1093/screen/hjn086.

Sedgwick, E. K. & Frank, A. (1995). Shame in the cybernetic fold: Reading Silvan Tomkins. *Critical Inquiry, 21*(2), 496–522.

Sharp, D. (2002). Introduction. Auteur theory/auteurs: 16 source guides. *British Film Institute*. Retrieved from https://web.archive.org/web/20120309164313/http://www.bfi.org.uk/filmtvinfo/publications/16+/pdf/auteur.pdf.

Sheridan, D. (2016, March 28). A maker mentality toward writing. Blog carnival 8: Makerspace and writing. Digital rhetoric collaborative [Web log post]. Retrieved from http://www.digitalrhetoriccollaborative.org/2016/03/28/a-maker-mentality -toward-writing/.

Shipka, J. (2011). *Toward a composition made whole*. Pittsburgh, PA: University of Pittsburgh Press.

Sirc, G. (1997). Never mind the tagmemics: Where's the Sex Pistols? *College Composition and Communication, 48*(1), 9–29.

Sirc, G. (1999). What is composition? . . . After Duchamp (Notes toward a general teleintertext). In G. E. Hawisher & C. L. Selfe (Eds.), *Passions, pedagogies, and 21st century technologies* (pp. 178–204). Logan, UT: Utah State University Press.

Sirc, G. (2002). *English composition as a happening*. Logan, UT: Utah State University Press.

Sirc, G. (2007, March). Writing classroom as Warhol's factory. Paper presented at Conference on College Composition and Communication, New York, NY.

Smith, D. (2007). Deleuze and the question of desire: Towards an immanent theory of ethics. *Parrhesia, 2*, 66–78.

Smith, D. W. (1998). Introduction: A life of pure immanence: Deleuze's critique et clinique project. In Deleuze, G., *Essays critical and clinical: Gilles Deleuze* (pp. xi–lv). New York, NY: Verso.

Solomon, S. J. (1974). Film study and genre courses. *College Composition and Communication, 25*(4), 277–283.

Spielberg, S. (Director). (2002). *The minority report*. USA. Twentieth Century Fox.

Spellmeyer, K. (1992). *Common ground: Dialogue, understanding, and the teaching of composition*. Upper Saddle River, NJ: Prentice Hall.

Spellmeyer, K. (1997). Inventing the university student. In L. Z. Bloom, D. A. Daiker & E. M. White (Eds.), *Composition in the twenty-first century: Crisis and change* (pp. 39–44). Carbondale, IL: Southern Illinois University Press.

Spinoza, B.B.de.(1677) *Ethics III. On the origin and nature of the emotions*. Library of Alexandria. (Trans. R.H.M. Elwes.) *The project gutenberg ebook of the ethics, by Benedict de Spinoza*. (2017). Retrieved from https://www.gutenberg.org/files /3800/3800-h/3800-h.htm.

Tarkovsky, A. (1989). *Sculpting in time: Reflections on the cinema*. London, UK: Faber & Faber.

Taylor, T. (2003). *Take 20*. Retrieved from https://www.macmillanlearning.com/catalog/static/bsm/take20/.

Taylor, T. (2005, December). *Coming soon to a writing program near you*. Modern Language Association Annual Convention, Washington, DC.

Trimbur, J. (1989). Consensus and difference in collaborative learning. *College English, 51*(6), 602–616.

Ulmer, G. (2002). *Internet invention: From literacy to electracy*. London, UK: Pearson.

Varda, A. (2016). Agnès Varda. Notes on the filmmaker. *Criterion*. Retrieved from https://www.criterion.com/films/28629-mur-murs.

Vitale, C. (2011). Towards a cinema of affects: A manifesto, part I— From film-world to film-art. Networkologies [Web log post]. Retrieved from https://networkologies.wordpress.com/2011/04/24/towards-a-cinema-of-affects-a-manifesto-part-i/.

Vitanza, V. J. (2003). Abandoned to writing: Notes toward several provocations. *Enculturation: A Journal of Rhetoric, Writing, and Culture, 5*(1). Retrieved from http://www.enculturation.net/5_1/index51.html.

Vreeland, A. V. (2015). Color theory and social structure in the films of Wes Anderson. *Elon Journal of Undergraduate Research in Communications, 6*(2). Retrieved from http://www.elon.edu/docs/e-web/academics/communications/research/vol6no2/04_Vaughn_Vreeland.pdf (For a more visually oriented display, see http://www.anothermag.com/art-photography/3586/wes-andersons-colour-palettes).

Warhol, R. (2003). *Having a good cry: Effeminate feelings and pop-culture forms*. Columbus, OH: Ohio University Press.

Watkins, M. (2010). Desiring recognition, accumulating affect. In M. Gregg & G. Seigworth (Eds.), *The Affect Theory Reader* (pp. 269–285). Durham, NC: Duke University Press.

Weisinger, R. (1948). The motion picture and the teacher of English. *College English, 9*(5), 270–275.

Wetherbee, B. (2011). Toward a rhetoric of film: Theory and classroom praxis. (Master's Thesis). Retrieved from https://etd.ohiolink.edu/!etd.send_file?accession=miami1313119045&disposition=inline.

Williams, J. S., Temple, M. & Witt, M. (Eds.). (2004) *Forever Godard*. London, UK: Black Dog Press.

Williams, P. (2002, July 3). The French new wave revisited. *MovieMaker, 47*. Retrieved from https://www.moviemaker.com/archives/moviemaking/directing/the-french-new-wave-revisited-3366/.

Williamson, R. (1971). The case for filmmaking as English composition. *College Composition and Communication, 22*(2), 131–160.

Wise, J. H. (1939). The comprehensive freshman English course—Reading, speaking, and writing—at the University of Florida. *English Journal, 28*(6), 450–460.

Worsham, L. (1998). Going postal: Pedagogic violence and the schooling of emotions. *Journal of Advanced Composition, 18*(2), 213–245.

Wysocki, A. F. (2007, July). Fitting beauties of transducing bodies. Paper presented at the Penn State University Conference on Rhetoric and Technology, State Park, PA.

Wysocki, A. F. (2010). A bookling monument. *Kairos: A Journal of Rhetoric, Technology, and Pedagogy, 7*(3). Retrieved from http://kairos.technorhetoric.net/7.3/coverweb/wysocki/.

Wysocki, A. F., Johnson-Eilola, J., Selfe C. L. & Sirc, G. (2004). *Writing new media: Theory and applications for expanding the teaching of composition.* Logan, UT: Utah State University Press.

Yancey, K. B. (2004). Made not only in words: Composition in a new key. *College Composition and Communication, 56*(2), 297–328.

Index

A

a bookling monument 31
Adams, Dale 34, 54, 147
aesthetics 114, 123, 128
aesthetic value 122, 133, 135
affect 3, 4, 13, 14, 15, 16, 18, 19, 20, 21, 22, 23,
    26, 27, 28, 33, 37, 38, 40, 43, 44, 45, 46, 47,
    49, 50, 53, 61, 63, 65, 66, 67, 68, 84, 85, 86,
    92, 93, 96, 98, 99, 100, 101, 102, 103, 104,
    105, 106, 108, 110, 111, 112, 113, 121, 126, 127,
    128, 129, 131, 132, 142, 147, 148, 150, 153,
    154, 156
affective intensities 3, 10, 15, 20, 22, 26, 28,
    30, 31, 32, 39, 40, 45, 50, 64, 93, 97, 98, 101,
    107, 110, 116, 127, 136
affective intensity 14, 18, 33, 42, 48, 53, 60, 84,
    87, 106, 107, 110, 113, 122, 124, 126, 133, 145
affective pleasure 122, 124, 129, 134
affects 3, 4, 13, 14, 16, 20, 26, 32, 40, 52, 72, 95,
    96, 98, 100, 104, 106, 107, 108, 127, 128, 129,
    130, 132, 142, 153, 156
affect theory 5, 11, 14, 15, 19, 28, 98, 99, 111,
    127, 129, 130, 131
affordances 10, 12, 14, 16, 17, 28, 29, 30, 53, 54,
    55, 56, 57, 60, 64, 69, 71, 72, 75, 91, 95, 98,
    100, 104, 106, 109, 115, 122, 125, 134, 145
Ahmed, Sara 108, 147
Alaei, Bahareh 147
Alexander, Jonathon 147
ambient 11, 21, 24, 50, 61, 62, 63, 73, 91, 110,
    116, 128
Anderson, Ben 104, 147
Anderson, Dan 147
Anderson, Wes 8, 42, 156
Aristotle 13, 30, 40, 51, 147
Arroyo, Sarah Johnson 147
Art of Noise, The 74
attachments 4, 5, 27, 41, 42, 52, 69, 108, 110,
    115, 129
attunement 20, 23, 47, 50, 70, 72, 106, 110
audiences 5, 11, 27, 28, 33, 39, 48, 58, 73, 85,
    100, 101, 106, 110, 114, 133
Aufderheide, Pat 147

auteur 5, 6, 8, 28, 61, 62, 63, 65, 66, 75, 77, 78,
    91, 93, 116, 152, 155
auteurist 5, 6, 8, 50, 52, 61, 64, 65, 66, 94, 111
auteurists 63

B

Baker, William D 147
Baker, William D. 58
Ball, Cheryl E 147
Banksy 30, 149
Barad, Karen 147
Barnes, Verle 66, 67, 68, 69, 70, 71, 147
Bawarshi, Anis 147
Bazin, André 7, 50, 51
Beck 48, 119
Bedford/St. Martin's 18
being with 45, 96, 102, 107, 108, 110, 122
Belliger, Andréa 147
Bergson, Henry 13
Berlant, Lauren 3, 22, 27, 37, 40, 148
Berthoff, Anne 19, 47
Berthoff, Ann. E. 148
Best, Stephen. 148
Best, Susan 128, 132
Bishop, Ellen 148
Blair, J. Anthony 138, 141
Blubaugh, Andy 119
body tracking 57
Boyle, Casey 148
Brand, Alice 14, 19, 43, 47, 148
Brannon, Lil 148
bravery 49
brave souls 49, 54, 55, 65
Brodkey, Linda 148
Burke, Kenneth 17, 26, 148
Burroughs, William S. 148

C

candlelight 87
Carter, Geoffrey. V. 148, 149

Cauoette, Jonathan 119

CCC 4, 32, 54, 114, 137

CCCC 4, 23, 47, 49, 73, 83, 138

Ceraso, Steph 39

Chion, Michel 149

Chopra, Deepak 149

chora 103

Christley, Jaime N. 81

Christley, Jaime. N. 149

cinematic arguments 16

cinematic rhetorics 3, 22, 26, 64, 122

cinematic value 124, 134

classrooms 3, 16, 17, 22, 24, 25, 29, 31, 36, 40, 41, 53, 54, 58, 70, 86, 97, 98, 111, 113, 134

Clough, Patricia T. 99

College English 37, 61, 148, 150, 153, 156

comic books 17

communication 7, 8, 9, 17, 23, 30, 33, 35, 55, 75, 86, 87, 97, 121, 123, 137, 138, 142, 149, 152

composition i, iii, 1, 4, 5, 7, 10, 12, 13, 14, 15, 16, 17, 18, 19, 21, 22, 23, 24, 25, 26, 28, 29, 30, 31, 32, 33, 34, 35, 36, 37, 38, 40, 42, 43, 45, 46, 47, 49, 53, 54, 60, 61, 66, 68, 70, 73, 74, 75, 76, 77, 78, 79, 81, 82, 83, 84, 85, 86, 87, 88, 89, 90, 96, 97, 98, 101, 102, 104, 105, 106, 109, 113, 114, 122, 124, 129, 130, 131, 135, 137, 138, 140, 145, 147, 148, 149, 150, 151, 153, 154, 155, 156, 157

compositionist 3, 13, 21, 49, 61, 76, 79, 80, 85, 89, 92

contemplative 74, 89, 116, 122, 125

conventions 6, 38, 48, 69, 75, 76, 77, 85, 86, 88, 91, 92, 136, 137

Cook, Roger 65, 149

cool rationality 14

Cox, Martha Heasley 23, 49, 149

creative 6, 7, 8, 13, 15, 18, 20, 27, 28, 32, 44, 49, 52, 57, 58, 61, 65, 75, 76, 90, 92, 94, 100, 101, 107, 109, 114, 115, 116, 120, 124, 128, 137

creativity 7, 8, 58, 63, 66, 81, 86, 87, 89, 114, 150, 153

critical analysis 128

critical practice 12, 120

Cronenberg, David 151

cruel optimism 3, 9, 22, 27, 40, 41, 50, 52, 114, 115, 116, 117, 118, 120

Csikszentmihályi, Mihály 108

Cultural Studies 4, 7, 90, 98, 150

cultural texts 4, 38, 52, 115, 116

Cushman, Ellen 149

cybernetics 130

D

Dargis, Manohla 149

Dart, Peter 149

Davies, Char 149

Davis, Diane 9, 103

Deer, Harriet 4

Deer, Irving 4

Deleuze, Gilles 20, 26, 82, 95, 96, 98, 100, 101, 102, 103, 105, 121, 123, 149, 154, 155

DeLuca, Kevin 149

DeLuca, Kevin Michael 29

Derrida, Jacques 150

design 6, 7, 21, 31, 43, 45, 71, 75, 135, 137, 139, 140, 143

desire 3, 5, 11, 12, 13, 18, 19, 20, 21, 23, 26, 27, 29, 31, 33, 37, 41, 52, 53, 58, 61, 64, 66, 69, 71, 73, 74, 75, 77, 79, 81, 82, 83, 84, 85, 86, 87, 88, 91, 92, 93, 94, 97, 98, 101, 103, 106, 107, 108, 109, 110, 111, 113, 114, 115, 116, 118, 119, 122, 128, 129, 136, 138, 140, 141, 142, 144, 155

desires 4, 10, 16, 20, 25, 26, 29, 30, 37, 39, 40, 44, 47, 52, 58, 66, 73, 74, 77, 87, 93, 94, 96, 97, 101, 103, 104, 105, 108, 111, 113, 114, 117, 120, 122, 123, 129, 130, 134, 140, 144

Detweiler, Eric 150

Detweiler, Eric N. 9

DeVoss, Danielle N. 94, 150

digital filmmaker 3, 5, 13, 19, 50, 51, 110, 129, 133

digital filmmaking 3, 5, 6, 10, 11, 22, 24, 27, 32, 57, 64, 94, 114, 115, 116, 117, 134, 142

digital media 10, 12, 14, 16, 19, 28, 29, 36, 38, 43, 53, 55, 75, 95, 104, 106, 111, 116, 122

digital scholarship 3, 5, 6, 12, 24, 61, 94, 96, 102, 104, 105, 108, 110, 114, 127, 130, 135

discursive attention events. See also turns

DIY 3, 5, 10, 12, 19, 22, 24, 27, 33, 35, 45, 50, 51, 58, 63, 94, 114, 116, 118, 119, 129, 133, 142

Dobrin, Sidney I 150

Dye, Robert 49

Dyer, Wayne 150

dynamic 7, 11, 14, 20, 22, 25, 29, 64, 75, 95, 96, 101, 102, 103, 111, 118, 125, 139

E

Edbauer, Jenny 28, 35, 85, 150, 154
ekphrasis 71, 72, 142, 143
Elbow, Peter 150
emotion 14, 15, 19, 33, 43, 44, 45, 46, 47, 99, 100, 106, 150
engagement 21, 28, 30, 33, 45, 59, 83, 84, 85, 87, 89, 130, 134, 137, 150
English Studies 40, 72
Erskine, Thomas 53
ethnography 3
ethos 12, 20, 42, 51, 59
experience 3, 5, 9, 10, 11, 12, 13, 16, 21, 27, 29, 37, 38, 45, 46, 51, 52, 55, 59, 64, 67, 68, 71, 72, 74, 75, 79, 81, 82, 83, 84, 85, 86, 98, 103, 109, 110, 111, 112, 113, 114, 115, 117, 119, 121, 127, 129, 132, 136, 143, 144, 148

F

Fair Use 32, 33, 57, 61, 114, 115, 116, 118
fantasies 108, 117, 118, 120
fear 3, 11, 19, 26, 37, 44, 49, 50, 52, 53, 54, 55, 56, 57, 58, 60, 61, 63, 64, 66, 68, 69, 70, 71, 92, 104, 113, 114, 115, 120, 128, 143, 145
film 3, 5, 6, 7, 8, 10, 11, 12, 13, 14, 15, 16, 18, 19, 20, 21, 22, 23, 24, 25, 26, 27, 28, 29, 30, 31, 33, 34, 35, 36, 37, 38, 39, 40, 41, 42, 43, 44, 47, 48, 49, 50, 51, 52, 53, 54, 55, 56, 57, 58, 59, 60, 61, 62, 63, 64, 65, 66, 67, 68, 69, 70, 71, 72, 73, 74, 76, 77, 79, 80, 82, 83, 84, 85, 86, 87, 88, 89, 90, 91, 92, 93, 94, 95, 96, 97, 98, 100, 101, 102, 103, 105, 106, 108, 109, 111, 113, 114, 116, 117, 118, 119, 122, 123, 124, 125, 126, 127, 128, 129, 131, 132, 134, 135, 137, 138, 141, 142, 144, 145, 147, 149, 150, 151, 152, 153, 154, 156
film analysis 34, 41, 42, 59, 60
film-composition 3, 5, 10, 13, 15, 16, 19, 20, 21, 22, 23, 24, 25, 27, 28, 29, 30, 32, 33, 35, 38, 40, 42, 43, 44, 47, 48, 50, 53, 55, 56, 57, 60, 61, 65, 68, 70, 71, 74, 76, 85, 92, 93, 94, 95, 96, 97, 98, 100, 102, 103, 105, 106, 108, 109, 111, 113, 122, 123, 124, 125, 126, 128, 129, 131, 132, 134, 135, 138, 142, 144
film-compositionists 6, 13, 18, 29, 30, 35, 37, 38, 39, 49, 52, 53, 55, 64, 72, 97, 105, 113, 122, 126, 127, 132, 133, 142, 145

filmmaker 15, 20, 28, 30, 51, 61, 63, 64, 65, 76, 79, 80, 81, 83, 85, 91, 101, 110, 115, 118, 119, 142
Final Cut Pro 11, 12
Fleckenstein, Kristie 15, 85
flourishing 27, 114, 115
Frank, Adam 129, 155
French New Wave 7, 50, 58, 63, 65, 74, 76, 79, 80
Freud, Sigmund 131

G

Galloway, Alexader 150
Galloway, Alexander Galloway 117
Gee, James 31
generative pedagogical practices 38
genre 6, 48, 65, 71, 75, 85, 120, 147, 155
George, Diana 4, 137
Godard, Jean-Luc 33, 63, 73, 74, 76, 78
Going Postal 15
Gonzaléz, Robert M. 7, 150
Gradin, Sherrie 150
Gregg, Melissa 19, 147, 149, 150
Grossberg, Lawrence 98, 150
Gross, Larry 137

H

hacking 57
Halbritter, Bump 17, 142, 145, 150
Hansen, Mark 13
Hansen, Mark.B 150
happy objects 108
Hardin, Joe M 151
Harmon, Gary 4
Harris, Joseph D 151
Harris, Joseph D. 32
Hawk, Byron 151
Hayles, N. Katherine 151
Haynes, Cynthia 121
heliotropic 117
Hesse, Doug 138, 151
Hidalgo, Alexandra 151
Hoggart, Richard 98
Holdstein, Deborah 151
Holmevik, Jan Rune 55, 151

hope 3, 5, 11, 12, 13, 16, 18, 19, 22, 23, 24, 26, 27, 29, 30, 33, 35, 36, 37, 41, 43, 48, 50, 57, 61, 65, 66, 71, 75, 76, 77, 79, 108, 110, 113, 116, 128, 134, 135, 137, 142, 143, 145
Howe, John 151
Hull, Glynda 151
hunches 19, 23, 31, 141
Huss, Roy 151
hyperdrives 102

I

identification 6, 7, 29, 50, 52, 53, 55, 77, 80, 83, 90, 119, 131
ideology 51, 148
images 15, 28, 29, 32, 44, 46, 52, 53, 66, 79, 94, 96, 102, 110, 111, 114, 121, 123, 124, 135, 136, 138, 139, 140, 141, 143
image work 45, 47, 110, 138, 139, 140
indeterminacy 33, 44, 99, 106, 141
Ingram, Brett 152
inventive 18, 76, 84, 86, 95
Ishaghpour, Youseff 152
iterative processes 22

J

Jarratt, Susan 152
Jaszi, Peter 147
Jeong, Seung-hoon 152
Johnson-Eilola, Johndan 31
Juhasz, Alexandra 152
jump cut 79, 80

K

Kairos 94, 124, 147, 148, 150, 152, 153, 157
Kantian aesthetics 133, 134
Kasl, Charlotte 152
Keller, Craig 78, 79, 152
Kellner, Douglas 152
Kent, Thomas 152
Kline, Robert 54, 147
Kress, Gunther 75, 152
Krieger, David. J. 147
Kuhn, Virginia 152
kyburz, bonnie lenore 152, 153

L

language is subtractive 113
Le Mepris 84, 87, 89, 90
Les Cahiers du Cinéma 51, 62, 76, 79, 89
Lessig, Lawrence 17
Lestón, Robert 153
liminal space 10
Lindemann, Erika 17
Lindquist, Julie 153
linkage 21, 25
Lopate, Philip 153
ludic ethics 55, 56
Luzi, Evan 153
Lynch, David 52, 111, 153
Lynch, Dennis 85

M

Macbook Pro 92
Maker Movement 22
making 5, 7, 8, 12, 13, 17, 20, 22, 24, 25, 27, 29, 31, 43, 49, 50, 51, 52, 56, 57, 59, 63, 64, 65, 71, 73, 74, 75, 77, 91, 96, 97, 100, 102, 103, 104, 105, 107, 108, 109, 112, 116, 123, 124, 126, 141, 143, 144, 148, 150, 154
Manovich, Lev 122, 124, 153
Manual Cinema 119
Marker, Chris 81, 149
Massumi, Brian 28, 31, 44, 80, 84, 133, 153
materiality 47
McComiskey, Bruce 153
McCullough, Malcolm 116
McLeod, Susan 19, 43, 153
Me and Earl and the Dying Girl 118, 119
melting snowman 111, 113
Metzger, David 153
Micciche, Laura 153
Miller, Susan 153
Milne, Tom 154
Mitchell, William J.T. 154
Modern Language Association 32, 36, 151, 156
MODs 7, 8
motion picture 34, 35, 38, 39, 40, 41, 42, 156
multiliteracies 31, 154

multimodal 11, 14, 16, 17, 25, 40, 43, 44, 47, 55, 57, 60, 61, 64, 83, 88, 91, 96, 97, 98, 102, 110, 116, 124, 154
multimodality 16, 26, 44, 45, 71, 97, 98, 119, 135
multipass 36
Multipass 36
Murphy, James 154
Murray, Joddy 28, 43, 154
mystic trance 52

N

Nancy, Jean Luc 96
Narboni, Jean 154
National Council of Teachers of English 4, 28, 32, 34, 37
neural turn 44
neuro-image 123, 154
New London Group 30, 55, 154
new materialisms 4, 45, 97
new media 17, 31, 40, 75, 76, 139, 157
Nolan, Christopher 30, 94
non-discursive 43, 44, 46, 47, 126, 128
North, Stephen M. 154

O

object oriented ontology 22
on-normative 58
overfull 40, 79, 112
overspill 48, 116, 143, 150
Oxford, vii–xv, 151

P

Palmeri, Jason 17
Parr, Adrian 154
pedagogy 3, 5, 6, 15, 16, 17, 22, 31, 32, 33, 35, 37, 39, 41, 56, 57, 60, 61, 68, 89, 93, 94, 96, 102, 104, 108, 110, 125, 126, 127, 134, 135, 137, 138, 140, 141, 142, 149, 150, 151, 154
Perl, Sondra 19, 47, 85
persuasion 9, 10, 30, 31, 34, 80, 141
Pisters, Patricia 122, 154
planeury. *See also* flaneur
Plato 44

pleasure 3, 10, 11, 19, 26, 28, 31, 37, 43, 45, 52, 55, 69, 70, 74, 94, 107, 108, 109, 110, 114, 119, 121, 122, 123, 124, 125, 126, 128, 129, 132, 133, 134, 135, 136, 137, 138, 139, 140, 141, 142, 143, 144
Poster, Mark 53
postmodern 7, 26, 33, 40, 43, 49, 58, 72, 88, 107, 130, 152
Poulakos, John 154
PRADAbility 143
Prensky, Marc 86, 154
producing 37, 40, 57, 85, 86, 117, 141
production 4, 5, 7, 10, 12, 13, 17, 20, 22, 24, 25, 26, 29, 30, 33, 34, 35, 37, 38, 40, 41, 42, 46, 53, 56, 58, 61, 63, 64, 65, 67, 68, 70, 74, 76, 77, 79, 83, 86, 88, 89, 91, 98, 101, 103, 110, 116, 117, 123, 124, 128, 133, 137, 138, 142, 149

R

Raaf, Sabrina 154
remediating 36
remix 4, 17, 45, 54, 57, 70, 116, 126
rhetoric 7, 8, 9, 11, 13, 21, 23, 29, 31, 43, 44, 46, 47, 55, 57, 59, 60, 66, 67, 68, 71, 75, 79, 85, 86, 90, 93, 94, 95, 100, 106, 111, 112, 113, 122, 126, 128, 133, 134, 135, 138, 145, 148, 149, 150, 151, 152, 153, 154, 155, 156
rhetorical craft 3, 12
rhetorical knowledge and skill 25, 26, 27, 29, 31, 38, 57, 61, 81, 88, 106, 111, 118, 134
rhetorical practice 3, 13, 52, 93, 94, 100, 105, 124, 134
rhetorical strategies 19
rhetorical velocity 94
rhetorician 3, 13, 20, 39, 41, 64, 71, 80, 95, 104, 105, 112, 114, 123, 124, 143
rhetoricity 5, 6, 9, 13, 16, 21, 47, 49, 52, 57, 59, 60, 72, 100, 101, 102, 108, 109, 110, 122, 127, 128, 138, 139, 141, 150
rhetors 6, 94, 95, 104, 125
Rhodes, Jaqueline 147
Rice, Jeff 154
Rice, Jenny Edbauer 154
Rickert, Thomas 21, 47, 107, 121, 154, 155
Ridolfo, Jim 94, 150
Rieder, David 12, 39, 155

Robbins, Anthony 155
Robinson, W. R. 53
Roen, Duane 32

S

scrubbing 81
Sedgwick, Eve Kosofsky 129, 155
Seigworth, Gregory 19, 150
Selfe, Cynthia 31
Senses of Cinema 78, 81, 149
serious play 53, 55, 56
Sharp, David 6, 155
Sheridan, David 155
Sheridan, David M. 125
Shipka, Jody 17, 25, 97, 155
Shor, Ira 17
Silverstein, Norman 151
Sirc, Geoffrey 31, 32, 35, 73, 77, 86, 153, 155
Smith, Daniel W. 28, 101, 123, 155
social process 83, 153
Solomon, Stanley J. 71
sound 7, 9, 14, 18, 38, 40, 74, 81, 86, 91, 110,
143
Spellmeyer, Kurt 155
Spinoza, Baruch Benedict de 91, 121, 155
storytelling 49
Strange, M Dot 119
Sundance 10, 13, 21, 31, 64, 115, 118
Szaniawski, Jeremi 152

T

Tarkovsky, Andrei 81
Taylor, Mark 21
Taylor, Todd 17, 25, 36, 74, 145, 153, 156
teachers 15, 17, 23, 34, 35, 37, 42, 54, 58, 59, 60,
65, 67, 68, 71, 72, 76, 82, 85, 113, 150
teacher-scholars 13, 26, 30, 31, 39, 71, 76, 122,
132
techné 56
television 17, 23, 122
text 10, 11, 12, 14, 17, 22, 27, 36, 40, 41, 44, 46,
59, 74, 75, 78, 80, 85, 88, 90, 91, 92, 95, 96,
98, 116, 132, 142, 150
textmaking 18, 28

The Art of Noise 74
the entire vibratory event 112
the missing half second 112
The Council of Writing Program Administrator's Outcomes Statement 26
the primacy of the affective in image reception 44, 110, 111
Tompkins, Silvan 128
Trimbur, John 156
Truffaut, Francois 5, 76
Truffaut, François 63

U

Ulmer 103

V

Varda, Agnès 63
video 5, 7, 14, 17, 29, 53, 55, 74, 82, 85, 103, 114,
115, 142, 150, 153
virtuality 106
Vitale, Chris 100, 156
Vitanza, Victor J. 156
voice 28, 32, 39, 51, 73, 77, 81, 103, 142
Vreeland, A.Vaughn 156

W

Warhol, Robin 156
Watkins, Megan 127, 156
Weisinger, Herbert 40
Weisinger, Robert 156
Wenders, Wim 65, 149
Wetherbee, Ben 156
Wilferth, Joe 29, 111, 149
Williamson, Richard 23, 34, 98, 156
Williams, Phillip 156
Wings of Desire 65, 149
Wise, J. Hooper 156
Worsham, Lynn 15, 85, 100, 156
Worth, Sol 137
writing 5, 12, 13, 14, 15, 16, 17, 21, 24, 25, 26, 27,
28, 31, 34, 35, 36, 37, 38, 39, 42, 43, 47, 49,
51, 52, 53, 54, 55, 57, 58, 66, 68, 70, 73, 76,
78, 79, 80, 81, 83, 85, 86, 87, 118, 126, 129,
130, 134, 138, 140, 141, 142, 147, 148, 150,
151, 152, 153, 154, 155, 156

Wysocki, Anne Frances 31, 73, 85, 153, 156, 157

Y

Yancey, Kathleen Blake 138, 157

Z

zone(s) of optimism 3, 9, 10, 13, 16, 21, 50, 52, 55, 56, 57, 58, 60, 61, 107, 108, 109, 116, 128, 141